The World of
FRANZ KAFKA

The World of
FRANZ
KAFKA

Edited by J.P. Stern

HOLT, RINEHART AND WINSTON
NEW YORK

First published in the United States in 1980 by
Holt, Rinehart and Winston, 383 Madison Avenue,
New York, New York 10017.

**Library of Congress Cataloging in Publication
Data**

The World of Franz Kafka.
Includes index.

    1 Kafka, Franz, 1883–1924–Addresses, essays,
      lectures.
    2 Authors, Austrian–20th
      century–Biography–Addresses, essays, lectures.
I. Stern, Joseph Peter.
PT2621. A26Z986 1980   833'.   912(B)   80–23689
ISBN 0–03–051366–9

First American Edition
Printed in United States of America

10 9 8 7 6 5 4 3 2 1

Contents

Introduction *J.P.Stern*   page 1

PART ONE   LOCAL AND BIOGRAPHICAL   9

1   A Chronology of Kafka's Life *Allan Blunden*   11

2   Kafka's Prague *F.W.Carter*   30

3   The Spirit of the Place *Sheila Stern*   44

4   The Rise and Fall of the Jewish-German Symbiosis:
      The Case of Franz Kafka *Felix Weltsch*   47

5   Two Recollections: Prague, 11 June 1924 and
      The Golem *Johannes Urzidil*   56

6   Under the Harrow *Rosemary Dinnage*   69

7   Kafka's Castle? *Klaus Wagenbach*   79

PART TWO   SUMMONSES TO INTERPRETATION   85

8   On Kafka's Novels *Martin Walser*   87

9   Endings and Non-endings in Kafka's Fiction *J.J.White*   102

10 Investigations of a Dog and Other Matters: A Literary
      Discussion Group in an American University *Erich Heller*   103

11 Kafka's Parables: Ways Out of the Dead End
      Roy Pascal   112

12 An Uninterpretable Radiance *Frank Kermode* 120

13 The Cunning of a Writer *Joachim Beug* 122

14 Kafka and Language *Anthony Thorlby* 133

15 Freud and the Magic of Kafka's Writing
    Walter H. Sokel 145

16 Kafka and the Muirs *Joyce Crick* 159

17 Challenges and Protests *Commentary by*
    J.P.Stern 175
    Walter Benjamin 175
    Bertolt Brecht 178
    Georg Lukács 181
    Günther Anders 183
    Karel Kosík 186

PART THREE   FICTIONS AND SEMI-FICTIONS 189

18 A Normal Enough Dog: Kafka and the Office
    Roy Fuller 191

19 'I always wanted you to admire my fasting', or,
    Looking at Kafka *Philip Roth* 202

20 A Triptych for the Jackdaw *Jerzy Peterkiewicz* 218

21 K. on the Moon *D.J.Enright* 220

22 Kafka Without a World *Wolfgang Fischer* 223

23 A Path in Autumn *Idris Parry* 229

24 The Matljary Diary *J.P.Stern* 238

List of Contributors 251

Index 255

Illustrations

(Between pages 72 and 73)
1 Kafka aged five
2 His father, Hermann Kafka
3 Franz Kafka with two of his sisters
4 Hermann Kafka's trademark
5 Příkopy (the Moat)
6 The Old Town Hall Square
7 Franz Kafka *c.* 1894
8 A Baroque monument (Pohořelec)
9 The family apartment
10 The schoolboy *c.* 1896
11 Handwritten entry in a friend's album
12 Children in the Jewish quarter of Josefov, *c.* 1900
13 Prague: a recent view of the Castle

(Between pages 136 and 137)
14 The building in Bílkova Street where Kafka moved in 1914
15 Kafka with Ottla, his favourite sister *c.* 1915
16 'The Golden Pike', where Kafka lived in 1915
17 Max Brod
18 Felix Weltsch
19 The Old Synagogue
20 Johannes Urzidil
21 Oskar Baum

22 Prague Jewish cemetery
23 The Worker's Accident Insurance Offices
24 King Charles IV's Bridge
25 Kafka and Felice Bauer
26 A view of Marienbad
27 Kafka in Prague, *c.* 1920
28 The John Hus monument and Týn Church

(Between pages 200 and 201)
29 and 30 Two drawings from Kafka's diaries
31 Kafka, 1921
32 His friend, Milena Jesenská
33 Prague: Hradčany Castle
34 Roofs of the Old City
35 and 36 St Vitus's Cathedral and its choir on the Castle Hill
37 Kafka's parents
38 Dora Diamant (Dymant)
39 The last photograph of Kafka
40 A recent plaque on Kafka's house
41 A drawing of Kafka by Friedrich Feigl

Illustrations are supplied or reproduced by kind permission of the following: 17, 20 Bildarchiv d. Ost. Nationalbibliothek; 5 Bilderdienst Suddeutscher Verlag; 25, 27, 37, 40 CTK, Prague; 41 from *Kafka* by John Hibberd; 29 and 30 from *Kafka and Prague* by Johann Bauer; 35 Klaus Lehnartz (Bavaria Verlag); 22 Joachim Messerschmidt (Bavaria Verlag); 19, 33, 36 Paul Popper; 9 Erika Schmauss (Bavaria Verlag); 13 Sheila Stern; 34 Ufa (Bavaria Verlag); 8, 14, 16 Ullstein Bilderdienst; 6, 12, 26 Roger Viollet; 1, 2, 3, 4, 7, 10, 15, 23, 31, 32, 38, 39 Klaus Wagenbach.

Introduction

J.P.Stern

'I hope you won't destroy the mystery,' a friend remarked when I told him of my plans for this volume.

There is little danger of that. The writings assembled in this anthology are intended to illuminate Franz Kafka's achievement – the 'world' which he created in his writings as well as the world in which he created them – but they do this as it were from the outside. The biographical contributions describe not palpable causes but (the distinction is Kierkegaard's) some of the occasions that gave rise to Kafka's fictions; the critical essays, including a few hostile ones, are as much concerned to point to the difficulties of interpretation as they are with interpretation itself; the poems and stories of the concluding section convey fleeting impressions of imaginary encounter; and the photographs (as always, steeped more deeply in the past they portray than any painting could ever be) distance the whole thing – 'the world of Franz Kafka' – in the perspective of history.

But as to 'the mystery' – there seems little agreement on where to look for it, let alone on how to get inside it. How could it be otherwise, the poet Rainer Maria Rilke asks – are we not always at odds with, always on the opposite side of, the object of our attention?

> Da wird für eines Augenblickes Zeichnung
> ein Grund von Gegenteil bereitet, mühsam,
> dass wir sie sehen. . . .
> 　　　　　　　　Wir kennen den Kontur
> des Fühlens nicht, nur was ihn formt von aussen.

There, briefly, for the sketchwork of a moment,
a ground of contrast is set up, painfully,
to make us see the sketch. . . .

We do not know
the contour line of feeling – only that
which forms it from outside.

Rilke (1875–1926) and Kafka (1883–1924) were fellow-townsmen and close contemporaries. They both came from the same Slavonic fringes of German-speaking culture, and they are among the half-dozen or so authors who constitute the greatness of modern German literature and give it a distinction it had not enjoyed since the age of Goethe; yet their contributions to that literature could hardly be more different.

Their biographical affinities are worth noting. Both went to the same kind of German schools in the heart of Prague and moved in roughly the same minority culture. Both were brought up on the same impoverished and threatened linguistic inheritance, 'Prague German', aware of its lifelessness and peculiar correctness, embarrassed by – yet sharing – the social kudos claimed by its speakers. (In its restriction, the medium reminds one of Anglo-Indian English.) One was born into the German minority of Prague, the other into the German-Jewish minority within that minority – a difference by no means as great as subsequent events and subsequent interpretations have made it appear; in reacting against their background both turned with warmth and sympathy towards their Czech surroundings. They were neither German nor Austrian, and though each for a time entertained socialist sympathies, neither was able to identify consistently with any national or political cause. They found their native milieu repressive and occasionally embarrassing, and looked for 'reality' and authentic life in the East: Rilke on his journeys to Russia (1900), Kafka in his contact with the Yiddish actors who visited Prague in 1910. Yet both knew that what they sought could only be found within, in what Kafka called 'the dream-like life of my soul'. His attitude towards all social and political solutions of personal problems is best summed up in his diary entry of 8 January 1914: 'What have I in common with Jews? I have hardly anything in common with myself. . . .' They made their escape from Prague, but the timing was characteristically different: Rilke left at the beginning of his career, as soon as he was confident of his poetic powers, Kafka at the very end, exhausted from the struggle, a year before his early death.

Above all, they were both wholly obsessed by their literary vocation, and apt to regard everything and everybody that stood in its way with anxiety and occasionally terror. Neither had any sustaining contact with the literary movements of their time, and both regarded isolation and solitude as the necessary condition of their creativeness – that is, of their lives. In biographical as well as in literary terms Rilke is for ever on the move, Kafka remains guiltily loyal to his origins: whether this is a difference in resilience and psychic energy or in sensitivity of conscience, who is to say?

Apart from an occasional sentence, perhaps, no paragraph written by one could be mistaken for a paragraph written by the other. What divides them may be made clear by looking at the different ways in which they treat a common theme.

Both are fascinated by the story of the prodigal son (Luke 15). Rilke devotes to it the last chapter of his only novel, *The Notebooks of Malte Laurids Brigge*; the chapter opens with characteristic indirection – 'It will be difficult to convince me that the story of the lost son is not the story of one who did not want to be loved' – and all that follows is designed to support this strange interpretation. The reason why the youth of Rilke's story has left his father's home and is afraid to return is his fear of a loving, all-too-loving family, of its paralysing embrace of sympathy and ready though inaccurate understanding. What ultimately decides him not to return – or 'to return, but not yet' – is his need to be himself, to explore his own feelings and imagination and creative gifts. His need is to be, and to remain, outside. There are a few sentences in Rilke's version of the story which could have been written by Kafka: 'All one had to do was to enter the house with its smell, and most things were as good as decided. Details might still change, but on the whole one was already what one was taken to be.' The experience of the familiar as prison is common to both, but beyond that Kafka's story moves in the opposite direction. It expresses not the fear of communion, but a dire need of it; not the excesses of familiarity, but the frozen world of isolation – a world whose very *things* ('a puddle ... useless implements ... a torn piece of cloth ... smoke coming from the chimney ...') signal hostility and rejection.*

Our comparison points to quests whose goals are at the opposite ends of experience yet *equally* unattainable, and the unattainable is seen – in Kafka, by implication – as something inexpressibly precious. Placed in the fuller context of Rilke's and Kafka's writings, this amounts to the view that the more difficult of attainment a goal, the more valuable it is. But of the two goals – liberation from communion on the one hand, breach of the isolation of solitude on the other – we are likely to recognize Kafka's as the less eccentric, as the more human goal.

'We do not know / the contour line of feeling – only that / which forms it from outside.' Rilke's Fourth Duino Elegy consists of a group of bold

---

* The full text of this reflection is to be found on p. 113 below.

metaphors constructed round a huge ontological assertion in historical time: *we* modern men are incapable of undistracted feeling, *we* do not know what it is to perceive one thing without being deflected towards perceiving quite another; 'humankind', as T.S. Eliot, of the same generaticn, puts it, 'cannot bear very much reality.' The poetic self-confidence of Rilke's assertions, the luxuriance of the metaphors from which he creates his metaphysics, have no equal in Kafka. Rilke's practice of encouraging his poems to burgeon into a 'project of the Being of Man', meaning modern, twentieth-century man, would have struck Kafka as an act of hubris, an undertaking beyond his moral and creative powers (for the two, with him, were one). Even the *minima moralia* Kafka conveys, either in his diaries and letters or through the reactions of his 'heroes', are hedged in with qualifications and expressions of diffidence.

Rilke's essential medium is poetry, Kafka's sole medium is prose. Two different kinds of literary creativeness face a profoundly similar experience of deprivation. Rilke hides the experience by building it into the foundations of his poetic *oeuvre*, he imposes on it his complex and vertiginous metaphoric structures. Chief among these is his myth of inwardness; and this myth, which informs some of his finest poetry, has in it elements of an ideology. He writes, a supreme lyrical poet, as one of the 'legislators of mankind', proclaiming a design for the right way of feeling, for the right kind of living in the world.

Kafka on the other hand remains faithful to that initial experience of deprivation. This is how he first captures our attention. And he retains it by staying close to the experience, the language in which it comes to him, and to the metaphors it dictates. Squeezing an unexpected wealth of meaning from these metaphors, he ties them closely into his scenes and actions; so much so that many of his stories take their entire structure from a central metaphor or image placed in a context which plays with the restraints of realistic expectation. Kafka's father described a friend of his son's as 'a verminous parasite'; in 'The Metamorphosis' the phrase is taken literally, the story consists in a sober and even laconic – realistic – exploration of the image turned fictional 'reality'. Rilke rejected the grey-in-grey of 'Prague' German and its world. Kafka remained its chronicler, and with its language drew scenes whose characteristic mixture of familiarity and strangeness has had many imitators but no exact parallel in modern literature; only the paintings of Edvard Munch, his contemporary, provide an illuminating comparison. Yet although the achievement is unique, it undoubtedly belongs to the literature and spirit of its age. Rilke provides a general statement of it. Commenting on the poems of Georg Trakl, Rilke challenges the customary prejudice against the poetry of lament, by which he means the reader's mistaken 'belief that in the direction of that poetry only lament is to be found: there too lies a world'. This is the subject-matter of our book.

Kafka's Prague is dead – more dead than Dostoyevsky's St Petersburg and Tolstoy's Moscow. The essays assembled in the first, biographical part of this collection set Kafka's life in a city and culture which two world wars, the German and Russian occupations and several major political changes make difficult to recapture. Our first attempt to do so is factual. Allan Blunden's chronology is largely composed of extracts from Kafka's correspondence. Frank Carter is interested in the data of the demography of Prague in Kafka's time, Felix Weltsch and Johannes Urzidil write as Kafka's contemporaries and friends, Sheila Stern contributes a nineteenth-century vignette of the city, and Rosemary Dinnage takes up the cudgels on behalf of 'Kafka's women'. At this point the reader may well feel that these sombre portraits need to be supplemented by such accounts as Roy Fuller's and Philip Roth's (in the third part), which are no less true to life for being built from fictional and semi-fictional material. In that section too he will find Idris Parry's and the editor's accounts, cast in the form of prose elegies, and capriccios by D.J.Enright, Jerzy Peterkiewicz and Wolfgang Fischer.

There is about the man Franz Kafka a charm, a good-natured resignation, an uncommon kindness and thoughtfulness for others, which come across in his letters and in the testimonies of his friends. (In all the hundreds of letters he wrote I have only found one in which Kafka is asking for a personal favour – a request to his friend Max Brod to make out a good case for extending of yet another of his many periods of sick-leave.) There is, every now and then, a mocking exasperation with himself and a gentle sense of humour at all the suggestions and retractions, the collapsing engagements (his own) and marriages (other people's), the slamming doors and misunderstood messages – a humour which should not be made to bear the brunt of 'deep' interpretation. Even Brod's account is not all gloom. He tells the story of Kafka's visiting him in his parents' apartment (Brod too seems to have been an incorrigible stay-at-home) and disturbing Brod's father's afternoon nap on the sitting-room sofa: tiptoeing through the room, Kafka said, 'Please look on me as a dream.' Addressing the fish during a visit to a Berlin aquarium, after he had become a vegetarian: 'Now I can look at you calmly, I won't eat you any more.' On a rainy day in Marienbad Kafka watches a famous rabbi with his solemn entourage in search of medicinal waters after the springs have all been shut for the day, the bottle brought for the purpose meanwhile filling with rainwater – a Marx Brothers scenario which Kafka ends with a comment on one of the rabbi's followers who 'tries to find or thinks he finds a deeper meaning in all this: I think the deeper meaning is that there is none, and in my opinion that is enough.' Or again, commenting on his job in the industrial workers' insurance office: 'In my four districts – apart from all my other chores – people fall off the scaffoldings as if they were drunk, or they fall into the machines, all the beams topple, all embankments give way, all ladders slide, whatever people carry up falls down, whatever they hand down they stumble over. And I have a headache from all these girls in porcelain factories who incessantly throw themselves down the stairs with mountains of dishware.'* The humour and the charm of such scenes is not diminished by our awareness that every one of them is a trying-out of the writer's pen, a literary rehearsal. In no letter or document, not even in his astonishing commentaries on factory acts and industrial safety regulations, was he anything other than a maker of literature.

In one of his many fragmentary reflections Kafka notes that in his writing 'life should both retain its natural, heavy rise and fall and at the same time and with equal clarity be recognized as a nothing, a dream, a hovering ...'; and he likens this to 'the wish to hammer a table together painstakingly and in a craftsmanlike way yet at the same time to do nothing: but not so that one might say, "Hammering is nothing to him," but "Hammering is real hammering to him and at the same time it is nothing."' How is this programme accomplished? In the second, critical section of this collection a number of answers to this question are offered. Martin Walser, himself a novelist, considers the ghostly groupings and attitudes of the figures round the 'heroes' of Kafka's three novels; Joachim Beug and Anthony Thorlby look for an answer in Kafka's ideas on art and language respectively, while Erich Heller throws a somewhat sceptical eye on the interpretative business and its conventions. Walter Sokel seeks enlightenment from Freudian analysis, Joyce Crick considers what the Muirs made of Kafka's German in giving it an English guise, and Roy Pascal uses an enquiry into Kafka's parabolic form in order to find an affirmation – that 'world' which Rilke affirmed – beyond the prevailing gloom. A selection from the criticism of the age of the Popular Front indicates something of the political significance that could not fail to be attached to Kafka's work at a time when beleaguered left-wing intellectuals fought each other almost as much as they fought the common enemy.

While in the thirties and forties Kafka's work was attacked by Marxists of various hues as a manifestation of bourgeois decadence and defeatism, its post-war politicization took on a very different and rather surprising

---

* From a letter to Max Brod, summer 1909: '... was man hinauf gibt, das stürzt hinunter, was man herunter gibt, darüber stürzt man selbst'. This use of 'gibt', taken from the Czech, is part of that 'Prague German' which Kafka took care to suppress in more formal contexts.

form. The indictment of decadence continued, mainly from East German critics. But in 1963 an official conference was organized by Eduard Goldstücker at the castle of Liblice near Prague; it was the first occasion when Kafka's native land took any notice of him. Seen as literary criticism, the papers delivered at that conference are not exciting. But by asserting the freedom of readers east of the Iron Curtain to read Kafka at all, and to make up their own minds about his qualities as a writer and his role as a critic or victim of the capitalist system, the speakers for the first time affirmed that freedom of expression which led to the Prague Spring five years later, in 1968, and was buried in the Russian invasion of August that year. One might hope that, for all his deep scepticism about the value of his work, Franz Kafka would look on this strange development with a mixture of astonishment and pleasure.

PART ONE

LOCAL AND BIOGRAPHICAL

A Chronology of Kafka's Life

Allan Blunden

1883

3 July: Franz Kafka is born in Prague, the first child of Hermann and Julie Kafka. Married only ten months previously, on the eve of his thirtieth birthday, Hermann Kafka had been born of Czech-Jewish parents in a tiny village in Southern Bohemia, where the family lived in the humblest of circumstances. His own father, Jakob Kafka, had been a butcher, and a man of legendary physical strength (it was said that he could pick up a sack of flour with his teeth). Hermann liked to boast to his own children about the hardships of his youth, recounting how he had had to walk from village to village, sometimes barefoot, delivering meat with a handcart even in the depths of winter. Franz will later recall some of these reminiscences, 'which must have ploughed deep furrows in my brain'.

Leaving home at the age of fourteen, Hermann Kafka made his living as an itinerant trader for a number of years, before settling finally in Prague. Shortly after his marriage to Julie – and with the aid of her family's money – he set up his own business selling fancy goods. His business emblem was a jackdaw – '*kavka*' in Czech.

Julie Kafka (*née* Löwy) came of a family of prosperous German-Jewish merchants of rather more orthodox background. Her ancestors on her mother's side included scholars, doctors, eccentrics, many of them characterized by their extreme religious devotion. Her mother Esther died when Julie was only three, and her father, Jakob Löwy, soon remarried; her grandmother, depressed by her daughter's untimely death, committed suicide shortly afterwards. Julie's stepmother bore her husband more sons, and Julie grew up in the company of five brothers. Two of them emigrated, one to the Congo, where he became a successful trader; the other, Kafka's Uncle Alfred, finally became head of the Spanish railways.

Kafka will later describe himself as 'a Löwy with certain underlying Kafka elements, albeit the spirit that animates the latter is not the traditional Kafka family appetite for life, business affairs and conquest, but a more subtle and secretive energy, characteristic of the Löwys, that inclines me in other directions – and often enough abandons me altogether. . . .'

1883–93

Franz's two brothers (born in 1885 and 1887) both die in infancy. Three sisters are born: Elli (1889), Valli (1890) and Ottla (1892). (All three will be murdered in Nazi concentration camps.) German is the language of the ruling class in Austria-Hungary, and Hermann Kafka's keen desire to advance his family socially is reflected in the fact that all his children are given an exclusively German education (although Franz also learns to speak and write Czech). Kafka's childhood has been described by his friend Max Brod as 'unspeakably lonely'. The experiences of his early life – the deaths of two brothers and six changes of address in as many years – are unsettling enough; but they are overshadowed by the deeply disturbed relationship that exists between Kafka and his father. Like any child, Kafka looks to his father as 'the measure of all things' while he is growing up; and like many fathers, Hermann Kafka aspires to raise his son in his own image. But father and son are so completely dissimilar in temperament that the robust ideals represented by the former seem hopelessly unattainable to the sensitive and timid child.

For the father is 'a real Kafka', the embodiment of all those 'manly' family characteristics that Franz – more Löwy than Kafka – feels he lacks: 'strength, health, a hearty appetite, a powerful voice, eloquence, self-satisfaction, a supreme sense of assurance, stamina, presence of mind, a knowledge of human nature and a certain generosity . . .' As a small child he was 'oppressed', Kafka recalls, by his father's 'sheer physical presence. I remember, for instance, how we often used to get undressed in the same cubicle at the swimming bath. I was skinny, weak and slight, while you were big, strong and powerfully-built. I felt then that I was a thoroughly miserable specimen . . .'

The demands of the family business undoubtedly leave Hermann Kafka little time or energy to devote to his children: but there are no indications that he would have wished it otherwise. Years later Kafka will recall his father's perfunctory interest in his upbringing: 'Since you usually saw me only at mealtimes, the instruction you gave me as a child was largely confined to teaching me correct table manners.' Instead of giving Kafka the guidance and reassurance he so badly needs, his father bullies and taunts him into frightened submission: 'The methods you used in our upbringing – which were highly effective, at least in my case – were abuse, threats, irony, mockery ...'.

What Kafka finds so disquieting is not the severity of his father's authority as such (as an impressionable and diffident child he would have respected, even welcomed, forceful direction), but the arbitrariness with which it is exercised. For he senses in his father a fundamental lack of principle, and a hypocritical failure to match precept with personal example. His only aim, it seems, is to belittle everything that Kafka does, everything that Kafka is – to isolate and subject him: 'It seemed as if the world was divided into three parts. In one part I lived as a slave, subject to laws which had been specially devised for me, and which for some unknown reason I could never completely satisfy. The second world, infinitely removed from my own, was the one in which you lived, occupied with running the business, issuing orders – and getting angry when they were not carried out. The third world was the one where everyone else lived happy lives, in which the giving and taking of orders played no part.'

Of all his father's 'methods', notes Kafka, none was more potent than irony: 'You were a great believer in irony as a means of instruction and correction. And it was the perfect expression of your superiority over me.' Indeed it was. For by masking the ironist's private feelings irony serves precisely to maintain a *distance* between him and his subject – or victim ('a second world, infinitely removed from my own ...'). And by refusing to be defined, or identified with a particular viewpoint or principle, the user of irony arrogates to himself the freedom to exercise his skill – or power – in an *arbitrary* fashion. He is accountable to nobody and to nothing.

Kafka's lifelong fear of his father has its deepest roots here. *The Trial* and *The Castle*, images of distant and arbitrary regimes, will later spring from the same soil: for this is no longer parental authority, but totalitarianism writ small: 'From your armchair you ruled the world. Your opinion was the only right one: every other opinion was idiotic. ... Sometimes you had no opinion at all about something – so all the opinions that could possibly be entertained on that subject were necessarily and without exception wrong. ... You acquired in my eyes that enigmatic quality common to all tyrants, whose authority rests not on what they think but on who they are. ...'

1893–1901

September 1893: Kafka enters a notoriously strict German grammar school in the Old Town of Prague, where he remains until July 1901. The curriculum includes a good deal of Goethe and Schiller. In his later school years he also reads Darwin and Haeckel, and declares himself both an atheist and a socialist (even wearing a red carnation to proclaim his political sympathies). His school friends include Felix Weltsch, the future philosopher and Zionist (and lifelong friend), and Oskar Pollak, whom he later describes as 'a kind of window through which I was able to look out on the streets'. Through Pollak Kafka is introduced to *Der Kunstwart*, a vigorous periodical for literature and the arts which bears the stamp of Nietzsche's influence. This in turn leads him to read Nietzsche's *Zarathustra* (in 1899) and the work of Hofmannsthal. June 1896: his *bar-mitzvah* is celebrated, although his parents preferred to call it a 'confirmation'. In later years Kafka is bitter about his father's perfunctory Jewishness: 'As far as I could see it was something non-existent, a joke – no, not even a joke. . . .'

November 1901: enters the German University in Prague. Studies chemistry for two weeks, then changes to law. He later claims that he was not interested in conventional career success, that he chose law because he wanted a safe job that would enable him to survive decently, 'without injuring my vanity too much. . . . Even as a small child I had a pretty clear notion of what all my studying and choosing a career would amount to: I expected no salvation from that quarter. . . .'

1902

During the summer term Kafka attends lectures in art history and German literature, including those delivered by the vociferous German nationalist August Sauer. End of August: he goes to stay with his favourite uncle Siegfried, who is a country doctor in Moravia. Evidently unhappy with the study of German literature as presented by Sauer – 'may it roast in hell!' he writes to Oskar Pollak – he contemplates studying the subject in Munich instead. He visits Munich briefly in October, but nothing more comes of the plan. 23 October: Kafka meets Max Brod after a talk given by the latter on 'Schopenhauer and Nietzsche'. They walk home together, Kafka defending Nietzsche against Brod's strictures.

1903

Resigned once more to the study of law, Kafka spends the early summer preparing for his university examinations in legal history, which he passes in July: 'I fed my mind on sawdust which thousands of others had chewed over before me. It was a tremendous strain on my nerves.' While working for the examinations he has a passing affair with a shop-girl. 'I was happy, but only because I had some peace at long last from the eternal complaining of this body of mine. ...' By now Kafka is working on a novel: 'God doesn't want me to be a writer. But I have no choice.'

1904

Kafka is reading Thomas Mann's short stories, including 'Tonio Kröger' (1903). In January he reads Hebbel's diaries (throughout his life he enjoyed reading biographical material), and tells Pollak, 'One should only read the kinds of books that bite and sting ... a book should be an ice-pick to break up the frozen sea within us.' In the autumn Kafka, Brod, Felix Weltsch and the blind writer Oskar Baum begin to meet together at weekends to read and discuss each other's work (although Kafka does not contribute work of his own at this stage).

1905

In July/August Kafka spends several weeks at a sanatorium in Zuckmantel (Silesia), where he has a love affair with an unknown woman.

1906

18 June: Kafka graduates as a doctor of law. In July/August Kafka returns to Zuckmantel and resumes his relationship with the unknown woman. 1 October: begins his compulsory year of practical legal experience (unpaid).

1907

August: Kafka stays with his uncle Siegfried in the country again, and meets two girl students who are ardent Social Democrats. He views their dogmatic political enthusiasm with a certain irony now, but continues to correspond with one of them until 1909. 1 October: begins work at the Assicurazioni-Generali, a privately owned insurance company in Prague. The hours are long, the working atmosphere is abrasive, and he complains that he has no leisure for writing. Soon he is looking for another job.

1908

March: Kafka's first short prose pieces are published in the magazine *Hyperion*. 15 July: leaves his job, ostensibly for health reasons. 30 July: begins work at the semi-nationalized Workers' Accident Insurance Institute, where his day ends at 2 pm. He quickly takes his place as a well-esteemed member of staff, and when his head of department is promoted to the directorship shortly thereafter Kafka gives a speech in his honour.

1909

4–14 September: Kafka, Max and Otto Brod spend a holiday together at Riva in northern Italy. They make an excursion to Brescia to see an air display; Blériot is there, after his historic cross-Channel flight in July. Kafka's account of the Brescia meeting subsequently appears in a Prague newspaper. At work he is reported to be 'untiringly diligent and ambitious, remarkably versatile . . . outstandingly able and eminently conscientious in the discharge of his duties.' A few weeks after this is written, in September/October, Kafka meets Michal Mareš, a Czech anarchist who works in the street where Kafka lives. He begins attending meetings of several anarchist and radical groups.

1910

8–17 October: Kafka is in Paris with Max and Otto Brod. 17 December, in a letter to Max: 'I can't write . . . every single word stops and has a good look round before it will let me write it down.' The same day, in his diary, he notes that he has scrapped nearly everything he has written during the year. 26 December: 'Solitude has a power over me which never fails. . . .'

1911

Late January: a business trip takes him to Friedland in Western Bohemia, where the castle, brooding on its hilltop in the winter snow, makes a strong impression (possibly reflected years later in *The Castle*). 19 February: the 'terrible double life' he is leading – working at the office, then writing at night – is beginning to tell on him. March: attends lectures by Rudolf Steiner (the founder of Anthroposophy), the Viennese satirist Karl Kraus and the architect Adolf Loos.

26 August: Kafka and Brod go on holiday together once more, to Zürich, Lucerne, northern Italy and finally Paris (until 13 September). On the way home Kafka spends a few days at a nature-cure sanatorium near Zürich. 4 October: he sees a Yiddish theatre group performing at Prague's Café Savoy. He attends many subsequent performances, follows the group's fortunes closely, and becomes very friendly with the players' leader, Jizchak Löwy. He finds the actors 'innocent and child-like' – although his father disapproves of his son's association with 'such vermin'. October: the family has decided to open an asbestos factory, and Kafka is

reluctantly involved in the enterprise. 16 December: he speaks of his 'lack of feeling. Between me and everything else there is a hollow space which I make no attempt at all to pierce.'

1912

3 January: 'I am a clear case of somebody whose powers have been channelled in the direction of writing. When my body realized that writing was to be my most productive bent, all my strength flowed into that activity and ceased to nourish whatever capacity I may have had for enjoying sex, food, drink, philosophical reflection, and above all music. My taste for all these things began to atrophy.' Early February: Kafka organizes an evening of Yiddish readings and songs in the Jewish Town Hall in Prague. He arranges everything – even ensuring that the key to the piano is available on the night – and gives the introductory address. His success as an organizer – not a role in which he normally sees himself – clearly gives him great satisfaction; but in his diary he ends the account of his triumph with the pointed observation that his parents were not there. (He no doubt wanted to believe that they would have been proud of his achievement: but the occasion itself – the uncompromising celebration of a Jewish cultural tradition – is hardly likely to have appealed to Hermann Kafka.) End of May: he hears a lecture on the colonization of Palestine. Earlier in the year he has attended a talk on the decline of the German Jews, while 'devouring' books on various aspects of Jewish culture and history.

28 June: with Brod he travels on holiday to Weimar (via Leipzig: here he meets the publisher Rowohlt, who offers to publish a book of Kafka's prose). In Weimar he falls in love with the daughter of the family who were looking after the house where Goethe lived; and throughout the first week of July the drama of this flirtation is enacted in and around the house of the writer whom Kafka never ceased to revere. 7 July: travels on alone to a health farm near Goslar, returning to Prague three weeks later.

13 August: while visiting Brod he meets Felice Bauer, a young woman from Berlin who is distantly related to Brod's family. 20 September: Kafka's first letter to Felice. 22/23 September: writes 'The Judgment' at a single sitting during the night, and subsequently dedicates the story to Felice. For Kafka this is an important break-through – although years later he views it as an equivocal triumph: 'It was then that the wound first opened up, in the course of a long night. ...' He then begins to write the second draft of his novel *America*, originally started in the spring. For two weeks in October he has to supervise the asbestos factory in the afternoons, when it has been his habit to sleep for a few hours in order to be able to write during the night; and he tells Brod he has contemplated suicide. Late

17

October: the correspondence with Felice begins in earnest, and by mid-November Kafka is writing twice a day.

17 November: begins to write 'The Metamorphosis' (completed in three weeks), then continues to work on *America*. The demands of office work, the effort of creative writing, and the emotional strain of his intense correspondence with Felice are all aggravated by lack of sleep. 'My life is essentially composed of attempts to write, and that's how it has always been with me. These attempts have failed for the most part, but if I didn't write I felt like a piece of garbage on the floor, ready to be swept out the door. ... Tomorrow I shall begin writing again, and I shall go at it full tilt: for I know that if I don't write I shall be thrust out from among the living without mercy.'

1913

In January *America* is not progressing well: 'Two evenings ago I confessed myself totally beaten. It's falling apart in my hands – I can't keep hold of it any more.' By March he has rejected all but the first chapter (subsequently published in May as 'The Stoker'). The mood of his letters to Felice darkens, and he becomes obsessed by the 'irrefutable' conviction that he is not meant for normal, happy married life: 'Tell yourself this, that you will never have pure joy of me – but pure sorrow as much as the heart can desire.' Pain and isolation, Kafka believes, are the necessary conditions of his writing. He has headaches 'nearly all the time now. I don't walk enough, I don't sleep enough: and when I do sleep I sleep badly. In short, I'm living as though I were writing something good – although of course if that were true it would bring me the cure to all my ills, and happiness besides.' He looks to exercise to improve his health – riding, swimming and rowing – and seeks therapy in gardening and joinery. (Years later he will write dismissively of these hobbies: 'My life has been filled with futile activities: first the study of law, then the office, and then various other futile pursuits which I took up later, such as gardening and joinery. ... These subsequent additions are like the behaviour of a man who throws a needy beggar out of his house in order to play the benefactor all by himself, transferring alms from his right hand to his left.')

Felice's letters to Kafka have not survived, but it seems clear that she did her best to see him in the conventional terms available to her. He in turn tries to dispel her illusions (as he says later, the trouble was not that he didn't tell her everything, but that she couldn't *believe* the things she saw and heard for herself). So at the beginning of March he writes: 'You asked me ... about my plans and prospects. ... Well, of course I have no plans, no prospects. I can't "move ahead" into the future; I can plunge into the future, lurch into the future, stumble into the future – I can do all that; and what I can do best of all is stay put where I am. ...' Nevertheless, a common future appears to be taking shape, and at Whitsun (11/12 May) he visits Felice and her family in Berlin. In mid-June Kafka and Felice become unofficially engaged.

Meanwhile the ominous warnings continue: 'I need solitude for my writing; not "like a hermit" – that wouldn't be enough – but like a dead man.' At the same time he writes in his diary of 'the prodigious world I have inside my head. But how to free myself – and liberate that world – without breaking apart? A thousand times better to break apart than hold it back or hide it away inside me. That's what I'm here for, after all – I'm quite clear about that.' In July he finds a flat in Prague where they are to live after they marry. But simultaneously he is listing arguments against marriage in his diary: 'I hate everything which doesn't relate to literature. Conversations bore me (even when they are about literary subjects), visiting people bores me, and the joys and sorrows of my relatives bore me to death.' Literature, he tells Felice, possesses him like a devil: 'I don't have "literary interests": literature is what I'm made of.'

Felice's letters grow less regular, and Kafka's are filled with tormented reproaches and self-reproaches – 'my cursed letters, like messages from the Underworld.' 13 August, in his diary: 'Perhaps it is all over now. ... It would be the best way, without a doubt. What she will suffer and what I shall suffer is nothing compared with the pain we would suffer if we were together.' Yet two days later he writes to Felice's father, formally asking for her hand. A week after that he drafts a second letter ('which I will send tomorrow, if I have the strength'), pointing out all the factors which make him unsuitable as a son-in-law. Clearly, the decision to get engaged was a desperate leap in the dark of this increasingly unreal and disembodied relationship. The situation is impossible, yet Kafka cannot bring himself to make the break; so he tries to elicit the initiative first from Felice, then from her father. He makes it impossible for them to accept him – or all but impossible: for he still clings to the hope that Felice will somehow refute the irrefutable and overcome all the obstacles he has raised.

6 September: travels to Vienna on business, then on to Italy. From Venice he writes to Felice (16 September): 'We must say goodbye.' Travel and the change of environment seem to break the deadlock, and for six weeks Kafka does not write to her. Analysing his condition, he tells her, 'I'm able to enjoy human relationships, but not to experience them.' 22 September–13 October: stays at a sanatorium in Riva, where he has a fleeting affair with a young Swiss girl (he subsequently tells Felice). End of October: Kafka ends their unofficial engagement. Felice asks a friend, Grete Bloch, to act as a go-between; Kafka meets Grete in early November

and they begin to correspond. 8 November: travels to Berlin to see Felice, but their brief meeting is unsatisfactory.

1914

In January Kafka proposes to Felice again. 28 February: he pays her a surprise visit in Berlin. Next day he writes to Grete: 'It couldn't have been worse.' A week later, in his diary, he admits to himself that 'F. doesn't love me very much – not with all the love at her command.' He considers moving to Berlin to work as a journalist: not, he says, in order to be near Felice – on the contrary, it might 'help to get F. out of my system. . . .'

But still the painful correspondence continues. Kafka tells Grete of the effort required to extract a reply from Felice: 'If one could only concentrate all the energy I've expended it would be enough to pull down the sun from the sky.' At Easter Kafka and Felice are unofficially engaged once again. 27 May (in a long diary entry containing several scenes and fragments of stories): 'Perhaps after all it is just a question of loosening up my wrist. I *shall* be able to write again.' Three days later he travels to Berlin with his father, and the official engagement is announced. In his diary he writes, 'Felt confined like a criminal. If they had tied me up with real chains and stuck me in a corner with a police guard, and only allowed me to watch [the family proceedings] on those terms, it couldn't have been any worse.' At the same time he writes to Grete, 'Each of us has his own way of escaping from the Underworld. I do it by writing.'

28 June: the Habsburg Archduke Franz Ferdinand is assassinated at Sarajevo. Europe prepares for war. 12 July: Kafka meets Felice, Grete and two others at a Berlin hotel. After a discussion the engagement is called off. He then spends two weeks on the Baltic coast, and contemplates giving up his job, moving to Germany and devoting himself to full-time writing. In these weeks he recalls the painful scenes in Berlin: 'The courtroom session in the hotel. . . . [I was] diabolical in my innocence;' his letter to Felice's parents is a 'speech from the scaffold;' and Grete is later called a 'judge'. A few days later, back in Prague, Kafka writes a fragment about a certain 'Josef K.', and then begins to write his novel *The Trial*, first mentioned by name on 21 August.

31 July: a general military call-up is announced in Austria-Hungary. Kafka is exempted from military service because he is performing 'an essential civilian function'. 5–18 October: takes two weeks' leave in order to write. At first it goes badly – 'Am I to conclude that I'm not worthy to live without the office?' – but at the end he looks back on 'a fortnight of good work'. As well as working on *The Trial* and *America* he has written 'In the Penal Colony', a story born of the same obsession with guilt and

punishment which nourishes the writing of *The Trial*. For this bizarre parable about 'death by writing' (literally: the condemned man's sentence is slowly engraved into his flesh) reflects Kafka's understanding of his relationship with Felice, whom he has 'tortured' beyond endurance by his devotion to writing ('no girl who was ever loved as I love you was ever tormented by her lover the way I am compelled to torment you'); and when the officer/executioner in the story embraces the fate of his victims, Kafka implies that the necessity of writing is a source of suffering for him too. In a long letter to Felice shortly afterwards he speaks of this suffering – but insists on the necessity as well: 'It was my duty to stand guard over my work, the only thing which gives me the right to live' – words which could well have come from the 'officer' who identifies himself so completely with the infernal machine in his charge.

1915

In January the need to attend to business at the asbestos factory every day poses a new threat to Kafka's work: 'Unless I can pursue my stories through the nights they break out and disappear.' 23/24 January: Kafka and Felice meet at Bodenbach (Ústí nad Labem) on the Czech-German frontier, but their aims remain incompatible: he wants a life shaped around his writing, while she has conventional middle-class aspirations. 'She insists on putting my watch right, when it's been an hour and a half fast for the last three months. ...' Kafka writes to her afterwards, 'Outwardly we have no quarrel, we go along peacefully side by side; but inwardly we find ourselves wincing, as though somebody were for ever slashing away at the air between us with a sabre.'

10 February: Kafka at last takes the plunge and leaves home for his first rented room. He moves again a month later, because of the noise and 'my own restlessness'. The new room is 'about ten times more noisy ... but incomparably more attractive', with a fine view of the Old Town of Prague. The husbands of Kafka's two elder sisters, Elli and Valli, have both been called up, and he is aware that his private anxieties must be seen against a larger background: 'Don't laugh, Felice, don't despise my sufferings. So many are suffering now, I know, and the cause of their suffering is more than the sound of whispering in a next-door room. But ultimately they are fighting for their very lives – or rather for the ties that link their lives to the community at large. So am I, so are we all. ...' 23–27 April: he accompanies Elli on a visit to Hungary, where her husband is stationed. They travel via Vienna – which Kafka once called 'an enormous village dying on its feet' – and Budapest. He returns to Prague alone, in low spirits: 'Incapable of living with people, talking to people. Totally

absorbed in myself, thinking about myself. Dull, mindless, fearful. I have nothing to say – not ever, not to anyone.' Clearly this brief excursion into a world at war had a disturbing effect on Kafka – possibly because his lack of involvement made him feel guilty. At all events, he tells Felice soon after his return that he hopes to enlist; but in August the army turns him down. 23/24 May: spends Whitsun with Felice, Grete and Felice's sister in the Bohemian mountains. He sees Felice again in June, at Karlsbad.

October – first public recognition: Carl Sternheim, winner of the 1915 Fontane Prize for Literature, offers to pass the prize money on to Kafka as a mark of his esteem, and during this month 'The Metamorphosis' appears for the first time, in a literary magazine. The story is published in book form a month later, and while the manuscript is being prepared for the press the publisher, Kurt Wolff, informs Kafka that he has commissioned an artist to furnish a frontispiece. Kafka writes back in alarm, 'It occurred to me ... that [the artist] might want to draw the insect itself. Please, not that – anything but that! ... The insect itself cannot be drawn. It cannot even be shown in the distance.' Kafka knows that the ambiguities of his fiction can only be accommodated in the mind, in the imagination: to *draw* his images is to resolve their ambiguity, 'take them literally' – and hence destroy them. Christmas: 'Always this one big fear: If only I had left [Prague] in 1912, at the height of my powers ...'

1916

March: Kafka now has to work longer hours at the office. He longs for release: 'I'm desperate, like a caged rat, ravaged by insomnia and headaches. ...' The headaches of which he has complained for years rarely seem to leave him now, and in April he consults a doctor about his nervous condition (despite an abiding mistrust of orthodox medicine: he once told Felice that his two younger brothers died 'through the fault of the doctors').

In May Kafka visits Marienbad on business, and tells Felice that it is 'unbelievably beautiful'. In July he takes three weeks' holiday there, sharing the first eleven days with Felice; they occupy adjacent hotel rooms. 5 July: 'The strains of living together. The forced product of strangeness, compassion, lust, cowardice, vanity: and only right down at the bottom is there – perhaps – a thin trickle that deserves the name of "love", too remote to be discovered – a flash of light glimpsed for the fraction of a second.' Yet he writes to Brod of their future plans in cautiously optimistic mood: 'What we've agreed, briefly, is this: to get married when the war is over and take two or three rooms in a Berlin suburb, with each of us being separately responsible for our own economic needs. F. will carry on working as at present, and I – well, I'm not sure about that yet.' It sounds an unlikely arrangement – a marriage and yet not a marriage. After Marienbad Kafka again begins to write to Felice almost daily, and he encourages her to become involved in the teaching work of the Jewish People's Centre in Berlin, of which Brod is a sponsor. He follows her work with keen interest, making detailed suggestions about the curriculum.

19 October: 'I cannot believe that any woman in any fairy tale has ever been fought for with such desperate determination as I have fought for you – right from the beginning, at every turn along the way, and perhaps for evermore.'

10 November: Kafka gives a public reading of 'In the Penal Colony' in Munich, where he stays for two days. Felice comes to meet him there. Later in the month he begins to write in the evenings in a tiny house which his sister Ottla has rented in the old Alchimistengasse, under the walls of the Hradčany Castle.

1917

Winter months of 1916/1917: Kafka writes 'A Country Doctor' and several other stories. March: moves to new rooms, where he plans to live with Felice after the war. His new quarters are unheated, and he continues to write in the Alchimistengasse until May; but coal is very scarce this winter. 'The Great Wall of China' probably dates from this period. In July Kafka and Felice become engaged for the second time.

9 August: Kafka wakes in the night and brings up blood from his lungs. Next day the doctor diagnoses bronchitis. Three weeks later he writes to Ottla (who since April has been looking after her brother-in-law's farm at Zürau [Siřem] in Northern Bohemia): although the doctor is non-committal, Kafka knows it is tuberculosis: 'And now it begins.' He sees the disease as the symptom and symbol of a more general failure: 'I sometimes think that my brain and my lungs must have conspired in secret. "Things can't go on like this," said the brain; and now, five years later, the lungs have agreed to help.' More particularly he sees it as the 'final defeat' in the 'battle' for Felice – a battle fought for five years between the warring principles of good and evil within him, and ending now with the triumph of evil: 'Deep down, you see, I feel that this illness of mine is not tuberculosis – or at least, not tuberculosis first and foremost ... the blood doesn't come from my lungs – it comes from a fatal blow struck by one of the two contenders. . . . I shall not recover.'

12 September: having obtained extended leave of absence from work – the doctor's certificate looks like 'a passport to eternity', he writes – Kafka goes to stay with Ottla in Zürau. Here he rests completely and relishes his

freedom. His long letters to his Prague friends are notably cheerful and full of wry self-mockery: 'Perhaps I shall be the new village idiot. ...' He enjoys village life, and observes it with affection and indulgence. He is well aware of being an outsider – 'My relationships with the people here are so loose, so vague: it isn't like normal earthly existence at all' – and Kafka will draw upon the memories of these months when he comes to write *The Castle* in 1922. 20/21 September: Felice visits him, ten days after he has told her of his illness.

25 September: 'Stories like "A Country Doctor" can still give me a passing satisfaction ... but real happiness will only come if I can lift the world into the realm of purity, truth, immutability.' In November he writes to Brod and speaks of his present circumstances as the logical sequel to a catalogue of failures: 'In the city, in family life, in my job, in society, in my love relationship (put that at the top of the list, if you like) and in the community at large – whether the one that exists or the one we are to strive after – in all these areas I have failed to stand the test. ...' Christmas: Kafka and Felice meet in Prague, and the engagement is dissolved. Their relationship ends.

1918

Kafka's sojourn in Zürau is prolonged until the end of April, when he returns to work in Prague. Two years later he will speak of the months in Zürau as 'perhaps the best time of my life.' Preparations for the publication of the collection *A Country Doctor* (comprising the story of that name and thirteen other pieces) continue throughout the year. In March Kafka calls it 'probably my last book'.

In mid-October he succumbs to the world-wide influenza epidemic (which killed an estimated twenty million people in 1918 and 1919): he is in bed for three weeks. The last days of October see the emergence of the new Czechoslovak state; and on 11 November a declaration by the Emperor Charles marks the formal dissolution of the Habsburg monarchy – the end of Austria-Hungary.

19 November: Kafka returns to work for a few days, but then falls ill again. 30 November: having obtained further sick-leave he travels to Schelesen [Želizy], north of Prague, to convalesce in a guest house. He spends Christmas in Prague.

1919

January/February: back in Schelesen Kafka meets Julie Wohryzek, the daughter of a Jewish shoemaker and synagogue attendant, and they enjoy each other's company in the almost deserted guest house. To Brod he writes (2 March): 'At a rough guess I'd say that I haven't laughed so much in the last five years as I have in the last few weeks.' Julie is already back in Prague when Kafka comes home at the end of March, and their relationship continues.

In the summer they become engaged. Kafka's father is furious (at the beginning of the year he had already opposed Ottla's plans to marry Josef David, a Gentile – and at that time an impecunious law student). He regards Julie's family as socially inferior (their orthodoxy is not likely to improve their standing in his eyes), and he humiliates Kafka deeply by insinuating that she is little more than a whore whom he is marrying for sexual gratification. Nevertheless, the wedding is arranged for early November. It falls through, ostensibly because of a last-minute hitch; but the real reason, clearly, was Kafka's abiding fear of marriage. 'The whole thing was a contest between the actual outward circumstances and my own inner weakness. ... My father's opposition ... was a distraction that took my mind off the real dangers ... in the end I couldn't go on, and I had to tell her.'

He returns to Schelesen. In the celebrated letter which he now writes to his father – but never sends – he attempts to analyse the deeply flawed father-son relationship. Mindful of recent events, he writes at length about his ambivalent attitudes to marriage: 'To marry and start a family, accepting all the children who are born, supporting them in this uncertain world of ours, and even giving them a certain amount of guidance: I regard this as the ultimate in human achievement. ... So why haven't I married? ... I'm obviously mentally incapable of marriage.' More specifically, Kafka reiterates the old argument that marriage might jeopardize his writing; more profoundly, he suggests that matrimony would be a form of filial hubris, a futile attempt to set himself up as his father's equal in the sphere of tangible social achievement: 'Marriage is not open to me for the simple reason that it is *your* territory.' 21 November: he returns to work, still engaged to Julie.

1920

Beginning of April: travels to take the cure at Merano in northern Italy. From here he begins writing to Milena Jesenská-Polak, a young, most unhappily married Czech woman, living in Vienna. A journalist and a translator, Milena has received Kafka's permission to translate some of his stories into Czech. They have met briefly in Prague. The correspondence soon develops a formidable momentum and intensity; and through the medium of the written word Kafka and Milena fall in love. (Two years later, when the high point of their relationship is long past, Kafka will write this: 'One could say that all the misfortune in my life stems from letters. ... I have hardly ever been deceived by people, but letters have deceived me without fail – not other people's letters, but my own.' One is reminded of an earlier aphorism, contained in a letter to Grete Bloch: 'Sentences have their own force of gravity. You can't escape from it.'

Under the strain of this emotional involvement his health fails to improve; far from being a rest-cure, his three-month stay in Merano is a time of trial and endurance. In May he complains again of insomnia, and in June he tells Milena, 'I am mentally ill, and the disease in my lungs is only the mental illness overspilling its banks.' 27 June: leaves Merano and travels to Vienna, where he sees Milena on five consecutive days. Thence to Prague – and the prompt dissolution of his engagement to Julie. In August Milena makes it clear that she will not leave her husband for Kafka's sake. He replies, 'I knew it all along, like a man who has passed the whole day behind closed shutters, lost in sleep and dreams and fearfulness, and who then opens the window when evening comes, and is not in the least surprised – for he has known it all along – to find that it is now dark outside – intensely, wonderfully dark.'

A week later they meet for a night and a day at Gmünd, on the Austrian-Czech frontier; but by mid-September Kafka accepts that their relationship cannot develop any further: 'We shall never live together, in the same house, side by side, eating together at one table, never. ...' In late August he has reverted to his old pattern of sleeping in the afternoons and writing in the hours of the night: 'A few days ago I went back on "active service" again – or back in training, at least. ...' But he knows that his health is no longer equal to this kind of strain, and has little hope of producing anything. In October the doctor recommends a three-month course of treatment at a sanatorium. 18 December: Kafka goes on sick-leave once more, to a sanatorium at Matljary* in the High Tatra Mountains. 'I am filthy, Milena, utterly filthy. That's why I am always going on about purity. Nobody sings with such a pure voice as those who are in the very depths of hell: what we take to be the singing of angels is really *their* song.'

1921

Early February: Kafka meets Robert Klopstock, a young Jewish medical student from Budapest, who soon becomes his principal companion at Matljary – a combination of friend, disciple and unofficial personal assistant. Kafka helps him unselfishly, trying to find him a job, lending him books,

* See below, pp. 238ff.

and even getting his girl-friend into art school. On medical advice Kafka's original three months' leave is twice extended, to a total of eight months. Although he feels deeply guilty about taking so much leave – he is still on full salary – he tells Ottla he cannot contemplate quitting his job for a new way of life: 'The Insurance Institute is like an eiderdown, heavy and warm. If I crawled out from underneath it I should immediately run the risk of catching a cold: they don't heat the outside world.' The winter is hard, and Kafka feels that his condition is worsening. The first six weeks in Matljary (he writes) have done him less good than three days and nights in Merano. But he refuses to complain: 'When it gets dark we will light a candle: and when the candle has burnt down we will lie quietly in the dark. In our Father's house are many mansions – and for that reason we should take care not to make any noise.' For the first time (he continues) he has looked his illness 'straight in the eye'. Late August: returns to work in Prague. But his health deteriorates further, and his hours at the office are merely a token gesture. Milena visits him from time to time and Kafka gives her his diaries, with instructions to give them to Brod after his death. At the end of October he obtains another three months' sick-leave.

1922

Kafka probably begins to write *The Castle* in late January. His leave is extended yet again, and he goes to Spindlermühle in the mountains of Northern Bohemia for four weeks. At the hotel he finds that his name has been entered as 'Josef K.': 'Shall I tell them? Or is it they who have something to tell me?' 15 March: reads early portions of *The Castle* to Brod. In June he retires on a pension (since doctors have ruled out any chance of an early recovery) and goes to stay with Ottla in Planá, in rural surroundings close to the Czech-German frontier in southern Bohemia. By now he has written 'A Hunger Artist'.

July: Kafka abandons plans to visit Oskar Baum in Germany because of a sudden attack of *Angst* – a state of mind he has described in his letters to Milena. It is, as he now tells Oskar, 'a dreadful fear of any kind of change ... the fear of attracting the attention of the gods.' He chronicles four such 'breakdowns' during the summer in Planá, and it seems clear that his extreme sensitivity at this particular time (underlined by an aversion to noise which now verges on the pathological) is bound up with his work on *The Castle*: the isolation which that novel depicts is also the condition of its writing. 'The writer's existence is totally dependent on his desk, and unless he wants to go mad he should never leave it; he must hold on by his teeth.' But in early September he writes, 'I've had to abandon the castle story for good, it seems. . . .' 19 September: Kafka returns finally to Prague.

1923

In the spring Kafka meets an old school friend who is visiting Prague from Jerusalem. For years Kafka has been applying himself to the study of Hebrew, and has toyed occasionally with the notion of visiting Palestine – perhaps even of emigrating there. Now he contemplates the possibility once more. Early July: accompanies Elli and family to Müritz on the Baltic coast for a holiday. Here he meets Dora Diamant (Dymant), a Jewish girl half his age, who is cooking for a party of children at the holiday home run by the Jewish People's Centre in Berlin – the same organization that Felice had worked for. He soon feels very close to this little Jewish community: 'For half of the days and nights the house, the woods and the beach are full of song. When I'm with them I'm not happy; but I stand at the threshold of happiness.' Clearly Kafka is searching for his own Judaic heritage at this time – the climax of a long process of reaction to that 'miserable scrap of Jewishness' bequeathed to him by his father; and in Dora, an accomplished student of Hebrew, whose family are adherents of the highly spiritual Hasidic movement, he finds a friend able to answer that need. They rapidly become very close. Mid-August: after a few days in Prague Kafka accompanies Ottla and her children to Schelesen, where he stays some five weeks. Having abandoned the Palestine scheme as 'a fantasy', he now conceives an alternative plan of escape from Prague (for such, plainly, was his aim). To Robert Klopstock he writes, 'Palestine would have been beyond my reach anyway, of course; but now that I have Berlin as a possible alternative it isn't even necessary any more. Mind you, Berlin is almost beyond my reach as well. . . .' On 24 September he moves to Berlin to live with Dora* He calls it 'a reckless move which can only be compared to some great historical event, like Napoleon's Russian campaign'. And to Ottla he writes, 'This whole Berlin business is such a fragile thing, something I grasped at with my last ounce of strength. . . .'

1924

Kafka's health deteriorates rapidly, and the high cost of living in Berlin causes him anxiety. Yet he remains cheerful: 'If only I could make some money! But around here nobody pays you for staying in bed until midday.' 17 March: Brod takes him back to Prague. In early April he is moved to a sanatorium in Lower Austria, then to a clinic in Vienna. Dora is with him

* For Kafka's last year, see below, pp. 203ff.

constantly; and Robert Klopstock interrupts his studies in Berlin to remain at his friend's bedside. A week later Kafka is transferred to a sanatorium in nearby Kierling. He now has tuberculosis of the larynx – a disease whose appalling effects he witnessed three years before in a fellow-patient at Matljary: 'It's far worse than an execution, far worse than torture even ... this slow funeral pyre, not actually burning, just smouldering away. ...' (The patient subsequently committed suicide – as Kafka knew.)

The doctors can do nothing to help Kafka, apart from giving him pain-killing injections. Because of the condition of his throat he can scarcely eat or drink, and instead of talking he converses by writing notes.* 11 May: Max Brod visits his friend for the last time. Kafka has just received a letter of refusal from Dora's father, from whom he has sought permission to marry Dora. 3 June: Kafka dies, one month before his forty-first birthday.

Kafka is buried in Prague's Jewish Cemetery on 11 June, at four o'clock in the afternoon.† When the funeral party returns to the Kafka family home in the Old Town a couple of hours later, Brod observes that the great Town Hall clock has stopped. The hands are pointing to four o'clock.

---

* See below, p. 248.
† See below, pp. 56–61.

2

Kafka's Prague

F.W.Carter

Und es werfelt und brodelt
und kafkat und kischt . . .
Parody of Friedrich Schiller's 'Der Taucher'

Prague at the beginning of this century was the provincial capital of
Bohemia. It had been part of the Austro-Hungarian monarchy since the
Provincial Constitution proclaimed in 1627, when the Czech throne was
made hereditary in the Habsburg dynasty. Prague's population, including
several suburbs, as recorded in the census of 1900, was a little over half a
million. In that year Franz Werfel was ten, Max Brod was sixteen, Kafka
was seventeen, Egon Erwin Kisch fifteen, and Rainer Maria Rilke twenty-
five. All these writers were born in Prague and although none lived there
continuously throughout his entire life, the social, intellectual and political
atmosphere of the city deeply influenced them, as it did other writers who
were active in it at different times.

It was not until the late eighteenth century that increasing industrial
progress led to an economic and political revival in the city, resulting
during the first half of the nineteenth century in its achieving an unrivalled
position as the central focus of Bohemia. This helps explain why, in 1837,
the Czech dramatist J.K. Tyl wrote, 'Once in his lifetime every Czech
must behold Prague, once he must come to its gates, like an unbelieving
Moslem to the bones of the Prophet.' This idea of Prague as the 'Mecca of
Bohemia' was enhanced by its position on the River Vltava (Moldau), just
where its valley begins to broaden and the plateau in which it has been
incised begins to sink towards the Labe (Elbe) plain. It lies close to the
junction of two physical environments and must, like so many foot-hill

towns of Europe, have derived some importance from this fact. The favourable factors which together produced the Prague environment are perhaps best seen through the eyes of a foreign traveller; an Englishman, George Hibbert, on his tour through Europe at the end of the eighteenth century, wrote,

North from Vienna, the Tourist usually made for Dresden by way of Prague. An extremely beautiful city, though much damaged in the Seven Years War, Prague seems to have delighted nearly every Tourist who visited it. Its white stone houses, the fruitful countryside around it, its copper-roofed churches glittering in the sun, the fine Italian-like buildings, the Gothic Cathedral, the Regal residence, the people so handsome, the shops so good and everything looking so happy and delightful, induced one appreciative Tourist to describe Prague as the 'handsomest city in Europe'.

New life came to the urban development of Prague during the last few decades of the nineteenth century. During the early 1880s, Austria had recovered from the after-effects of the great Viennese stock exchange crash of 1873. The centre of Austrian industry remained as before in Bohemia, Moravia and Silesia, and contained three-fifths of all industrial establishments and production. Once industries had been firmly established in such centres as Prague, migration from country to capital placed greater pressure on the old city area, which rapidly became too small to shelter its new inhabitants. Symptomatic of this migration trend were Kafka's own parents; his father, Hermann, came to Prague from Osek, a village near Strakonice in Southern Bohemia, whilst his maternal ancestors lived in the Poděbrady region, fifty kilometres east of Prague.

Building construction within the city received great impetus from the demolition of its walls and the dismantling of fortifications in about 1875, while by the turn of the century the historic Jewish quarter, Josefov, one of the oldest parts of the mediaeval town, was pulled down. Only a few of its most valuable buildings were saved. Much of the area vacated by this demolition policy, both in 1875 and in 1896, was replaced by high blocks of flats, erected on land parcelled out schematically, without regard for the historic structure of the street pattern. Some measure of this building growth may be seen from the fact that in the last third of the nineteenth century the number of houses in the city increased by more than eighty per cent.

Such building activity reflected rapid population growth. Over the thirty-year period the number of inhabitants living in Prague more than doubled, from 239,790 in 1869 to 514,345 in 1900. The Jewish element in the Prague population rose from 20,508 in 1880 to 27,289 in 1900, yet the overall percentage of Jews in the total population declined from six to five per cent, and the German element too declined from thirteen to six per cent of the total population. Both groups showed a strong tendency to inhabit the central parts of the city, and many industrial establishments were owned by them. Migration from other parts of Bohemia was high; of every 1,000 members of the city's population 631 were not born in the city.

Another noticeable factor was the increase in personal movement in the city, resulting from improved means of communication. In the last decade of the century in Prague the speed of the horse trams could no longer compete with the tempo of industrial production. As late as 1896 the tram network was still best suited to movement within the single city nucleus, although it had expanded considerably over the previous decade. The large-scale introduction of electric tram services after 1896, however, meant that the average speed of local transport was more than doubled. Surprisingly, the volume of passenger rail traffic did not grow at such a rate, in spite of the centralized situation of the numerous railway terminals; and it was not until the end of the second decade of the twentieth century, when Prague was the new republic's capital, that the impact of rail travel really began to be felt. These facts are also reflected in Kafka's own life-style, for, according to his diaries, his personal mobility increased noticeably as the twentieth century progressed.

Into the fabric of Prague's urban society was also woven another factor – namely, the ethnic problem. It has justifiably been called a 'City of Three Peoples' and this ethnic juxtaposition helped give Prague a particular character. This mixture led to manifold national and social tensions, and gave the Jews a special status as bearers of German culture amidst an overwhelmingly Czech majority. It is factors such as these which help to explain why, through transmission, assimilation and development, the writers of 'the Prague-German School' came to occupy a wholly individual and characteristic place in early twentieth-century German literature.

Against this more general backcloth we may now look at those strands in the city's life and environment which were more closely connected with Franz Kafka's work. Our attention must therefore be focused more intimately on Josefov, or the Jewish Town, where the Prague Jews have lived for over a thousand years. It is known from extant documents that two Jewish settlements already existed in the city by about 1091 AD. Today, if you walk along Maislova Street towards the Old Town Square, you come to the corner house of the street which is now called U radnice ('at the Town Hall'). The original house on the site was the prelature of the Benedictine Monastery; you will see that Franz Kafka was born on this spot on 3 July 1883, but only the portal from the later Baroque house, in which the writer was born, still exists.

Kafka was born in the mediaeval heart of the city, with its narrow streets and compact structure. The 'Spring of Nations' movement, culminating in the 1848 revolution, had meant that Prague's Jews were granted civil and political rights. In 1852 the city's ghetto was abolished and united with four other wards to form the fifth district known as Josefov (in German, Josefstadt). Here Franz Kafka spent his earliest years, but growing discontent throughout the city at the unhygienic conditions in the former Jewish quarter led the Prague municipal council to agree to its abolition in 1896. After this date the whole quarter was subject to the rigours of urban renewal, although the most important historic sites were left intact. Only the Jewish cemetery, the synagogues (the Pinkas, Klaus, Maisel and Hoch) and the Town Hall, along with a few other places of historical interest, were spared, and extensive demolition encouraged the exodus of the quarter's inhabitants to other parts of the city.

Although central Prague remained a strong magnet for Kafka throughout his years in the city, the ever-growing suburbs also attracted him for short or longer sojourns. By 1900 only one-third of Prague's total population was living within the central city areas (that is, those formerly enclosed by the city walls), compared with two-thirds in 1869. Two factors appear to have contributed to this situation: higher rents and improved public transport. With the rapid growth during the second half of the nineteenth century, both private and commercial rents rose significantly in the central parts of the city. In many of the surrounding suburbs much lower rents and house prices prevailed, and these areas were subject to high immigration both from central Prague and from the surrounding Bohemian countryside. Several suburbs which originally had Czech working-class populations now attracted increasing numbers of Jews, many of them from the smaller provincial communities. Many joined in the industrial growth of these suburbs, especially the textile, clothing, leather, shoe and food industries, and through wholesale and retail trade they gradually accumulated considerable wealth. From Kafka's diaries one learns that his visits to these inner suburbs after 1900, when city travel improved, became more frequent. Throughout the summer of 1919 he lived in the suburb of Vršovice; he frequently visited the village of Roztoky in the Vltava valley north of the city, and went for long walks in nearby Sedlec. Also to the north of the city is the suburb of Troja, where the environment was thought to benefit Kafka's health; at its renowned 'Pomological Institute' he spent the last summer of the First World War.

In spite of these occasional excursions to the suburbs, it was undoubtedly the city centre, with its varied social life, that attracted him most strongly. In fact, though he changed residences many times, Kafka continued to live in old Prague, even after he had left his parents' house and moved into his own apartment. 'Every ancient city has a high erotic tension; this is as true of Prague as of Vienna, of Venice as of Paris', writes Pavel Eisner, a younger contemporary from the same milieu; the point is underlined in Kafka's diaries, when he describes the appearance of strange girls whom he happened to see in Wenceslas Square (*Václavské náměstí*), the city's main thoroughfare. This may have been one side of the city's attraction for him, but the people of Prague also liked to gather for conversation in coffee-houses. Vilém Haas writes about city life in 1912: 'Prague seemed to be a dead city. The windows of the old palaces were blind and dark; grass grew on the pavement of the narrow lanes ... the porter on his small bench sat and smoked his pipe and breathed the evening breeze. The lanes were empty. The city seemed empty and mute. We sat in our café and talked.'

Much has been written about the various meeting-places in the city, the most important of which was the Café Continental. Max Brod saw this as 'one of the citadels of German Prague', favoured by the local representatives of German literature and much visited by Kafka. Younger writers preferred the Café Central, where no nationality predominated, but this later lost its popularity to the Café Arco in Hybernská Street. Franz Werfel was a regular visitor, Kafka less so. A smarter clientele frequented the Café Louvre, where Kafka went with Max Brod in 1905. Other coffee-houses of note in Prague at that time were the Café Edison, situated on the old Town Moat or Ditch (*Na příkopě*), a popular meeting-place frequented by Kafka; the Café Geiringer, where the Zionists congregated; and still others, such as the Café Savoy, Café City, and Café Paris, all conjuring up Brod's image of such places as 'free and open to ideas, crammed together in four or five rooms, smoky, stifling, thick with the fumes of mocha coffee'.

Closely associated with this development of social integration was the growth in importance of the local press, clubs and literary societies. Prague in the second half of the nineteenth century witnessed a genuine growth in literacy; demand from an increasingly literate society was reflected in the establishment of daily newspapers and journals, which all played an integral part in the 'knowledge explosion' of nineteenth-century Austria-Hungary. By 1877 there were thirty-eight journals and newspapers in the city, of which twenty-four were published in the Czech language. Increased literacy is a major aspect of the national revival; it is reflected in book-borrowing from Prague's libraries, which, towards the end of the century, averaged one book a year for every ten people in the city. Greater literacy also provided increased outlets for the city's writers, but again the three-fold nature of its society clearly emerged in the printed word. During the 1860s several new daily newspapers in Czech were founded, including *Čas* (*Time*) and *Národní listy* (*National Journal*); the former, which was certainly read by Kafka, had T.G. Masaryk among its contributors. Jews who felt themselves to be Czech had founded at the turn of the century the assimilationist newspaper *Tribuna*. It had a forthright liberal voice and a notable literary supplement, in which Milena Jesenská-Polak published the first translation of one of Kafka's stories; after the First World War, Jaroslav Hašek, author of *The Good Soldier Švejk*, was among its contributors. Other Czech journals having Kafka connections included *Rozvoj* (the Czech-Jewish assimilationist paper), *Kmen* (where Jesenská published a collection of his reflections), and the monthly *Umělecký měsíčník*. The two major German-language dailies were *Prager Tagblatt* and *Bohemia*. At the turn of the century the latter (the official organ of the German Progressive Party) had been overtaken by the former in numbers of subscribers, but both had a substantial Jewish following, and Max Brod and Kafka himself read them and wrote for them. In 1907 the Prague Zionist weekly *Selbstwehr* had been founded and quickly attracted Kafka's attention for its serious articles about anti-Semitism and the courts' attitude to Jewish defendants. The other weekly journal founded by the Eastern Jewish group in Prague was the *Prager Jüdische Zeitung*, which appeared simultaneously in the German and Yiddish languages. Numerous journals from Austria and Germany were avidly read and discussed in the coffee-houses, among them Expressionist periodicals like *Die Aktion* and *Die Weissen Blätter*, the Catholic journal *Das Hochland*, *Hyperion* (largely devoted to poetry), and Karl Kraus's satirical magazine *Die Fackel*.

An obvious outlet for much of the written word were the discussions held, not only informally in the coffee-houses, but in the more serious literary meetings and clubs. In the 1880s a group of Prague German-Jewish authors founded a club known as the 'Prague circle' ('Der Prager Kreis'), which was later to achieve international recognition and included Kafka, Max Brod, Franz Werfel, Oskar Baum, Ludwig Winder, Leo Perutz, Egon Erwin Kisch, Otto Klepetář and Vilém Haas. In his reminiscences of the year 1912 Haas writes, 'I like to revive the memory of a little magazine (*Herderblätter*) that I edited together with the poet and journalist, Otto Pick. We had what seemed to us quite a lot of money from a club in Prague.' And he continues, 'The third issue contained the first contribution by Franz Kafka and Max Brod – a joint work; it was the story "Richard and Samuel", a journal of Brod's and Kafka's trip to northern Italy. Kafka's publications were rather personal and intimate and not the sort he liked to submit to a larger circle of readers. We had about one hundred subscribers only', but, Haas adds, 'our club awoke once more from its lethargy during that year.' Some of the literary meetings were held in cafés and Haas describes how 'Franz Kafka smiled silently. ... He seemed elusive. But a tender word in a poem, even a bad poem, could move him profoundly.'

There were also clubs with more political leanings. Kafka frequented the Czech Young Men's Club (Klub mladých) in Prague, an association of Czech literary radicals, and there made the personal acquaintance of such young socialists and anarchists as Karel Toman, S.K. Neumann, Fráňa Šrámek, and Jaroslav Hašek. This club agitated for socialist ideals and protested against the increasingly militaristic attitude of the state. In 1912, in the working-class suburb of Žižkov, Kafka attended a meeting of Hašek's famous spoof club, the 'Political Party of Moderate Progress within the Law'.

The majority of Jewish students were members of the German Student Debating and Reading Club, a German liberal organization, known as 'die Halle' for short. It contained a section for literature and art, where authors, many of whom were natives of Prague, read their own works at meetings. Towards the end of the first decade of the twentieth century many students at the University joined the Bar Kochba. The organization had its origins in 1893 as a Jewish-national students' union founded in Prague; after 1899 it was dominated by Zionists, who gave it its Hebrew name. In 1913 a collective volume (*Vom Judentum*) was published for the Bar Kochba by the Leipzig publishers Kurt Wolff and Ernst Rowohlt, who in that year also listed Max Brod and Kafka in their author catalogue. (The students' union was named in memory of the revolutionary who, in 132 AD, led an uprising of the Jews against their Roman masters. In 1897 Jaroslav Vrchlický, the greatest of contemporary Czech poets, wrote a grandiose Romantic epic to commemorate Bar Kochba as a Jewish national hero and thus as an exemplar to the Czechs in their struggle for national independence. Vrchlický's poem has been mentioned as evidence of Czech philo-Semitism, yet, paradoxically, the Hebrew nationalism which the poem celebrates is the least characteristic aspect of Bohemia's most ancient minority, its Jewish population.)

One of the side-effects of late industrial development in the Habsburg Empire was that Prague, culturally, was an almost classless society; while noted class distinctions existed as far as occupation, income and living standards were concerned, culture created no barriers. Nevertheless, ethnic divisions still presented themselves. Perhaps this was most clearly illustrated by the city's theatres. In 1881 the Czechs built their own National Theatre, opening with a performance of Smetana's patriotic opera *Libuše*; four years later the German drama club built their equivalent, the German Theatre, under the direction of Angelo Neumann. He initiated the annual May Festival, in which the greatest German actors and singers took part. This festival contained such productions as the complete operatic works of Wagner, Verdi's operas, and cycles of classical dramas. It was also very popular among Prague Jewry, where (at the very end of Kafka's life) actors such as Ernst Deutsch were among its most celebrated performers. Cultural life flourished. Haas describes how 'in that same year, 1912, ... Nijinsky danced at the Prague Opera in Stravinsky's new ballet, *Petrouchka*, in *Le Spectre de la Rose*, in *Pavillon d'Armide*, and in Rimski-Korsakov's *Schéhérazade*. We seemed to live in a Paradise.'

At the turn of the century changes were also taking place in the amount of recreational space available in the city to its ever-growing number of inhabitants. It was becoming increasingly difficult to harmonize the mildly undulating hills on which the city stood with the straight lines and the great unbroken areas of modern dwelling-houses and official buildings which were regarded as the ideal of city planning, and which already in the nineteenth century were arising practically overnight. This planning process was the doing of the 'bestia triumphans', as the Czech writer Vilém Mrštík, at the end of the nineteenth century, called that conglomerate of administrative forces and speculators which tore down not only individual houses but entire streets, and replaced charming architectural corners by monotonous rows of houses. Many of these changes inevitably followed on the industrialization of the city, which brought the epoch of hustle and bustle, and ruthlessly threw away the heritage of the past without creating a style and expression of its own. This meant that the enclaves of green space in the city, the parks, became even more precious to the local inhabitants – Kafka mentions them frequently as meeting-places. Perhaps most popular was the open space around the castle and the left bank of the Vltava River, the earliest part of which, known as Chotek's Park (named after a Bohemian noble family), was founded in 1833. Nearer to the city centre was Městský sad (to which the Germans referred as Stadtpark), one of Kafka's favourite walking areas, together with the Rieger Park (named after a Czech nationalist politician) in the district known as the Royal Vineyards (Královské vinohrady), which had been created from the amalgamation of several former farms. Kafka was also able to appreciate some of the cultural legacies inherited from the past and set in these open spaces, like the 'Rudolfinum' palace, or the 'Mozarteum' – that is, the Bertram Villa in the suburb of Smíchov – where Mozart wrote his *Don Giovanni* for the city, after the triumphant success of *The Marriage of Figaro* in Prague in 1787.

A strong ethnic division was apparent in Prague's educational system. The very basis of the Austrian educational policy was the ideal of the universally educated person, and this fundamental theme ran through the whole school curriculum. At the elementary level most Jewish children went to the German Piaristenschule (a foundation of the Counter-Reformation), where, paradoxically, many of the teachers were Czech clergymen. The children, the great majority of whom were Jewish, were taught in German and encouraged to understand and appreciate German culture. (Strangely enough – as Felix Weltsch* later remarked – nobody thought this combination unusual.) The secondary or middle school was the Gymnasium, where the emphasis was on Greek and Latin, although natural sciences and mathematics were also well taught; no form of specialization was encouraged at this level. In September 1893 Kafka began attending the Altstädter Deutsches Staatsgymnasium (an exacting school designed for the academic élite), situated on the second floor of the Kinský Palace in the Old Town Square; his father had a shop on the ground floor. Kafka was one of twenty-four pupils in his class, of whom only two were non-Jewish, although there were no Jewish teachers, except for religion. Kafka was respected and liked by his teachers and a pen portrait of this time has been left us by his classmate, the painter Fritz Fiegl† : 'It was in the year 1894. . . . He was about ten years old, a thin, frail boy with very big, black eyes, a long skull and pointed ears which gave him a degenerate look. The reason why I remember him so clearly is that his mother always came to fetch him after school, which struck us other children as strange.'

Access to the university was through the *Matura* (matriculation) examination. Again, the concept of universal culture – the idea of *Allgemeinbildung* – was inherent in the higher educational system; even those candidates who wished to enter university to pursue such specialized courses as law or medicine had to show evidence of their appreciation of the humanities through an interest in music, art and literature. Accepted candidates then entered the privileged world of the *Akademiker* who, irrespective of his chosen subject, had to confirm his status with a knowledge of the classics, and be a regular attender at the opera, theatre, art galleries and musical concerts. Kafka entered this rarefied atmosphere in November 1901, to study chemistry under Professor Goldschmied; this course was followed by courses in Roman, Church and German law, and philosophy. Kafka's parents, like other Jews, had eagerly availed themselves of the opportunity to give their children a secular higher education. In 1882 the famous Charles University, established in 1348, was divided into two universities, German and Czech. (The Czech university was shut and many of its teachers and students executed by the Germans in 1941, and the process reversed, without the executions, in

* See below, pp. 47ff.
† See his portrait of Kafka, facing p. 217.

1945. Now there is only a Czech university in Prague.) In 1890 the Jewish students made up two-fifths of the German University students and less than one per cent of the Czech, a ratio which by 1925 had changed to 30 : 10 per cent.

Life within the university student clubs has been fully described by Max Brod. He talks of the various fraternities, some with their strict regulations and colours, similar to their counterparts in Germany, Vienna and Graz; in contrast, there were those students who belonged to no particular section, did not wear colours or distinctive caps, and refrained from any ceremonial drinking sessions. Kafka, like Brod, belonged to the latter group within 'die Halle', and it was in the Literary Section that the two first met and became friends – a friendship that was to have a decisive influence on Kafka's whole life, for Max Brod was to become 'his squire and herald'. Kafka's university career ended successfully in March 1906, with the award of a doctorate in law based on a thesis entitled 'German and Austrian State Law, Common Law and Political Economy'. His education was not yet over, however, for in 1909 he attended a course in mechanics at the Prague Technical High School, in connection with his growing interest in the factory work covered by the industrial insurance company for which he worked.

Underlying much of the discussion in this essay has been the importance of the Jewish community in Prague. Jews may have arrived in Prague during late Roman times, but the first documentary evidence is contained in reports by the Spanish Arabic-Jewish merchant Ibrahim ibn Jakub in 965–6. His information suggests that Jews had either settled in Prague or carried out business there without necessarily being permanent citizens. It is safe to assume that the ancient Jewish community in Prague dates back to the first Přemyslids, the Czech ruling dynasty in Bohemia, from the ninth to the early fourteenth centuries. Jews came to Prague from the south across the Alps, and through the Balkans from the east. The theory of the eastern origin of the earliest Prague Jews, combined with the legacy of Slavonic language traditions, has been fortified by Roman Jakobson's discoveries that the first Czech grammarian was a Talmudist from the Prague ghetto. Between the thirteenth and sixteenth centuries Prague Jews increasingly spoke German, many new arrivals coming particularly from Bavaria and Franconia with the new wave of German colonists invited by the Bohemian rulers. Protection provided by these kings (for example, by Přemysl Otokar II, in 1254) through special privileges, made it possible for larger numbers of Jews, especially those from Germany, to settle in the city. They suffered considerable hardship and persecution during the thirteenth and fourteenth centuries, while at the beginning of the fifteenth century they found themselves entangled in the religious and national conflicts associated with the Hussite wars. Their position remained insecure throughout that century, to be followed in the sixteenth by repeated attempts at expulsion; these failed to achieve their aim and the number of Jews in the city rose from six hundred to twelve hundred between 1522 and 1541. Successful attempts to found new communities in the New Town (Nové Město) and the Little Quarter (Malá Strana) were relinquished in about 1500 in order to consolidate and extend the Jewish quarter in the Old Town (Staré Město); this was accompanied by the rebuilding of the Altneuschul (the Old-New Synagogue – the oldest extant synagogue in Europe) and the construction of the new Pinkas Synagogue, completed in 1535; Kafka had connections with both, for in them he met such Jewish intellectuals as the satirist Kurt Tucholsky and the artist Kurt Szafranski, and also studied the Talmud under Dr Jeiteles.

A noticeable contribution to the progress of the Jewish community was the founding of a Hebrew printing works. One Gershom Kohen came from Italy in 1512, and founded a printing business in the city. His first book was a collection of miscellaneous prayers. Although not the first in Europe, it became one of the Continent's most important printing works. The seventeenth century was to witness the steady development of Jewish culture in Prague under the influence of several notable rabbis, while David Gans, the chronicler and astronomer, lived there during this period. By 1600 Prague contained about six thousand Jews, and in 1627 the area occupied by the community was almost doubled with the purchase of the so-called Lichtenstein houses (named after the man who made a census of Prague houses in 1805). Plague was to reduce the number of Jews by half in 1680, while the anti-Semitic policy of Maria Theresa led to their expulsion in 1745–8. Further tragedy struck in 1754, when a large part of the Jewish quarter was devastated by fire, but, in spite of all these setbacks, Jewish culture continued to flourish in the city, being fostered by some famous rabbis during the Baroque period.

According to Ruth Kestenberg-Gladstein, 'Throughout the eighteenth century, in fact from 1650 to the beginning of the nineteenth century, the Prague Jewish quarter was by far the largest Jewish settlement to exist anywhere. The circumstance that its population over this long period was stated as a mere 10,000 souls was doubtless connected with legitimate fears about restriction; the actual numbers must have been far higher.' The reign of Joseph II was one of conciliation toward the Jews, as expressed in his 'Toleranzpatent' of 1782. Nevertheless, restrictions on their freedom still remained. For example, only the eldest son of the family could marry; no son meant family extinction. Thus, Kafka's paternal grandfather, a second-born, had to wait until 1848 (when Jews obtained equal civil rights) before he could marry; he was then thirty-five. Conversely, some more enterprising Jews gained considerably from Joseph's reforms. This was particularly noticeable in the textile industry. Some of the first Jewish industrialists, having founded much-needed industrial establishments in the city, were now permitted to live outside Prague's Jewish quarter.

The reigns of Maria Theresa and Joseph II had seen concerted efforts to Germanize the Habsburg lands. The process of Germanization was greatest in the city, and, with the abolition of the Prague ghetto in 1852, the Jewish inhabitants with their more liberal style of life now attached themselves to the German element of the city's population. This seemed to them quite natural, for German was, according to the Viennese government, the 'language of the land'. By 1848 Prague's Jewish population of ten thousand was certainly much larger than that of Vienna (four thousand); perhaps Prague now deserved the eighteenth-century accolades of 'the metropolis of Israel', 'the Mother of Jewry' and 'the City and Mother in Israel'. Nor was the increase of Jewish inhabitants in the city to decline, for in 1880, three years before Kafka's birth, there were twice as many (namely, 20,508) as in 1848. Thus the process of Germanization (Jews were even officially required to attend German schools), combined with the rapid growth in their numbers, helps to explain how Kafka was regarded as being a German Jew coming, not from Czech but from German Prague; in this sense he was a product of the time in which he lived and wrote his works.

The detailed statistics of the time show the numerical development of the Jewish population in Prague, which included suburbs incorporated into the city, some only after the First World War. The period roughly corresponds to Kafka's own residence there, and illustrates the movement away from the old quarter (which in 1870 contained over half of Prague Jewry), to disperse throughout the city (leaving less than a quarter in the central area by 1900). Although there was a steady numerical increase of Jews in Prague over the period, more significantly, their percentage of the total population – as well as that of the non-Jewish German element – declined in the face of a growing Czech majority.

At the same time, however, the small Jewish community in Prague became economically comfortable, and by 1900 many of its members had joined the ranks of the city's middle classes. On leafing through a Prague directory at the turn of the century, one could see Jewish names among the lawyers, doctors, chemists, technicians, teachers, writers, university professors and bank officials. Similarly, several had become successful industrialists and merchants, while others became skilled artisans and shop-keepers. Kafka was the product of such a Jewish middle-class family, whose father, through hard work and with the support of his wife's parents and their money, had gradually built up a business on which he could comfortably support his family and himself. This 'self-made man' image, common among many Jewish businessmen of the period, was to bedevil Franz Kafka's thoughts throughout his life.

The first decade of the twentieth century saw an awakening of the Jewish consciousness in Prague, in which Kafka participated in his own way. Many of the German-Jewish intellectuals (Max Brod, Egon Erwin Kisch, Franz Werfel)* who became associated with Kafka were also aware of this new trend, expressing an increased interest in and sympathy for a socially conscious type of Zionism. Much of this was no doubt part of a subconscious attempt to reject the growing Gentile environment of the Western Jew and to seek a chance to return to the Eastern Jewish way of life, of which the orthodox wing of Zionism was an offshoot. The way these intellectuals perceived their environment – the Prague milieu – may have encouraged their efforts; with its old palaces and royal castle without a king, it contained the right atmosphere to nurture a strong belief in the past and pride in one's individual identity. One of Kafka's class-mates, Hugo Bergmann, together with his family, provided the driving force of Prague's Zionist movement, interpreted through the activities of the Bar Kochba. Cafés offered the ideal meeting-places for members of the Zionist movement, which led Max Brod to remark, 'If the ceiling of a certain café collapses, then that's the end of all Prague Zionism.' It is quite remarkable how the young movement gained success, for already by 1918 the Zionists on the Prague municipal council had commanded two mandates, and thus obtained a position of political power.

The world of 'old Prague' was to change for ever. To any observant citizen it must have been clear that during the first decade of the new century the Austro-Hungarian Empire was being allowed to slide towards a severe crisis. Haas and his fellow-intellectuals were well aware of this situation: 'The voices of the fighting nations sounded from afar, echoed in the Viennese Parliament. The Imperial Cavalry officers still walked proudly with their shining helmets and red breeches, their swords under their arms. But Austria was dying'; and, Haas continues, 'From the heart of the city another voice sounded ... the voice of the Czech nation who rallied round their standards.' The First World War terminated the life of the Austro-Hungarian political-economic unit, and in 1918 an independent Czechoslovak Republic was proclaimed. The desperate food situation and increased social radicalism were more strongly felt in the industrialized western part of the former empire than in Hungary. In Prague they had already manifested themselves during the last year of the war, when the city was rocked by mass rioting caused directly by reduced

* See the epigraph to this essay.

food rations, with outbreaks also occurring in the smaller Bohemian cities. Kafka, like other Prague citizens, had to acclimatize himself to a new environment, which was no longer a rather large provincial city in the Austro-Hungarian monarchy, but a European capital which was inevitably becoming a centre of wider political and economic interest.

Kafka, we can see, lived in Prague through an interesting phase of its history. The city had gradually made a transition from being a political, administrative centre of the Austro-Hungarian monarchy, where handicrafts predominated in trade and where emphasis had been placed on Germanization and adoration of German culture, to the new political, administrative capital of the Czech nation, where factory-based industrialization and commercial expertise came to be the hallmark of continued success. Outwardly, Prague still bore the characteristics of an Austrian provincial capital, but things were changing, for not only did the ethnic differences between German, Czech and Jew undergo a change of balance, but the intellectual controversies within the city became sharper and more intense. When, in 1923, a year before his death, Kafka left Prague for Berlin, there were profound personal reasons for his move. It may be however that the increasingly tense atmosphere of national and social conflict, which included an increase in anti-Semitism, helped to decide him to spend the last year of his life beyond what he had once called 'the sharp clutches of Little Mother Prague'.

3
The Spirit of the Place

Sheila Stern

Prague is not mentioned in any of Franz Kafka's major stories, yet it is the clearly implied location of most of them. Nobody doubts that Chapter 9 of *The Trial* takes place in St Vitus's Cathedral, next to the castle that overlooks the city. Such assumptions are made even by critics who have little interest in the 'real-life' equivalents of Kafka's fiction, if only because the unnamed streets and squares and bridges described in his stories are obviously the same as the streets and squares and bridges named in his letters and diaries. However, the 'Kafkaesque' quality of these descriptions is not confined to Kafka. Here is a nineteenth-century example:

So immediately did the imperial hill tower over the spot on which Balatka lived, that it would seem, at night, when the moon was shining ... that the colonnades of the palace were the upper storeys of some enormous edifice, of which the ... merchant's small courtyard formed a lower portion. The long rows of windows would glimmer in the sheen of the night, and Nina [the heroine] would stand in the gloom of the archway counting them till they would seem to be uncountable, and wondering what might be the thoughts of those who abode there. ... The windows of the palace look out ... from a thousand rooms. But the rooms have seldom many tenants, nor the tenants, perhaps, many thoughts. Chamber after chamber, you shall pass through them by the score, and know by signs unconsciously recognized that there is not, and never has been, true habitation within them. Windows almost innumerable are there, that they may be seen from the outside.

Later in the story in which this passage occurs, we are told of a young man, Ziska, who has entered a part of his own city where he has never been before, uncertain whether the people there will allow him to proceed about his dubious business. He is seeking Anton, his rival for Nina Balatka's love, who lives in that quarter and whom he hopes to outwit by a mean stratagem; two girls direct him to a public building where Anton may be found: 'Ziska would have escaped now from the project could he have done so without remark; but he was ashamed to seem afraid to enter the building, as the girls seemed to make so light of his doing so.'

There is just enough of a glimpse here into the uppermost layer, as it were, of Ziska's motives in intruding on what turns out to be a ceremonial occasion:

He could see that those inside the building were all clothed in muslin shirts of different lengths, and that it was filled with men, all of whom had before them some sort of desk, from which they were reading, or rather wailing out their litany. . . . There was no ceiling, and the high-pitched roof, which had once probably been coloured, and the walls, which had once certainly been white, were black with the dirt of ages. In the centre there was a cage or iron grille, within which five or six old men were placed who seemed to wail louder than the others. Round the walls there was a row of men inside stationary desks, and outside them another row, before each of whom there was a small movable standing desk. . . . There seemed to be no possible way by which Ziska could advance, and he would have been glad to retreat had retreat been possible. But first one and then another moved their desks for him, so that he was forced to advance, and some among them pointed to where Anton was standing. But as they pointed, and as they moved their desks to make a pathway, they still sang and wailed continuously, never ceasing for an instant in their long, loud, melancholy song of prayer. At the further end there seemed to be some altar, in front of which the High Priest wailed louder than all, . . . and even he was forced to move his desk to make way for Ziska. But, apparently without displeasure, he moved it with his left hand, while he swayed his right hand backwards and forwards as though regulating the melody of the wail. . . .

After asking Anton to follow him outside, 'Ziska turned to make his way back, but he saw that this was not to be his road for retreat. Behind him the movable phalanx had again formed itself into close rank, but before him the wailing wearers of the white shirts were preparing for the commotion of his passage by grasping the upright stick of their movable desks in their hands. So he passed on, making the entire round of the building. . . .'

In this accumulation of visual detail Ziska's embarrassment is left to our imagination, but we are subjected with him to the compulsion of the manoeuvres his presence brings about – the opening of a way through the throng and its closing up again behind him, desks and all. The incipient misery of his situation is swallowed up in its strangeness, and the matter-of-factness with which those present encourage him to disturb the ritual paradoxically transforms the strangeness into mystery.

Ziska is almost, though not quite, without a clue to the behaviour of those he encounters. Elsewhere in the story the intrigue set up by his mother, Sophie Zamenoy, and her maid causes Anton, Nina's betrothed, to behave in a way that she finds unfathomable. In the midst of assurances of his love he keeps returning to insistent, even bullying questions as to the whereabouts of the deeds of the house she lives in with her bankrupt father, who is on his death-bed. The deeds are Anton's by right, and she knows them to have been retained by her cousins the Zamenoys. But Ziska and his mother have told Anton that Nina has the deeds 'in her possession', implying that she distrusts his intentions and will try to keep them until he marries her. The truth is that the Zamenoys have secreted the title-deeds in Nina's desk among other papers; so she has them without knowing that she has them.

Nina's helplessness and bewilderment in the face of Anton's questions and, ultimately, of his accusations, are similar to the helplessness we are familiar with in Kafka's stories, but since the reader has been enabled to guess where the document is and who put it there, this is a Kafka story *en clair*. If it had been written by Kafka, the lovers would no doubt have parted finally in the intolerable atmosphere of distrust and resentment brought about by the conspiracy. As the author is Anthony Trollope, good sense and good will prevail.

The Zamenoys are inspired by their profound loathing of all Jews and their determination to prevent Nina's marriage to the Jew Anton. It is to the Prague ghetto that Ziska goes as a stranger and the worship he interrupts is of course taking place in the synagogue. The uninhabited but many-eyed and baleful palace is the Hradčany Castle, on which 'the moon was shining as it shines only at Prague'. At the end of the story the destitute Christian girl marries the wealthy Anton, but they leave Prague to live in Frankfurt, where a mixed marriage will be accepted.

Trollope, who had visited Prague shortly before he wrote *Nina Balatka*, rated this novel highly enough to accept philosophically its relative lack of success. Writing of the popularity of *The Eustace Diamonds*, he says, 'I have done better things – *Phineas Finn* and *Nina Balatka* for instance. ...' His intention and experimental style in this work were connected with his sense of the injustice inherent in the warm reception accorded to each new product of the established writer, while a new author is mercilessly criticized: 'I determined ... to begin a course of novels anonymously, in order that I might see whether I could obtain a second identity. ...' The intensity with which the topography and atmosphere of Prague are evoked may be considered the great virtue of *Nina Balatka*: it strongly conveys Trollope's perception that Prague, more than other cities, puts the stamp of its physical being on its inhabitants – even to the point, as it seems, of causing Anthony Trollope to anticipate something of the manner of Franz Kafka.

4

The Rise and Fall of the Jewish-German Symbiosis: The Case of Franz Kafka*

Felix Weltsch

I A Centre of Thriving Assimilation: Prague at the Beginning of the Twentieth Century

The city is Prague, the period is the first quarter of the century, the man is Franz Kafka.

The strange fate of this city, where Germans and Czechs had confronted each other since time immemorial, had made the Germans aggressive and nationally conscious. Oddly enough, the same historical evolution had, for the most part, made the Jews of the city into nationally conscious – Germans.

The influx of the Jews from the times of Moses Mendelssohn onwards into German cultural life in the whole of that area where the German language predominated is an event of very great historical significance, but it does not belong within the scope of this essay. Here we are only concerned with the case of Prague Jewry. Its peculiarity lies in the fact that here the authorities, the Austrian Government itself, guided their emancipation into the path of German culture. Because it corresponded to the Habsburg policy of centralization, the authorities were entrusted with the task of 'Germanizing' the Jews ever since the reign of the Emperor Joseph ii. The Jews in no way opposed this policy. It seemed to them quite natural. The transition from the Judeo–German language of everyday life to the German language of the state schools presented few difficulties and the German culture of Prague seemed to them *the* secular

*From *Year Book I*, Publications of the Leo Baeck Institute of Jews from Germany, London 1956, pp. 255–65.

culture. After marking time for centuries, the Czechs were only beginning to recreate their own culture and literature. Most of the Jews hardly noticed the initial steps. The cultural revival of the Czechs led naturally to political demands and, later, to a passionate struggle for their national independence and sovereignty, *vis-à-vis* both the Habsburg state and their German fellow-inhabitants of Bohemia and Moravia. A situation then developed that was characteristic for the Jews of these provinces and particularly for the Jews of Prague. It gave to their relations with the Germans a character altogether different from that of the Jews in Germany. They became in fact the natural allies of the Prague Germans in their struggle against the Czechs.

This development did not take place as a result of deliberate policy, as though the Germans had consciously sought out the Jews as allies and welcomed them as adherents of the same culture. It arose spontaneously without either of the two parties to this strange alliance being fully alive to the situation. People are not too particular where the choice of allies is concerned. The advantages which the Germans enjoyed through the adhesion of the Jews were obvious, all the more so – and this is a second highly significant factor – because the Germans in Prague were a small minority compared with the Czechs. The addition of the Jewish Germans enabled them to represent a far stronger cultural and, above all, economic factor both in Prague and throughout the whole country.

This alliance was so close that the Jews did not feel themselves to be allies at all but simply identified themselves with the Germans. This also meant that the Czechs often enough made no distinction between Germans and Jews so that anti-German riots and street fights had – and to an increasing extent – an anti-Semitic character. The Germans were relatively farthest removed from this feeling of identity. This aloofness grew in proportion with the increasing influence of the Sudeten Germans in German policy. The Germans from the border areas of Bohemia, where only the one language was spoken, sent their sons to the German University at Prague. They brought with them their native anti-Semitism which they eventually also disseminated amongst the Germans of Prague. They were strangers to the German culture that had evolved through collaboration with the Jews in Prague and were less interested in intellectual life. Thus there were two strictly separate trends in the student body of the Prague German University, its clubs, fraternities and corps. There was, first, the so-called *voelkisch* (racially nationalist) trend, which was anti-Semitic, refused to accept Jews and in many fraternities would not give Jews 'satisfaction', i.e. even in the case of insults it was not prepared 'to rehabilitate honour with the sabre'. There were, second, the so-called 'liberal' corporations which did not only accept Jews but also mostly had a Jewish majority. Only through their absence of anti-Semitism did they differ from the other student bodies. In any case they yielded to none in their German sentiment.

The cultural centre of the 'liberal' German student bodies was the Lese-und Rede-Halle (Debating and Reading Club of the German Students) to which Jews belonged in the main.* Here it was that Kafka met Max Brod.

The predominant part taken by the Jews in the work of the Literary Section of the 'Halle' was paralleled at this time in the whole of German cultural life in Prague. The leading lights were mainly Jews; the public was mainly Jewish and to a decisive extent material support came from Jewish manufacturers, merchants and bankers.

This applied with especial force to the German Theatre, which stood on a remarkable level of artistic achievement. The public, patrons, box-holders and Theatre directors were mainly Jewish. Angelo Neumann, the most famous of all, who had raised the theatre to its high level and whose role as a populariser of Wagner has earned him a place in musical history, was a baptized Jew. One of his successors was Heinrich Teweles, who was in literary contact with Theodor Herzl, and was the author of a well-known book, *Goethe and the Jews*. J. Rosenheim, for many years the secretary of the Theatre, was also a Jew. The German Theatre in Prague, which presented both drama and opera and had at its disposal two large buildings, was not only an influential centre for the dissemination of German culture amongst all Prague Jewry. It was also a meeting place where the Jews of all classes felt at home and, it might almost be said, on their own. To be sure, it was the German Theatre, it was German drama and music that was presented. There were also, of course, Christian Germans in the theatre. But the verve, the resonance, the criticism, which made the Theatre into a living force, were to an essential degree Jewish.

For many years there was an annual May Festival. ...† It can be said without exaggeration that these May Festivals were days of rejoicing for Prague Jewry, eagerly looked forward to and discussed in every family circle. When the Jewish paterfamilias read out extracts from his morning paper, he did not choose political items but preferably news about the German Theatre. Such was the atmosphere of the time. It was certainly an idyllic time – for the Jews and also for the world in general – those years at the turn of the century. But they were also years marked by a strange aloofness from reality, by a surprising lack of consciousness of the past and of history, especially amongst the Jews.

The cultural symbiosis expressed most strikingly in the role of the German Theatre developed in literature on analogous lines. The

---

* See above, p. 36 [Ed.].
†See above, pp. 36–7

overwhelming majority of the leading poets in the German world of Prague and Bohemia at the end of the nineteenth century were Jewish. There is *one* great exception – Rainer Maria Rilke, who came from a district of Prague inhabited by Christian Germans. However famous Rilke later became, he was little known in Prague itself. He held himself aloof from Prague literary life and soon, indeed, left his native city.

At the end of the nineteenth century both the representative German poets of Bohemia, Hugo Salus and Friedrich Adler, were Jews. Salus was a subtle and sensitive lyric poet. Adler was best known as a translator of plays. Nevertheless, both were rather local worthies. However, a new generation of Jewish poets and writers followed them whose works permanently enriched German literature and in some cases achieved world-wide fame. There were, amongst others, Max Brod, Franz Werfel, Franz Kafka, Oskar Baum, Leo Perutz, Ernst Weiss, Paul Kornfeld, Rudolf Fuchs, Ludwig Winder, Hermann Ungar, Otto Pick and Egon Erwin Kisch.

The mention of these names takes us of course somewhat beyond the period of which we were just speaking and a little closer to the phenomenon that forms the main theme of this essay – the revival of Jewish consciousness in the midst of assimilation. This revival, in one form or another, took place in many of these writers. But at the period described earlier their awareness of themselves as German writers was naive and all but untroubled.

The same situation prevailed to an even greater extent, if that were possible, in the lower reaches of literature – amongst critics and journalists. The German newspapers of Prague, headed by the *Prager Tagblatt*, whose chief editor was for some time the former theatre director Heinrich Teweles (later Sigmund Blau) were almost exclusively edited by Jews. In all simplicity the Jewish journalists spoke on behalf of the Germans, politically, socially and artistically. It is significant that the acknowledged political leader of the Germans in Bohemia was a Jew, Bruno Kafka, who happened to be a cousin of Franz Kafka. The social centre of the Germans in Prague was the 'German Casino', their stronghold, and a thorn in the side of the Czechs. Here also the Jews played a large part. They would meet there in the afternoon to read the paper or have a game of cards. And all this took place – which is its most interesting feature for us today – in the most unselfconscious way in the world, with the untroubled sentiment of feeling absolutely at home.

The school-room was the scene of one of the most interesting aspects of the symbiosis. The Jews, of course, attended the German schools. (Not till later did this change slightly.) As a consequence, the Jewish pupils of these schools were in the majority. ... It seemed to everybody natural and in no way out of the ordinary that [in the German elementary school, the Piaristenschule] Catholic clergymen of Czech origin should teach Jewish children to appreciate German culture. The children had no complaints nor had their parents. They did not see that the path they trod led to the loss by both parents and children of something essential – their self-awareness as Jews and their identification with the Jewish past.

It must once again be emphasized that in the most naive way they felt themselves to be Germans. Perhaps the present writer may be allowed to adduce himself as an example. By chance I still have in my possession the draft of a speech I delivered in one of the upper forms of the Gymnasium. It is entitled 'The German Folk-song'. It ends with an enraptured nationalistic German quotation that still re-echoes in my mind: 'A strange magic lies buried in these folk-songs. There one feels the heart-beat of the German people, here there thunders German wrath, here there whistles German scorn, here is the kiss of German love, here sparkles true German wine and the true German tear.' And who wrote this? None other than Heinrich Heine. And a soft voice reminds me that it was my late father who drew my attention to this quotation. Heine and Schiller were the most quoted poets. Such was, as I remember it, the intellectual world of the generation that lived at the end of the nineteenth century.

The loss in Jewish consciousness can best be understood by recalling what Prague had still meant to the Jewish world a century earlier. In a city, once known as a 'Mother in Israel' and once a centre of Jewish intellectual life, there hardly remained anything left of Jewish knowledge. The number of observant Jews had shrunk to a small circle centred on the Lieben family. One could sum it up by saying that over a few decades Schiller had ousted Rashi.

Prague Jewry was more remote from Judaism than its co-religionists in Germany. The reason was undoubtedly its rapid and uninhibited entry into the world of German culture in the special circumstances prevailing in the city, as described earlier. The process was so fast and it encompassed intellectual life so thoroughly that in a very short time, perhaps in one generation, the religious life of the vast majority of the Jews was almost completely devitalized. It was condemned to lead a pseudo-existence, the consequences of which will be further discussed below.

II Language – Ancestry – Religion

... Our present problem is the mutual relationship of these three basic orders of historical consciousness. How do they co-operate to form an ultimate unity? Are they dependent on each other? Can they in fact collaborate at all? Must they collaborate? Can they perhaps fall apart?

Could each in isolation produce a historical consciousness? Or does a uniform consciousness demand the co-operation of all three?

These questions are here posed generally. They emerge of their own accord from any consideration of human destiny. But it is none the less Jewish history that has made these questions particularly topical. For it was in the history of the Jews that for the first time consciousness of history and of the past became a driving force capable of giving meaning to Jewish life. Yet the Jews are the very people in whom the three basic principles of a common tradition have again and again fallen asunder.

This development of itself undoubtedly reveals the existence of the very intimate relationship amongst the three principles of cultural evolution. The historical experience of an ethnic group finds its expression in the language of the group. It is here that its significant experiences are preserved and transmitted to later generations in the form and colouring characteristic of the language. Conversely the fate of the group will influence its language. Events will demand of language that it represent and describe them, give them firm shape and hand them down to posterity. Through this demand the language itself will be developed in a characteristic way. Here is an example of a clear inter-action, a shaping of the one by the other. In its language the history of the tribe finds its native melody. Language pursues its way, led by history. The historical consciousness of language and of common descent exercises a mutually formative influence, becomes creative through mutual contact.

There can be just as little doubt of the creative relationship between religion and language. The Bible is the proof. It was the Hebrew language that gave it its form. The Bible in its turn formed the language. The ability of the Bible to shape language is so powerful that through the medium of Luther's translation it was even able to make its impact felt on the German language.

The relationship between religion and ethnic grouping is of interest. There is no necessary relationship. There are religions which deny it. They make their appeal to the whole of humanity, to every man, no matter what his ancestry. It is precisely in this that they see a basic principle of religion in general, as does, for example, Christianity. The connection between religion and ancestry is far closer in Judaism. It needs no further exposé here. God's covenant was made with Abraham and his seed. The Jewish people, as already explained, was the first to make consciousness of the past an essential part of the existential consciousness of man in general. This consciousness had from the very beginning a religious sub-structure. In no other people is there such a close bond between religion and ethnic consciousness. At many periods of their history it even led to their complete identification.

Yet despite the close relationship in Judaism of the three basic factors in historical consciousness, fate has decreed that it is precisely the Jews whose history shows the repeated alienation of the three principles. This has had the most varied cultural, moral and political consequences.

The feature of the period of assimilation was the constant strengthening of the linguistic to the gradual detriment of the ethnic factor in their capacity as components of historical consciousness. In the present case the language was German. This finally led – although only later and then not everywhere – to a weakening of the religious factor. Thus the stage was reached when the Jews, undisturbed by the missing elements in their own historical consciousness, were able to participate with devotion and success in the cultural life and endeavours in art and literature, of the peoples whose language they spoke.

It would be a much over-simplified judgment utterly to condemn at the outset this state of disunited principles as a pernicious symptom of decay and devoid of any value. The course of events is not so simple. New creative power in intellectual life can everywhere assert itself where it succeeds in making a new unity of a new situation, i.e. even of disharmony. This is precisely what happens to a large extent at a time of assimilation. Admittedly, the dissolution of consciousness can lead to the collapse of the existing unity, but it can also inspire a creative reaction to disharmony. It depends on the ratio between the consciousness that is present and the fresh influx from outside, that is, on the degree of disharmony and on the individual's capacity to handle it and shape it anew. This was present to a large extent, giving rise to the creations of assimilation and of the cultural symbiosis. Jewish historical consciousness was widened and reshaped by its experiences in foreign linguistic territory in the same manner as German linguistic consciousness was enriched by inter-action with the Jewish mind.

Yet these are the blossom and fruit of a transitory phase without a future. The blossom and the fruit will fall. The future will then depend on the strength of the trunk of the tree, on the united and *full* consciousness made up of all three factors. The blossoms of the symbiotic relationship are transitory phenomena. A historical consciousness of which the basic factors are no longer in harmony knows no stability and no equilibrium. It is in a state of flux, striving to regain its lost harmony. The history of assimilation shows continual and repeated efforts in this direction – above all the attempt to compensate for the loss of normal linguistic con-sciousness. The result here was the creation of a two-fold substitute – linguistic consciousness: the creation of a jargon, of different language enclaves inside the foreign language; and the language of prayer and the Talmud. The impact on language of tribal and community relationships is so extensive that in certain families an individual linguistic 'colour' can be observed. There are fixed expressions and family anecdotes that have penetrated everyday conversation, as a form of 'thought-shorthand', and given it a special character of its own.

National consciousness in the midst of linguistic assimilation does, of course, receive powerful support from a strong religious awareness. This explains how the Jewish people, despite its lack of a genuine common linguistic consciousness and the repeated penetration of alien linguistic influence, has been able to preserve over long periods its own historical consciousness. This situation did not change until, on the one hand, the impact of the Enlightenment, modern science and, above all, an alien language began to weaken religious consciousness. On the other hand, even those remnants of an individual 'substitute linguistic consciousness' vanished. An isolated tribal consciousness had thereby to bear a double and even a triple burden. And then there set in at last that period of transition – the period of total assimilation.

The characteristic feature of this condition of the historical conscious-ness is, as already mentioned, its instability. It has no equilibrium of its own and thus leads to confusion and to lashing out wildly in different directions. Many people simply become converted, completely changing their historical allegiance. The new linguistic awareness eases the path; in many cases perhaps it misleads the person concerned into complete conversion, even though the reasons are in general not a changed linguistic awareness but political or economic calculations. It is a violation of the historical consciousness, but not an impossible one. It is something akin to a self-mutilation of the historical consciousness. Experience shows, however, that the wound heals in one or two generations.

Such escapes from an unstable equilibrium are, as experience again shows, only possible on an individual scale. They cannot be universal, social solutions, cannot genuinely re-establish the equilibrium of a disturbed national consciousness. There are two reasons for this, one internal, one external.

First, the foreign community which is the object of conversion will defend itself against newcomers if the influx has a mass character or even if it is only too perceptible. The manifestations of defence are well enough known. They range from social ostracism to mass murder. Second: the internal and essential reason is that the individual's feeling for the past protects itself against dissolution. Almost, it might be said, along unknown paths. A new ethnic, religious and linguistic consciousness arises.

Ethnic sentiment revives simply because it has a vitalistic basis whose kernel cannot be destroyed. It rests on the emotional relationship between parents and children reaching deep down into the realm of physiology.

Love and the genuine relationship between man and man are admittedly more than an instinctual-vitalistic sentiment of solidarity. But as a basis, or to employ again the illuminating image of the tree-trunk on which the blossom of genuine human relationship grows or can grow, this vitalistic connection is indispensable. It refuses to be killed. It asserts itself and takes hold of a man by means over which he has no control.

Religion revives as well – even if only on negative lines, should it receive no other help. A religious vacuum is not a situation with which man can rest content. Religious consciousness will arise as questioning, yearning, task, demand, sin, guilt.

Both orders seek to win back their missing partner, linguistic consciousness; they rediscover the language with which they were once creatively united.

This awakening, this threefold awakening is at work in the outstanding case of Franz Kafka.

5

Two Recollections

Johannes Urzidil

Translated by Chris Waller

Prague, 11 June 1924[*]

The morning of Wednesday, 11 June 1924, in Prague began amiably enough. The city, already bathed in summer light, was beginning to be caught up in a holiday mood. The republic, its affairs conducted by wise Thomas Garrigue Masaryk, had been in existence now for five-and-a-half years and its essential character seemed secure, in spite of all internal conflicts and external problems. At any rate, the people of Prague (and the Germans among them) felt this to be so. The inhabitants of the historic city, with its gleaming gilt roofs and, beneath, the deep-cast shadows of timeless national and religious contrasts, were waking from the snug comfort of their beds and making ready for the sedate industry of a late spring day, which, as always, would be permeated by the emerald splendour of the gardens, with the chords of popular Bohemian music resounding in the background and, on the air, the aroma of smoked meats and the smell of beer and a contentious buzz, which, restrained at first, grew in intensity as evening approached.

The times were not straightforward, it's true, but where *were* the times straightforward? In Italy the Fascists were hatching their black schemes, but Italy was a long way away. In Russia Lenin had died in January and Trotsky had been exiled; but Russia, too, was remote and had long ago ceased to be the all-embracing Slavonic mother of the pan-Slavonic times of the legendary past. In America Woodrow Wilson had died on 3 February and with him had died one of the principal architects of the new

[*] From *Da geht Kafka*, Artemis Verlags, Zurich 1965, Chapter 10, pp. 98–103.

peace; but, again, by now Europe saw itself as very, very distant from America. In Germany an obscure ranter was busy writing *Mein Kampf.* But of what interest was Germany to us? In Prague most people were interested in the fact that the bob-cut was back in fashion with the ladies – an event of world-shattering significance, an enormous change.

For the German poets and writers of Prague, and for the German Jews of the city above all, 11 June was a melancholy, painful day. Eight days before, Franz Kafka had succumbed to his long, agonizing suffering in the Kierling sanatorium in the Wienerwald near Vienna. He had been brought to Prague and was to be buried that Wednesday at four o'clock in the afternoon. The servant of God had gone, the aphorist of prose had apparently seen his life in aphoristic terms, too. News of his death struck family, friends and acquaintances like a bolt from the blue. They found it impossible to believe, though most people had known for a long time that it was inevitable. But all of us – even the poets among us who from an early age had contemplated and extolled death – were unfamiliar with its direct reality in our very midst. I had been the only one to see the young poet Karl Brand die in his hovel in Prague. Apart from that, the war had snatched relatives and friends from us and also another poet (the highly gifted Franz Janowitz), but we thought of war as murder, which man in his callousness inflicts upon himself and his neighbours. That was not death, not the death decreed by God, but a death directed against God. The German Prague poets and writers, including Kafka, never accepted death brought about by human agency as death in the proper sense.

Kafka had not completed his forty-first year. I think that there cannot have been anyone who, knowing him personally, did not love him. And it must be said that all who loved Kafka loved his friends, too, for his sake, and that he created an invisible bond between all who felt that his presence, his life and influence granted them access to something higher and better, so that they were encouraged and strengthened in their innermost selves. Kafka had been the source of this fortifying, harmonizing influence. Was it now suddenly to cease to exist? At that time he was not 'famous' in the usual sense of the word. Other Prague writers were. Outside his Prague circle of friends only the more discerning connoisseurs of literature – those rare pioneering spirits among publishers, editors, writers and intellectuals – appreciated him. But we in Prague knew who was passing through our daily lives in those old lanes, who it was we hailed across the street – and his very response had all the magic of a special event – or walked the length of a few houses with or somewhere, for an hour or two, sat over a cup of coffee with. Not that he would ever say much himself, yet each of his sentences, whatever the circumstances, every casually proffered word, always penetrated deep to the core of the earth.

But how it came about that his words had such an effect no one could explain, not even those who were most closely related to him, not even that source of constant illumination and inspiration, Max Brod; nor the philosophically minded Felix Weltsch, nor the idealistic historian of religion, Hugo Bergmann, nor Oskar Baum, beloved of us all, robbed of the light of the sun by a boy's carelessly flung stone, but now able to peer, unblinking, into the luminous rays of the soul. They could explain what Kafka might mean, and one was then free to agree with their interpretations or put forward one's own. But how it came about that Kafka said what he said; how it came about that he said it the way he said it; how it came about that one never ended up in direct conflict with him or with what he said – none of them could explain that. This was because Kafka was the beginning, not the end, of an era. This was the reason, too, why a very special deep anguish filled us young writers at his death.

Franz Werfel, who had lived away from Prague for some years and came home only occasionally on family visits, once said to me, 'I should love Kafka much more if he were not so nihilistic.' Nihilistic? An opinion wider of the mark than this can rarely have been expressed, although it seemed to make sense coming from Werfel, 'the friend of the world'. His two volumes of poetry, *Wir sind* (*We Are*), and *Einander* (*One Another*), involuntarily balked at the unfathomable and fundamental tragedy of existence. There was nothing Danaidean about Werfel; he still believed – at that time at least – in the possibility of the golden mean and was trying – at the very time Kafka was dying – to achieve the ultimate reconciliation between the great antitheses in Verdi and Wagner, Juarez and Maximilian. We all loved Werfel's genius for its affirmation of the world and life, for we all wanted the world and life. Kafka, too, wanted these. Indeed, no one fought so fiercely and desperately for them; no one confronted, as he did, the continual disappointments and insoluble problems which life, the world and people placed in the path of anyone who proclaimed wholehearted belief in them. For Kafka was just such a believer; he was not a nihilist. The imperishable value of his genius lay in the fact that he demonstrated, for all to see, an incorruptible awareness of his own private weaknesses, so that each of his works represented an act of deliberate self-disintegration, and then he would begin all over again, subjecting the very essence of his self to humiliation.

But now he had left us, and in the afternoon we were to bury him, in the garden of 'peace' where 'the dead rest'. Wrong! They do not rest. In some way the body is reunited with the earth, but what significance does that have in comparison with the eternal survival of the spirit? We who had moved in his orbit did not merely have a presentiment of his greatness: we were convinced of it, though not all of us, of course, knew how far it would spread, how evident it would be. In the world of German literature outstanding minds were still active and creative, shaping and reviving the face of that literature; to the north, in a Germany racked by inflation, and to the south, in Vienna, robbed of the bearings by which it had lived its life for so long, was a glittering array of aspiring poets, who, for the convenience of reviewers, were assembled under the unwieldy collective term 'Expressionism'. Some of us Prague writers, including Kafka, were considered part of this movement. Yet we knew ourselves to be an autonomous community, our purity guaranteed by our language and well tested during the long years when we had experienced the ebb and flow of an extremely close symbiotic relationship with the Slavs. So we were special Germans, special Austrians, special Bohemians, and, moreover, most of Kafka's friends were also affected by the special problems of being Jews. Now, suddenly, with Kafka's death, a corner-stone had been removed from this community, a gaping hole had appeared in the roof. Could it ever be repaired again, or would it fall in? Would the storms undermine the building completely? The storms did not fail to materialize. The building collapsed.

In fact, Kafka's death meant the end of the intellectual Prague of that Czech-German-Austrian-Jewish synthesis which had sustained the city as a metropolis and inspired it over the centuries. At the time, the Czechs, whose interest in the intellectual life of their compatriots writing in German was casual, inadequate and lukewarm, were the slowest to realize this. The one exception to this, however, was the youthful Milena Jesenská, who had loved Kafka and translated some of his shorter prose pieces into Czech. (Milena Jesenská wrote the only Czech obituary of Kafka in the Prague newspaper *Národní Listy* on 6 June 1924. For more about this wonderful woman, who met her death in a German concentration camp, see the book *Kafka's Friend Milena*, by Margarete Buber-Neumann, published in Munich in 1963.) But almost all the other Czechs interested in literature knew far more about the most mediocre French hacks than about their neighbours in the next street, though their names might be Rilke, Kafka, Werfel or Max Brod, who himself had done so much to bring Czech culture to the attention of the rest of the world. In a way, it is possible to understand why at the time the Czechs were so indifferent – after all, they were, for the time being, still quite giddy, quite intoxicated, even disconcerted by the national independence and bewildering hegemony over other nations* which had unexpectedly come their way. How could they have known at the time that the name of the German-Jewish writer who was hardly known elsewhere and who was to

---

* i.e. Slovaks, Ruthenians, the German minorities of Bohemia and Moravia as well as the Hungarian minority of Slovakia. [Ed.]

be buried that afternoon, would remain indissolubly linked with the name of Prague, their charismatic capital? How could they have even begun to suspect that one day, all over the world, people, at the mere mention of the name 'Kafka', would, in a kind of reflex action, instantly think of 'Prague' – indeed, that in three decades the only significance which this historic city, of European importance, would have for countless people all over the world would be as Kafka's home town?

And yet Kafka was Prague and Prague was Kafka. Never had it been Prague so perfectly, so typically, as during Kafka's lifetime, and never would it be so again. And we, his friends, 'the happy few' – if such an expression was admissible on the day of his burial – we knew that the smallest elements of this Prague were distilled everywhere in Kafka's work. Every line that he ever wrote enabled – indeed, still enables – us to visualize this city, however much his work over the years has contracted to its essential substance and apparently shed its local and personal connections. Almost as if he were a satirical writer, Kafka has ensured that the Prague which ended with him was not buried with him, although no one, not even any of that 'band of brethren', knew that at the time.

Everyone made his own way, on foot or by vehicle, to the Jewish cemetery at Strašnice, a suburb on the outskirts of Prague. The weather, so pleasant in the morning, had grown gloomy in the meantime. The majestic city, with its towers and bridge-spanned river, is no longer visible from the Strašnice plateau. Here the terrain, already stretching away into the Bohemian countryside, is set aside for the silent orders of the departed ones whose kingdom begins in the north, if it is possible to speak of worldly regions for dead people. That Kafka was now to be given a home here was strange, incredible, because we were sure that he had a more permanent existence (here, there and everywhere) and that he would always be meeting us unexpectedly, in different guises; the nearer we came to the cemetery, the more the sensation of finality faded.

I was in the procession of mourners which accompanied Kafka's coffin from the hall where the formalities had taken place to the open grave; I walked with his friends behind the family and the pale Dora Dymant, companion of his last year, who was being supported by Max Brod. They were all still young then: the eldest (Brod, Hugo Bergmann and Oskar Baum) only in their early forties; Felix Weltsch, Ludwig Winder, Rudolf Fuchs and Friedrich Thieberger (my brother-in-law and Kafka's Hebrew teacher) still in their thirties; I was twenty-eight. Only a few of the hundred or so people who that day took part in the procession beneath the willows and cypresses are still alive today; only a few lived to see Kafka become the classic example of a writer's assuming world-wide importance. When the coffin was lowered, Dora Dymant gave an agonized, piercing cry, but her sobbing, the true significance of which could be assessed only by the person for whom it was intended, was drowned by the echo of the Hebrew prayer at the graveside, proclaiming God's holiness and the fervent hope of redemption. 'Writing as a form of prayer!' that had been Kafka's definition of the art of a writer; and 'Even if no redemption is forthcoming I want to be worthy of it at every moment': that was his belief. We threw earth into the grave. I have a precise memory of that earth. It was pale, lumpy, loamy, interspersed with crumbled fragments of stones and pebbles, and it fell on to the coffin with a clatter. Then the group of mourners dispersed. I walked away between the graves with my wife, who had been friendly with Kafka ever since she was a child, and with the poet-translator Rudolf Fuchs. Not a word was spoken. At last rain began to fall from the dismal sky.

The Golem*

For a time during the First World War, in 1917, Kafka lived in a little house in Alchemists' Lane, the tiny street of the goldsmiths on the Prague Hradčany, behind the castle, above the Stag Moat, which used to be part of the Imperial castle grounds. This extremely romantic, ancient corner of Prague, steeped in the atmosphere of past ages, occasionally attracted visitors at that time; yet there were not so many tourists in Prague then as were to come later, and none came at all during the war. Indeed, for some ludicrous reason, Prague was not regarded as a tourist city. People went to Berlin, Vienna and Budapest, towns which Cook's Travel Agency had in its brochures, but Prague did not seem important enough to this international travel organization, and so it was ignored. Similarly, prosperous tourists from Moravian Brno, or even from provincial Bohemian towns, if they were not Czechs, thought it smarter to go to Vienna than to Prague, a contemptible piece of irresponsibility and inanity which contributed to the subsequent collapse of the Austrian monarchy. However, this was all to the good of Alchemists' Lane, for it remained quiet and mysterious. In the evening the smallest noise was plainly audible in this lane made for loving couples, and, therefore, doubtless also for poets, for nothing about it at that time was artificial or contrived. Its tiny houses, which looked as though they had been glued together, had served the alchemists of the melancholy Emperor Rudolf II as workshops and homes; now they were inhabited by poor people who would show their minute household possessions to visitors for a minute sum and would also, at a pinch, rent out a tiny room. These houses, during the Renaissance, in the days of Tycho Brahe and Kepler, contained the laboratories in which

* From *Da geht Kafka*, Chapter 7, pp. 65–75.

the mystical search was going on: for the stone of the Magi, for artificial gold and for artificial man. Of course, the 'Golem' was not born up here on Castle Hill in the shadow of St Vitus's Cathedral, but down below in the old Jewish Ghetto, on the other side of the River Moldau. Kafka lived for a short time in just such an alchemist's cottage. It was at the time he was working on the stories in the book *A Country Doctor*, shortly before his tragic illness was diagnosed.

To see Prague from the top of the Castle Hill (Hradčany), or from the Little Quarter below, is something completely different from experiencing the city in the midst of the Old Town. If the Hradčany gives a regal, imperial, panoramic impression, the Old Town provides a bourgeois, popular one. Between the left and right banks of the Moldau there were always more than topographical differences – deep differences in people's ways and habits, even in the language they spoke. The 'Little Quarter German', with its sharp 's' and its short vowels, was different from the softer, somewhat heavier German of the Old Town. The luxurious palaces of the regal and imperial vassals on the slope of Castle Hill gave this part of the city the unruffled conservative tone to which the officials' and middle-class citizens' houses, slotted between the palaces, conformed. Later – in 1878 – that excellent Czech story-teller, Jan Neruda, in his *Stories of the Little Quarter*, fascinatingly recaptured the world of the left bank of the Moldau in what is, incidentally, one of the very few truly poetic books about Prague written by a Czech. Not only the Hradčany, but also the ambience of the Little Quarter, is part of Kafka's world. For a short time he had a room there, in the ducal Schönborn Palace.

To get from the world of the alchemists, high up by the castle, to the Jewish world of the Golem, all around the Old-New Synagogue, one had to cross the Moldau by the famous Charles Bridge and pass along its avenue of Baroque statues of the Catholic saints. It was with these statues that the triumphant Church symbolized the victory of its Counter-Reformation over the Bohemian (Czech-Bohemian and German-Bohemian) insurgency of the Thirty Years War, as well as with the statue of the Madonna, which stood in the middle of the Old Town Square. This statue stood there until the establishment of the republic in 1918, when, in order to give the bronze gaze of the religious and national martyr, Jan Hus, a free field of vision, it was at long last destroyed. Kafka's experience of the Old Town Square, the centre of his life in Prague, underwent three changes: first there was only the statue of the Madonna; then there was the paradoxical combination of Catholic Madonna and Hus monument, proclaiming to everyone in clear terms: 'Pravdy každému přejte', which amounts to 'Equal rights for all'; and finally there was only Jan Hus.

But the world of the Hradčany alchemists and the rabbinical world of the Golem in the Prague ghetto, which began just behind the Old Town Square, were linked together by more than the Charles Bridge: they shared an intimate historical connection. And in whichever direction Kafka moved between the Old Town and the Hradčany, whether up or down, he found himself right in the midst of a remarkable atmosphere which always had something eerily other-worldly about it and was mirrored in every sentence of his own writing. Indeed, this reflection of the old city in Kafka's work is a great deal more compact and convincing than in, say, Gustav Meyrink's novels about Prague, even though Meyrink, with his *Golem* (1915), had greatly influenced the picture which people who did not live in Prague, as well as many who did, had of the city. In the same year Max Brod's novel, *Tycho Brahe's Way to God*, considerably more profound and (from a narrative and historical viewpoint) more important, had also been published. The picture of Prague it presented was a good deal more convincing, but Meyrink ruled the day.

Meyrink's fictions about the Prague ghetto, its inhabitants, cabbalistic rabbis and the Golem itself, were widely read, filmed and dramatized, but they were only imprecise variations on the Golem legend or tradition. Prague's seething retort of national and religious elements, from which at times homunculi were distilled, requires us to delve further back into history. Johannes Faust, although not born in Prague, at least had a temporary lodging-place there, which is still shown to sightseers today. Goethe may well have known something about this from the twenty-sixth chapter of the Frankfurt Faust *Historia* of 1587, which appeared during the time the alchemist-emperor Rudolf II resided in Prague. In it, during the description of the necromancer's third magic journey, Prague is depicted with topographical thoroughness: 'This capital in Bohemia is large and is divided into three parts, namely Old Prague, New Prague and Little Prague. Little Prague is the left bank of the river, with the King's court and St Vitus's Cathedral. Old Prague (the Old Town) lies on the plain. From here you get to Little Prague (i.e. the Little Quarter) over a bridge with twenty-four flying buttresses. The New Town is separated from the Old Town by a deep ditch or moat (and "The Ditch", in Czech *Příkopy*, is later used as a designation for one of the main thoroughfares of the city), and is guarded all round by walls. The College of the High School is likewise there' (what is meant is the first Central European University, founded by the Emperor Charles IV in 1348). All this comes from the Faust *Historia*. Prague appears in it only as a sort of relay station. The homunculus in the second part of Goethe's *Faust* is not created by Faust himself, but by the latter's amanuensis, Wagner. Nevertheless, the homunculus belongs to the world of the scientific experiments of the sixteenth-century alchemists who lived in Prague. Then, in 1616,

Paracelsus, in *De generatione rerum naturalium*, provided a practical recipe for the creation of homunculi, probably drawing on the recent experiments of the Prague alchemists (Rudolf II died in 1612). Prague was, therefore, the city where a man-creating mysticism prevailed, which over the years could not fail to influence both the Czech and the German Prague writers, particularly when the Jewish Golem legend supervened as a magic counterpart to the 'scientific' activities of the alchemists. Of modern Czech writers, Karel Čapek became world-renowned for his science-fiction drama *R.U.R* (*Rossum's Universal Robots*), in which, as early as 1923, modern artificial machine-people appeared, called 'robots', a designation which became widely used and derives from the Czech word *robota*, meaning "forced labour". The ancestor of these robots was the Golem of the Prague Renaissance, Rabbi Liwa ben Bezalel, the 'High Rabbi Loew'. I have no doubt at all that Kafka's story 'The Metamorphosis' derives from this mysterious ancestry, in the same way as the endless research undertaken in the quest for the stone of the Magi may well represent, in its dogged but ultimate futility, an anticipation of that search for security which is so characteristic of Kafka's outlook. To the objection that the quest for gold is a quest for power, it must be said that the quest for power is after all only an over-compensation for deep-seated fear and insecurity. If alchemy is the refuge of a man left dissatisfied and sceptical by traditional religious certainties, the Emperor Rudolf II was just such a man. . . .

It has been proved that Jews have lived in Prague since Roman times. Moreover, the earliest traveller's account of Prague is by a Jew, Ibrahim ibn Jakub, who in the second half of the tenth century journeyed through Bohemia and the lands of the Slavs and noted down his observations in *The Book of Roads and Countries* (Codex Cordova). Even at that time he depicted Prague as an extremely busy junction of east-west and north-south link roads, as a many-faceted metropolis. The vigorously pulsating city created its myths (for example, the myth of Libuše, her foundress) and the myths in turn created the city. The Golem legend is an integral part of Prague's mythology. The Hebrew word *golem* means 'lifeless, unformed matter'. Golem is not a personal name, but the designation of a thing. Egon Erwin Kisch once maintained that he had located the attic of the Old-New Synagogue and had discovered the remains of the Golem there. But Kisch, whose intrepidity as a reporter cannot be disputed, could possibly have found were just decomposed, dried-out clay relics – that is, golem. Whether these bits of clay were in fact the remains of the High Rabbi Loew's artificial man is difficult to prove.

The legend itself is rooted in the earliest cabbalistic work, the *Yetzirah*, which the Babylonian Talmud corroborates. There (in the treatise

Sanhedrin) we find an account of the possible ways of animating lifeless matter – that is, the golem. The cabbalists believed that the person with the right qualifications could animate not only golems, but also a human corpse, if he affixed the Shem, the strip of writing with the symbol of the divine name on it, on the forehead or under the tongue. The spirit – that is, life – is everywhere, immortal, and matter is only its substratum. The duly qualified person can, under certain conditions, commune with the spirit and reawaken life in apparently dead matter. But who is qualified and what are these preconditions?

Golem-myths originated in Prague in early modern times, especially in the sixteenth century, when the city became the place where the wise Rabbi Liwa ben Bezalel taught and exerted great influence. It was said that he had the power to master space and matter and, therefore, time. His life and influence have been described by Friedrich Thieberger in a book which has hitherto appeared only in English and whose principal theses I adopt in this study. He had made a lifelong study of the subject, I have frequently heard him talk about it, and there is no doubt that in his close dealings with Kafka he discussed in great detail the highly significant golem-myth, which had a profound effect on anyone who lived in Prague. This incursion into the supernatural, rooted as it was in realism *and* religion, was bound to fascinate Kafka. The best known and most visible historical evidence of the High Rabbi Loew is his gravestone, covered with many inscriptions; it is to be found in Prague's Jewish cemetery, where he has lain buried since 1609 and is surrounded by the graves of his thirty-three favourite pupils, rather like a bodyguard. Where Liwa, or Loew, came from before settling in Prague is not known for certain. The general theory is that he was born in Posen, and he was reputedly still so vigorous in his hundred-and-fourth year that the angel of death did not dare approach him directly and, in order to reach him, had to hide in the scent of a rose. However, his magic powers continued to work after his death. For when, sixty years later, they wanted to bury his grandson near him and there was no ground to spare around the grave, the Rabbi, together with his monument, moved several yards over during the night.

The three main preconditions for possessing magic powers are, according to the *Cabbala*: first, an untrained religious spirit, and this, according to Judaic tradition, is a requirement which can be fulfilled only by virtue of God's immeasurable grace and by a chosen person who, at the same time, lives his whole life in the ways of God; secondly, a perfect intellectual disposition, which is, of course, humanly attainable, but only if that person has a wide-ranging mind and can practise the rare talent of critical discrimination when confronted by the world's phenomena and sources of knowledge; thirdly (but by no means least, because this is the basis of all that has gone before), the most intimate knowledge of God's word – that is, the *Thora* and the *Talmud*. But knowledge of this kind means such an intensive, unstinting effort of concentration that it absorbs all other aspects of an adept's life and turns it into a life of eternal learning. The first step, and of course the most important one, is knowledge of Hebrew, and Kafka tried this first step by beginning to take Hebrew lessons with Thieberger. Tradition has it that all three great requirements necessary (according to the *Cabbala*) for the development of supernatural powers were gloriously fulfilled in the High Rabbi Liwa ben Bezalel. We must take his religiousness for granted; his intellectual training and his knowledge of the scriptures are borne out by the great number of important Jewish writings he left behind. They are extremely difficult to understand and would be a mystery to any non-Jew. Many of them bear highly memorable and significant titles, like *The Dance of the Just*, *Pharaoh's Hard Heart*, and *The Tears of God*. Of course, Rabbi Loew, as head of the religious community, was also its supreme judge, against whose decision there could be no appeal. But his verdicts were considered to be truly Solomonic and motivated by the wisest humanity and the highest sense of morality as instilled by the scriptures. He was an astonishing psychologist who interpreted sin as 'a disorder of the soul' and not as the primitive consequence of spontaneous viciousness; he was a deep-probing theologian who saw in 'Jacob's struggle with the angel the struggle of the incorporeal in Jacob with an incorporeal messenger from God'; and he was – in the middle of the sixteenth century – an amazing philosophical-theoretical physicist who proclaimed, 'Time is only a form of matter and consists of movement.' That was a bold assertion.

It was natural enough that the Emperor up there on the Hradčany, this brooding and contemplative seeker after truth, collector, lover of the arts and experimenter, should hear of the celebrated *zadik* [pious teacher] down in the town and should want to be acquainted with him; there are in existence contemporary accounts of their meetings and of how the monarch was given lessons by the Rabbi. Nor is it surprising that a series of legends should be woven around these encounters. For example, the Rabbi is supposed to have made the Emperor's garden bloom in deep mid-winter. On another occasion, at Rudolf's behest he conjured up the Jewish patriarchs (we think of similar invocations in *Faust*). Once, when the Emperor visited the Rabbi in the latter's modest apartment, the Rabbi suddenly transformed it into a spacious and magnificent hall. Whatever the truth of this may be, the fact of the relationship and of its highly unusual nature remains. The Emperor existed, the Rabbi existed, their characters are firmly delineated in history, and we know as much about Liwa ben Bezalel from his writings and the influence he had as about any other man of the time. 'There are only miracles,' Kafka once said. The world of the spirits is not shut off. The power of magic is always a transforming power. The snow-bound garden blossoms forth. The scholar's cell becomes a magnificent hall. Time and space are conquered, and the patriarchs appear, as Helen appears. Magic is realism raised to an abstract extreme. Animals speak. Dead matter springs fo life. Man becomes an insect. There is basically nothing new about this; it is the age-old reality and wisdom of fairy-tales and parables. Who else, if not the Rabbi, should possess such wisdom? To whom should he communicate it, if not to the Emperor? And Franz Kafka, if one thinks about it, should in fact not be buried in the modern cemetery at Strašnice above Prague, but in the old one alongside the favourite pupils of High Rabbi Liwa ben Bezalel. If they had tried to bury Kafka there, the great teacher would undoubtedly have shifted to one side to make room for him.

The authentic account of the Golem has come down to us in a version written by the Rabbi's son-in-law, Yitzchak Bin Simson Cohen, who assisted personally at the creation and animation of the artificial man. The account runs: 'We clothed him in everything which a servant of the synagogue needed. He would always sit in a corner of the yard, with his head propped on his hands. The people in the streets thought he was a poor dumb man whom the Rabbi had taken in out of compassion.' A poor dumb man in the corner of a yard, with his head propped on his hands. 911 Broad Street. The animated lump of clay could see, hear and understand everything: the only thing he could not do was speak. He had a body and a real head, therefore a forehead, too, which he could tap with his hand. A silent symbol of naked defencelessness. He chopped wood, swept the floors, walked many a mile, hauling up water. Yet he was more than animated matter, for he could be brought into a prayer group as the prescribed tenth male member, although only in a silent role, a 'silent servant'; but he was much, much more than a mechanized broom. His duties extended a great deal further, for his main task was to put a stop to acts of violence against the Jews. His appearance was enough to deter the pogromists, of whom there was never a shortage in Prague, whether the predominant mood was sympathetic to the Catholics, Hussites or Protestants. 'Mažte židi!' – 'Thrash the Jews!' – is *not* a translation from the German, but a battle-cry which the present writer has had to hear often enough in the streets of Prague during his childhood and youth, a good three hundred years after Emperor Rudolf II.

According to accepted custom, the Golem had to rest on the Holy Sabbath. Then the Rabbi took away his supernatural powers from him by removing the Shem, the magic formula, which otherwise he carried under his tongue. Shem – or, more precisely, 'Shem ha-meforasch' – really means no more than 'the name' and is the designation for the unspoken and unspeakable name of God, whose grammatical phonetic spelling is the tetragram (four-letter symbol) JHWH, formulated by Philo of Alexandria – that is, Jahveh. The Golem took part with the Jewish congregation in the most important ceremony of the Jews, the hallowing of the Sabbath. Even if violent acts against the Jews took place on that day, he could not intervene. But every legend, if it is to be completely validated, needs to be spiced, indeed actuated, by human weakness. And so it is said that the Rabbi, for all his great wisdom, forgot one Sunday to remove the Shem from the Golem. So the latter, in a savage fury, began to hurl everything around, probably not only because he had apparently been deprived of the right to participate in the ceremony which incorporated everything Jewish, but because he resented the fact that his master had, for an instant, proved to be less than a true master. The people raced to the Old-New Synagogue, where the Rabbi was just beginning to sing the Sabbath psalm. Horrified by the mob and by what had happened, the High Rabbi interrupted the ceremony and hastened home, where he pacified the Golem by removing the Shem. Then he went back to the synagogue and continued the ceremony. Since that Sabbath the psalm has always been sung twice in Prague's Old-New Synagogue.

The end of the Golem is connected with a decree passed by Rudolf II, prohibiting all atrocities against the Jews. The High Rabbi, who had undoubtedly been one of the initiators of the Emperor's charity, thereupon decided to change his artificially produced assistant back again to lifeless matter, to a mere golem. This was achieved not just by removing the Shem, but at a ceremony at which – as on the occasion of the initial animation – the Rabbi's son-in-law was again present. Afterwards they laid the lifeless substance to rest in the attic of the Old-New Synagogue. There the remains lay forgotten for two hundred years. Not until the end of the eighteenth century did the very conservative Prague Rabbi Ezechiel ben Juda Landau (1713–93) dare to approach the mythical Golem again, having first fasted and donned his shroud. Yet he kept silent about what he had seen and, by solemn decree, placed the attic of the synagogue henceforth out of bounds.

6

Under the Harrow

Rosemary Dinnage

We know Kafka to have been sensitive, gentle, shy. 'One felt good with him,' friends have recorded; silent in company that intimidated him, he could be an ironically humorous talker and a patient listener. Towards the workmen whose insurance claims he handled in office hours he felt great sympathy. He was a staunch friend, an affectionate brother and a meek, though inwardly rebellious, child to his parents. He was incapable, in day-to-day life, of bluster, aggression, or self-assertion, qualities he left to his loved and hated father.

He was also a torturer. He invented a machine that gripped a man in a press and incised words on his body with spikes dipped in acid until, very slowly, he died. Characters in his stories suffer a series of random shocks, dangers, and rejections; punishment is the very stuff of the narrative. In his letters and diaries images of torture appear over and over again – whips, knives, screws, spurs, gags. With few exceptions, all this ferocity is of course directed to one person: himself. ('*Miserable creature that I am!* Just whip the horse properly! Dig the spurs into him slowly, then pull them out with a jerk, but now let them bite into the flesh with all your strength.') The exceptions are the women to whom he was drawn and on whom he therefore felt dependent, before whom he whipped himself into such a frenzy of self-torture, self-division, and self-deception that they were perforce caught up into the violence: as if, it might be, you were to approach a flagellant too closely, and catch the sting of the lash as it swung.

He was willing and eager to declare that a close relationship with him meant torture for a woman. 'She is an innocent person condemned to extreme torture; I am guilty of the wrong for which she is being tortured, and am in addition the torturer,' he wrote of his fiancée Felice Bauer. Perhaps it is a pity that the story of that long-drawn-out and dreadful relationship is documented in such detail; it cannot be ignored, it has to be attended to like the slow death under the harrow of the torture machine in the penal colony; but in talking of Kafka and women, we also have to remember his affection for his sister Ottla, the peaceful relationship at the end of his life with Dora Dymant, some fugitive early love affairs, and even his relationship with Milena Jesenská, desperate enough but just a little less agonized. Nevertheless, it is the relationship with Felice,* which overshadowed five years of his life, led (he believed) to his fatal illness, and summed up his central conflicts, which has to be looked at and learned from.

Are we justified in anatomizing a writer's private agonies? As human beings moved by the marvellous imaginings of our fellows, we cannot in honesty switch off our interest just where their private experiences begin. And it could be argued that Kafka's diaries and letters are as extraordinary, as much part of his work, as the fiction, that in spite of the difference between the subjectivity of the one and the marble objectivity of the other, they continually illuminate each other. And then Kafka himself was deeply interested in fellow-writers' personal lives, and found consolation, when he was struggling for a way of life, in comparing himself to Kierkegaard or Grillparzer or Kleist.

He met Felice Bauer in August 1912, when he was twenty-nine, at his friend Max Brod's home; jolted out of indecision by Brod, he had submitted his first collection of short pieces to a publisher, was about to have them accepted, and has come to discuss the future of the book. He had been writing well. He had been on holiday with Brod, and been much taken up with a girl in Weimar. His sister Valli was about to get engaged ('Love between brother and sister – the repeating of the love between mother and father,' he notes in the diary). How much any of these factors influenced his extraordinarily sudden capitulation to Felice Bauer we cannot know – though he says later in a letter that he would not have dared approach her if he had not been writing well. Their engagement photograph of 1917 shows a plain, simply dressed, competent-looking woman; she was executive secretary in a business firm. We can hardly doubt that it was at least partly her very strength and straightforwardness, qualities he felt he so totally lacked, that attracted Kafka.

Two days after their meeting he notes in his diary that he is thinking about her. A few days later: 'I was not at all curious about who she was, but rather took her for granted at once. Bony, empty face that wore its

* I do not call Felice Bauer by her first name in order to patronize her as a mere appendage of Kafka. I do so simply because it is conventional and convenient.

emptiness openly. .... As I was taking my seat I looked at her closely for the first time, by the time I was seated I already had an unshakeable opinion.' On 20 September he wrote to her for the first time. This letter contains the first of the many evasions and contortions that were to follow, for he says that he never expects a quick reply: even when he has to wait days for a letter, he says, he is never disappointed that it does not arrive. This was to be proved blatantly and defiantly untrue.

Two days after sending this first letter Kafka sits up throughout one whole night to write 'The Judgment' at a sitting. In his diary there is the beautiful, exultant entry:

This story, 'The Judgment', I wrote at one sitting during the night of the 22nd–23rd, from ten o'clock at night to six o'clock in the morning. I was hardly able to pull my legs out from under the desk, they had got so stiff from sitting. The fearful strain and joy, the way the story developed before me as if I were advancing over water. Several times during the night I heaved my own weight on my back. How everything can be said, how for everything, for the strangest fancies, there waits a great fire in which they perish and rise up again. How it turned blue outside the window. A wagon rolled by. Two men walked across the bridge. At two I looked at the clock for the last time. As the maid walked through the ante-room for the first time I wrote the last sentence.

It was a terrible exultation: his most splendid expression of joy in writing was at the same time a prediction of his fatal defeat in living. 'The Judgment' foretells the twelve years Kafka had left to live. It tells, in essence, of a young man engaged to be married whose father turns on him and sentences him to death, and of how the son complies, calling to his parents as he dies to tell them how much he loves them. 'Just take your bride on your arm and try getting in my way! I'll sweep her from your very side, you don't know how!' says the father. Kafka dedicated the story to Felice: to poor Felice.

The ending of the five years of their relationship has, therefore, already been foretold. Now Kafka writes his second letter to her. This is a more honest one; he makes a first attempt at explaining who he is. 'Oh, the moods I get into, Fräulein Bauer! A hail of irritability pours down upon me continuously. What I want one minute I don't want the next.' But he is brilliantly happy and writing well: Brod at this time notes in his diary, 'Kafka in unbelievable ecstasy', 'Kafka still greatly inspired.' Then comes the first in what is to be an interminable series of agonies, the situation he has so explicitly denied in his first letter: Fräulein Bauer does not reply at once, and so desperate notes are sent to her and to a mutual friend until the situation is put right.

The early exultation passes very soon. Though the correspondence is to last for years, the next few months encapsulate the whole relationship, a relationship between Kafka and everything that he reaches for outside himself. Felice, he says in the diary later, is only the occasion for a torment which would inevitably have presented itself in due course: 'F. simply happens to be the one through whom my fate is made manifest.' For the moment he can make her into pure writing; flesh and blood threaten, but, as yet, not imminently. However, even the written-to, invented Felice very soon indeed begins to become more than he can control. He writes more and more often, demands more and more replies and gets less and less satisfaction out of them, caught in the addict's vicious, masturbatory vortex:

When at last a letter arrives, then I think for a while I can be calm, that I shall be satisfied by it and that the day will go well. ... I read the letter once, put it aside, and read it again; I pick up a file but am really only reading your letter; I am with the typist, to whom I am supposed to dictate, and again your letter slowly slides through my fingers and I have begun to draw it out of my pocket when people ask me something and I know perfectly well I should not be thinking of your letter now, yet that thought is all that occurs to me – but after all that I am as hungry as before, as restless as before, and once again the door starts swinging merrily, as though the man with the letter were about to appear again.

A letter arrives; but it is no more than a letter after all, no sooner gobbled than the long day's wait begins for the next one – which will be seized and gobbled in its turn. Voracity increases, satisfaction decreases, in a dreadfully precise ratio; insatiability destroys what it longs for. Nothing she writes – and clearly she has been moved by the storm that has broken over her – can ever be enough. He knows it, and already the key word – torment – appears and reappears. 'How horribly I torment you!' He sees himself as a ghost sucking out her life-blood; but if he fattens, engorged, on the ritual of frantic demand and grovelling apology, he keeps it secret.

He knows that the future is going to be insoluble: 'When I want to draw close to someone, and fully commit myself, then my misery is assured.' The question of meeting again cannot be shelved for ever; Felice's letters evidently hint at it. He replies, many times, that he is a worm, a nothing, that there is no question for him of marriage or fatherhood – and yet again, 'When I read your letter, I feel I could overlook even what cannot possibly be overlooked.' He tries to explain the question of his writing, the nocturnal habits and special diet, the state of his inner world: 'If I arrived in person you would find me insufferable.' But the impossibility he faces is more than the practical difficulty of translating their communication into physical nearness, more than overthrowing the oedipal ban of a contemptuous father; it is the impossibility of establishing an exquisitely adjusted and absolutely safe relationship with the outer world while working from within his inner world – something that was only achieved,

Kafka aged five

His father, Hermann Kafka

Franz Kafka with two of his sisters

BELOW Hermann Kafka's trademark: *kavka* is Czech for jackdaw

Příkopy (the Moat) – one of the city's main thoroughfares in 1892

A contemporary picture of the Old Town Hall Square (with Týn Church) where the family moved in 1889

LEFT On entering High School, c. 1894

RIGHT A Baroque monument (Pohořelec) commemorating a fire in the Castle Square

BELOW The family apartment during his school days

ABOVE The schoolboy *c*. 1896

RIGHT Children in the Jewish quarter of Josefov, *c*. 1900

BELOW Es gibt ein Kommen und ein Gehen/Ein Scheiden und oft kein – Wiedersehen. Prag, den 20.November. (There is a coming and a going/a parting – often for ever.) Entry in a friend's album

Prague: a recent view of the Castle

perhaps, during the triumphant first few weeks of the correspondence with Felice.

For, without the 'real' world, what is there to populate the inner world? Much later, replying cruelly to Felice's suggestion that she will sit up and keep him company through the night while he writes, he says that no solitude is solitary enough for writing, that he would like to be locked in a soundproof cell, with pen and paper and food passed anonymously through a hatch. But what is there to write about, whom to write to, in a vacuum? Nothing, as he knows. Yet the 'real' world, the mere contiguity of another person, always carries the threat of crushing the inner world.

Only two months after his first letter he is writing a desperate proposal that they stop the correspondence. He does not send it. 'Accidentally', he nearly walks under a carriage; he wishes it had killed him. He proposes that Felice only writes once a week; but then again, 'Let us abandon it all.' And with honesty he concludes a letter: 'Did I think of signing myself *Dein*? No, nothing could be more false. No, I am forever fettered to myself, that's what I am.' (Later, he sent her a letter with part of his own address on it instead of hers.)

At this point Felice must have written to Max Brod in some distress, for a letter to her from Brod asks her to make allowances for Kafka's 'pathological sensitivity'. He is an idealist, an absolutist, but a 'unique and wonderful human being', needing special care and tenderness. So Felice writes to him in the *du* form; he is overjoyed; from now on she is 'dearest'. And another actor intervenes in the drama: Kafka's mother, 'by chance' reading Fräulein Bauer's letter (Felice had advised him in it to confide his troubles to his mother), begs her to persuade her son to eat and sleep 'like other young people of his age', so that his pastime of writing will do him no harm. (Later, after the couple have become engaged and then broken it off, his mother makes clearer her view of her son's writing: 'I was counting on Felice's intelligence, for I said to myself that a clever woman is able to change a man. Now all my hopes are dashed.' The threat that the two women pose to his work is not only in Kafka's mind.)

Three months after their one brief meeting Kafka is still writing twice a day, and Felice replying at almost the same rate, for if a letter of hers is delayed by so much as a day his anxiety mounts to a pitch of near-insanity. He has a dream: a postman brings an inexhaustible letter, page after page from an envelope that never empties. There are spells of calm and tenderness, but they always lead back to contradiction: 'If I were with you I'm afraid I should never leave you alone – and yet my craving to be alone is continuous.' 'I am frightened when you tell me that you love me, and if you didn't tell me, I should die.' Again, in desperation, he proposes that the spate of letter-writing should slacken: 'It can't go on like this. We are lashing each other with all these letters. They can't create a presence, only a mixture of presence and distance that becomes unbearable. . . . Let us put an end to this flood of letters that produces nothing but delusion, that makes one dizzy. . . .' Yet now he is writing 'The Metamorphosis', while Felice, evidently, is writing of tears and headaches and palpitations (he too has cried, says Kafka – over a passage in his book). As he remarks in a letter to Brod that is full of complaints, the beginnings of such letters cease to be true by the end: 'I feel a great deal better than I did when I began.' And Felice, perhaps, felt a great deal worse at the end of one of his letters than at the beginning. Kafka seems almost to experience a certain pride in transferring his torments to her. He sums the whole thing up in an answer that he imagines her making to an enquiry about her love affair.

Yes, he loves me, but for me it is a great misfortune. For he thinks that because he loves me he is free to torment me, and takes full advantage of this imaginary privilege. Almost every day comes a letter tormenting me to death, but then of course there comes another which is meant to make me forget the first; but how can I forget it? He always talks in riddles; one can't get a candid word out of him. It is possible that what he wants to say cannot be written, but then, for heaven's sake, he should stop it altogether and write like a sensible person. He doesn't torment me deliberately, for he loves me, I know, beyond all measure, but he ought to stop tormenting me and making me so miserable with his love.

Torment . . . torment . . . torment . . .: the word rings like a cracked bell from beginning to end of the letters.

It is not necessary to follow the excruciating story through four-and-a-half years more, to 1917, when Kafka coughed blood and knew that 'I will never be well again. . . . Tuberculosis is a weapon compared to which the countless others used earlier, ranging from "physical incapacity" up to my "work" and down to my "parsimony", look expedient and primitive'; nor to recount later relationships that followed the same pattern. There is enough – almost too much – in these letters of the first few months after the brief meeting with Felice Bauer. Even within these hundred thousand or so words the reader comes to feel trapped, transfixed, exhausted: yet condemned to go on, caught in the participants' torture machine.

It is the intensity of frantic, unassuageable need that so pierces the reader. Since we know Kafka was writing to an invention rather than to a known other person, it is need screaming into a vacuum. It is of course not accidental that in *The Trial* Kafka called one of K's warders Franz. Franz is to be whipped, on K.'s own half-unwilling instigation: 'Then the shriek rose from Franz's throat, single and irrevocable, it did not seem to come from a human being but from some tortured instrument, the whole corridor rang with it, the whole building must hear it.' These first letters are one great shriek of pain and appeal: an appeal not to disappear, not to desert him; above all, not to *become unreal* to his imagination. For it is more than a question of writing letters to an invention; he is trying, in Felice's person, to reinvent the whole outside world to suit his need. To say that, for this, he regresses to the dependence of childhood is an understatement. He supplicates in the posture not of a lover, but of an infant clinging to a capricious mother: 'my face resting on your shoulder, my talking, partly smothered and indistinctly, to your shoulder, your dress, to myself, while you can have no notion of what is being said.' He has no communication to make other than need and suppliance.

When a letter of Felice's ends, a mother has abandoned a child for ever: 'Finally I have to admit that it does have a full stop, that you got up and disappeared, as far as I am concerned, into the dark.' And when it is delayed there is no hope, there is an entire absence of hope, that it will ever come. When it does arrive he holds on to it in his pocket all day to convince himself that she exists: 'Stay with me, don't leave me.' Indeed, he cannot bear that she has any independent reality of her own at all, any existence that he cannot control: 'Oh God: I wish you were not on this earth, but entirely within me, or rather that I were not on this earth but entirely within you; I feel there is one too many of us; the separation into two people is unbearable.'

Once again we feel: should we not be looking the other way? Is there not something too frightening, too unbearable in the spectacle? Probably Felice Bauer, who sold the letters, and Kafka, whose project was continually to offer himself up for trial, would not have felt so. And I think Kafka's invention of Felice-as-world not only tells us about a pattern behind his work and a preoccupation in his life, but also about the way in which all writers turn to words in order to solidify their apprehension of things, to fill some empty socket in the mind by gestures of evocation.

What Kafka asks Felice over and over again is not, usually, what she thinks or feels, but what she wears, does, says, where she sits and stands and is, and at what time – and in particular, what exactly she is doing while he is writing to her or reading her letters – as if he were endlessly trying to fix an image from a faint or smudged negative, trying to establish a ground against which he can be a figure, rather than to talk to a real person. In choosing Felice and giving substance to her absent existence through letters, he is trying to perform some impossible therapy upon himself, to fill up a deep flaw that runs through his confidence in the world's reality. At its best, it does work, and banishes unreality: 'Before we met I also had these unpredictable moods; but then I seemed to lose all contact with the world; my life seemed disrupted; I rose to the surface and dived to the depths; now I have you, my dearest, I feel myself to be benevolently supported, and when I collapse I know it will not be forever, at least I think I know it. ...' At its worst, when a letter does not arrive, his whole existence is threatened with annihilation.

As therapy it *was* impossible, however, not only because Felice was a real and not an imaginary person, but because the whole fragile, agonizing project always balanced on a knife-edge. We can see that Kafka's earliest experience in life must have been of a world that alternately crushed and abandoned him, because the imprint of it is on his writing, with its images of suffocation and isolation. And the letters, in the end, could not 'create a presence, only a mixture of presence and distance that becomes unbearable'. Felice was not only the mother whom, as he says in 'The Married Couple', he 'lost when he was still a child' (lost in imagination); she was everything that was not him, that he wanted ravenously to absorb and fearfully to flee from, that either withdrew from him or engulfed him, that could scarcely ever be kept at just the right distance. But because she did after all have her own real, limited existence, 'the outside world' – she herself – was 'too small, too straightforward, too truthful to hold all that is contained in one man'. Nothing she did could ever have been right.

To make any comparisons between these obsessive, life-preserving preoccupations in the Felice letters and Kafka's portrayal of women in fiction is not a straightforward matter (is the castle, for instance, a woman?). We can, at the least, see from the fiction that Kafka was not a simple hater of women; the pain he inflicted was only incidental to his own. Women characters in his stories are not grotesque or ugly figures, but more often generous, erotic, elusive yet at home in the world; there is often a suggestion of the whore about them, and this whorishness is part of the fact that they have connections with the law, are 'owned' by the authorities – as, Kafka made it clear, all women were in a sense owned by his father.

When he was young, Kafka did have passing involvements with prostitutes, Brod reports – in striking contrast to the uncompromising ideal he had of marriage. The accessible woman's body was enticing but not good enough, the good woman too good to be desirable. ('The body of every other girl tempted me, but the body of the girl in whom I placed my hopes [for that reason?] not at all ... I can love only what I can place so high above me that I cannot reach it,' he wrote to Brod.) For marriage and family life, as the religious man's goal and duty, he did have the deep Jewish reverence: 'the infinite, deep, warm, saving happiness of sitting beside the cradle of one's child opposite its mother,' says the diary. He often quoted, says Brod, the solitary Flaubert's remark about his married friends: 'Ils sont dans le vrai.' And yet – there is the repugnance recorded in the diary at 'the sight of the nightshirts on my parents' beds, laid out for the night'. The very stringency of his ideal of marriage made the barriers so formidable (could one imagine Kafka, for instance, adopting Rilke's solution of marrying, leaving wife and child, and cossetting himself with the platonic attentions of elderly countesses?). He saw the dreadful, unattainable commitment as absolute.

To establish himself in relation to a woman – legally, totally, unconditionally – meant establishing himself in the world of nightshirts on the bed, of stability and comfort and fruitfulness; it meant establishing himself in his father's world:

> Why did I want to quit the world? Because 'he' would not let me live in it, in his world. Though indeed I should not judge the matter so precisely, for I am now a citizen of this other world, whose relationship to the ordinary one is the relationship of wilderness to cultivated land (I have been forty years wandering from Canaan); I look back at it like a foreigner, though in this other world as well – it is the paternal heritage I carry with me – I am the most insignificant and timid of creatures and am able to keep alive thanks only to the special nature of its arrangements.

And settling in the ordinary world where his father ruled presupposed first establishing himself securely within his own boundaries, able to reach out to real objects outside those boundaries – as he tried so desperately to do in the early letters to Felice. The closest parallel in his fiction to that relationship, a relationship to all women and the hope and dread they represented, is perhaps 'The Burrow', almost the last thing he wrote. The account of an animal's attempt to dig itself a home is, like the Felice story, a labyrinth of burrowing and defending, of agonized stratagems, of ruses and counter-ruses, menacing encroachments, wild joy and dreadful vulnerability, suffocating captivity and lonely exclusion; an oscillation between peaks of happiness and troughs of terror, between attack and withdrawal, impingement and depletion, as the animal attempts to mark out its territory and establish itself in the world.

Kafka demanded judgment – so long as he could pronounce it himself, on himself. He has put the case against his treatment of women in a 'protocol' which he 'quotes' in a deleted fragment of *The Castle*: 'It is clear that the Land Surveyor did not love Frieda, and that it was not for love of her that he wanted to marry her; he knew quite well that she was an insignificant hectoring girl, a girl, besides, with a past; he actually treated her accordingly, and went about his affairs without troubling about her. That is the gist of the matter. ...' The passage within which this was 'quoted' continues: 'That was the end of the page. There was also on the margin a childishly scrawled drawing of a man holding a girl in his arms; the girl's face was hidden in the man's breast, but he, being much taller, was looking over her shoulder at a paper in his hand on which he was gleefully entering some figures.'

Kafka suffered atrociously under the harrow, there is no doubt. But he was the taller figure, the one who could free himself from pain through writing over the girl's shoulder. He was the one, like the animal in 'The Burrow', 'privileged, as it were, not only to dream about the spectres of the night in all the helplessness and blind trust of sleep, but also at the same time to confront them in actuality with the calm judgment of the fully awake'.

7

Kafka's Castle?

Klaus Wagenbach
Translated by Sheila Stern

We can be fairly sure that the first pages of *The Castle* were written in January 1922. That February Kafka went to Spindlermühle in the North Bohemian mountains, then returned to Prague for four months. The last chapters of *The Castle* were composed, from the end of June 1922 onwards, in Planá on the River Lužnice in Southern Bohemia, near Tábor, where Kafka was staying with his sister Ottla and from where he wrote to his friend Max Brod at the beginning of September 1922, 'I have had to abandon the castle story for good, it seems . . .'

The description of the real-life correlatives of this unfinished novel must begin with a mention of the fragment of a so-called 'family-book' of the county-lands to which belonged the little village of Osek (Wossek); the village lies roughly a hundred kilometres south of Prague, and had about a hundred inhabitants. The 'family-book' is now in the City Archive of Prague. It is almost the only source for Kafka's paternal forebears, whose domicile at Osek can be traced back to the eighteenth century. The Kafka family belonged to the Bohemian Jewish provincial proletariat. They were butchers at first, and later, after the Emancipation of the Jews in Austria in 1848, shopkeepers. The fragmentary nature of the Osek 'family-book' is the result of historical circumstances; these books listed the Jews more or less as property and kept track of who occupied the position of family head, and thus possessed a formal permit to work and the right to a marriage-licence (without which no marriage was permitted). After the Emancipation, 'family-books' were no longer kept. The position of head of the Kafka family had fallen to the elder brother of Kafka's grandfather. Jacob Kafka, Franz's grandfather, who was able to marry only after the Emancipation, wed his neighbour Franziska Platowski, who was thirty-three, two years younger than himself. The couple moved into house No. 30 in Osek and it was there that the six children of the butcher's family were born: four sons, including Kafka's father Hermann, and two daughters.

The village of Osek consists of two parts. The larger is situated in a depression, beside a mere; the smaller, a few hundred yards away, is on a rise. The whole village is small: at present there are about 150 inhabitants. Coming from the direction of Radomyšl, you first enter the lower village, a ribbon of a few houses on either side of the road, which comes out on the village green. On the green there has always been an inn. Beyond the green the road divides. On the corner stands a little chapel, and the mere flows out beneath the road that forks off to the right. This road leads to a castle standing on the rise. The other road, half-left, runs in a curve through the open fields, then up the rise into the upper village, which surrounds the castle, and then on to Kbelnice.

From the village green two lanes also lead off to the left. The Kafka house is in the first of these lanes: a typical Bohemian village dwelling, hardly above the height of a man, now roofed with tiles, formerly thatched. You have to stoop to enter. The house has now had two rooms built on, but originally consisted only of one large ground-floor room, in which the whole family – two adults and six children – lived in the most primitive conditions, as Kafka's father was continually reminding his son Franz.

In the mid-nineteenth century the lower village was exclusively peopled by Jews, and even today is still called 'the Jewry'. It was a fairly large community, as the 'family-book' confirms, with its own cemetery and synagogue, the ruins of which can still be seen. The Osek community was indeed at that time a kind of educational centre and maintained its own school; the nearest Jewish school was at Tábor, some fifty kilometres away. By about 1890 this community had dwindled to a few families, and they too left Osek in the next few years, when the school and the synagogue were closed. The Christian peasants, who had previously lived only in the upper part of the village, round the castle, gradually moved into the lower village.

The Jewish cemetery is in the forest, about a quarter of an hour's walk from the village; it has been deserted for decades. The last Jew was buried there in 1889 and his gravestone has a Hebrew inscription at the top, and under it, in German:

> Here lies
> Jakob Kafka
> of Wohsek
> died 10th December 1889
> Peace to his ashes!

Kafka's grandfather died on a winter's day, the last member of what had been a large Jewish community but had been diminishing ever since the Emancipation, following the general pattern of the retreat of the Jews, in the middle years of the last century, from the provinces to the 'liberal' big towns. Jacob Kafka's sons and daughters – Franz's uncles, aunts and father – had also joined this exodus and were already living as traders in nearby Strakonice, Prague, Kolín and Litoměřice.

Kafka must have known Osek, most probably from visiting his grandfather, but he certainly saw it on the occasion of the funeral, when he was six-and-a-half years old and a pupil at the Prague German primary school on the Fleischmarkt. As the eldest son of the family, he would be obliged by Jewish custom to attend his grandfather's funeral. In the next few years he probably visited Osek on various other occasions during his school holidays, which he often spent with an aunt in Strakonice. After his schooldays Kafka probably never visited Osek again, for obvious reasons; it was his father's place, the geographical fixed point of those accounts of childhood sufferings the retelling of which represented his father's principal educational method.

The upper village consists of only a few houses, grouped round the castle and a farmyard. Seen from the lower village, the castle looks like this:

It was neither an old stronghold nor a new mansion, but a rambling pile consisting of a few two-storeyed buildings and many small ones standing close together; anyone who did not know it was a castle might have taken it for a little town. K. could see only one tower and it was impossible to tell whether it belonged to a dwelling-house or a church. . . .

K. continued on his way with his eyes fixed on the Castle, thinking of nothing else. But as he drew nearer he was disappointed in the Castle; after all it was nothing but a wretched-looking little town, a collection of village-houses, its only distinction the fact that it seemed to be built of stone; but the plaster had long since fallen off and the stone looked as if it was crumbling away. . . . Mentally he compared the church-tower at home with the tower above him. . . . This tower – the only one he could see – the tower of a house, as it now appeared, perhaps of the principal building, was uniformly round and in part softened by a mantle of ivy.

Thus Kafka describes the castle in his novel. It is only the castle tower at Osek that does not quite correspond to this description – it is square and topped by a four-sided gabled roof – but the other details are exact: an unimpressive tower, not a church-tower or belfry but like the little towers sometimes seen on dwelling-houses. As far as the rest of the castle is concerned, Kafka's account corresponds precisely to this one: neither an old feudal castle nor a splendid new building but a 'straggling collection of buildings dating most likely from the end of the eighteenth century, two-storeyed and surrounded by numerous low structures standing close together. One might indeed, from the lower village, take this assemblage of buildings for a small town, and indeed the closer view is disappointing; it is rather a wretched-looking castle, and the 'town' is composed of village dwellings. In addition to this, the castle offers no 'front view' towards either of its gateways. The façade itself turns towards the garden, which is enclosed and hidden by high walls.

The Osek castle has two gates, the main one facing the upper village. The gate to the lower village is more of an entrance for farm traffic, which can reach the courtyard only from this side. From the lower village there are three routes to the castle. One is the short, straight one, that leads directly from the village green to the lower gate. The second is the road that leads half-left from the green, passes the upper gate after a kilometre or so and continues to Kbelnice. The third way from the lower village to the castle is only a field path; it curves and winds its way to the Jewish cemetery at the edge of the forest, and from there one can walk on beside the high castle wall to reach the upper gateway. They are complicated routes: the shortest does not even lead to the right gate, the others go a long way round to get there. They would be particularly complicated for a child in his first year at primary school, a city child not at home in the village, one, moreover, having a child's perspective and sense of proportion, in whose mind minor topographical puzzles would seem to represent immense distances.

The two oldest inhabitants of Osek remember that period, and we asked them about the castle and the village; they are a lady of eighty-three and a man of nearly the same age. The first question was about the castle itself, and we quote the answer verbatim: 'The castle, you know, had an enormous administrative staff.' We were then given an exact picture of this 'administration', with its bailiffs, secretaries, gamekeepers, tree-wardens, foresters, indoor menservants, grooms and many maids; there was uncertainty as to whether there were more or less than a dozen housemaids. When we asked about the bailiffs, the word 'bailiff' was literally translated into Czech, but, nonetheless, in answering, they said 'castellans', the term Kafka uses in his novel: 'The castellans were always changing: they used to arrive with one carriage and drive away with several.'

In brief, we were given the image of a manorial castle with an administrative staff out of proportion to its modest estate, and with corrupt officials – just as Kafka described it. The owner of the castle was Eduard, Knight of Doubek, a man of low stature, belonging to a newly-rich Prague family ennobled only in the nineteenth century. Our two informants were unable to agree as to whether he was kind or unpleasant, but they both said he had always 'had a lot of women about'.

The land was entirely owned by the castle and all the peasants worked exclusively for it. Even the inn by the village green was castle property.

Kafka's grandfather Jacob, the butcher, was, we were told, a village character, very popular with the children, to whom he always offered sweets, but also generally respected, almost feared, on account of his size and physical strength – he was summoned to the inn if there was a fight. When he died many relatives came to the funeral, we were told – some of them from Prague, in a coach.

Kafka often refers to himself as having been a singularly helpless child. Memories of childhood and youth – not only his own – were for him always examples, documents, proofs. Especially for the period shortly before the composition of *The Castle*, there are many autobiographical notes in his diaries and letters. The most important references are in the *Letter* to his father, written in November 1919, two-and-a-half years before he began *The Castle*. Kafka writes there,

You have always made it a matter of reproach to me (either when we were alone or in front of others, showing no feeling for the humiliation this caused – your children's affairs were always public affairs) that thanks to your hard work I lived in peace, warmth and abundance, never wanting for anything. I am thinking here of remarks that must have positively traced furrows in my brain, like: 'When I was only seven I had to push the handcart round the villages.' 'We all had to sleep in one room.' 'We were glad when we had potatoes to eat.' 'For years I had sores on my legs because of not having enough warm clothes.' 'When I was only a little boy I was sent away to Písek to work in a shop. . . .' 'But in spite of all that, Father was always Father to me. Nobody nowadays knows what that means. What do you children know! Nobody's been through all that! Does any child understand that these days?' Stories like these might under other circumstances have been very instructive and might have encouraged me and given me strength to undergo the same sufferings and privations that my father had contended with. But that wasn't at all what you wanted, the whole situation had been changed as a result of your efforts, there was no opportunity to prove oneself in the way you had done. . . .

The phrase Kafka uses about his father's words having 'traced furrows' in his brain is not only strange but incomparably more vivid than any other comment he makes on his childhood. His father's reminiscences all referred to a single locality – Osek itself. Such admonitions, which still seem traumatic to the almost forty-year-old writer of the *Letter*, must have been all the more frightening to the six-and-a-half-year-old travelling with his father to his grandfather's funeral.

A village, a castle, a one-roomed house, a butcher's shop, a grandfather who was 'always the father' to Kafka's father, half-understood Jewish ritual that seemed to originate in this village, a school, an inn, the grandfather as peace-maker – for a boy who arrived there on 10 December

1889 and stayed a few days, all this must have been well known, 'stories he knew by heart', endlessly repeated as moral warnings, now experienced only as threats.

On the boy's arrival in snowy weather the proportions must suddenly have seemed to him to have shifted. A strangeness has come over the place he had thought he knew. The life of the peasants is incomprehensible to the city child, especially as it is winter-time, when there is obviously no sense in it. The school is small, with very few pupils, and the children speak Czech instead of German, as they do at the school in Prague. Judaism, towards which Kafka's father had always enjoined an attitude of reverent 'piety', is scarcely recognizable and unglamorous; the synagogue is half empty, quite unlike the one in Prague. The villagers too think the Jews are odd and avoid them, although they all, Jew and non-Jew alike, speak the same language. The castle everyone talks about – 'the old stories he knew by heart' – can hardly be seen; it is hard to reach and the gates are shut; children are not allowed in, least of all Jewish children. The owners are not in residence, for it is a summer castle. Only the bailiffs, keepers, secretaries, servants are there. And, anyhow, the castle is not at all impressive when you get nearer.

A forty-year-old remembers the school, with its two rooms and the teacher who lodges at the butcher's. He remembers an ostracized family, paths in the snow, stories of the castle, a funeral – for the novel *The Castle*, according to Max Brod, was to have ended with the death of the land-surveyor K.

A forty-year-old tries to survey a dream, a story, a recollection. But he does so – this is where the differences begin – with the instruments he has acquired in the previous thirty years. The survey comes to nothing, and the novel *The Castle* is the account of this failure.

All I have put together here are hints, circumstantial evidence. But they may serve as a warning against merely speculative metaphysical interpretations, and also as evidence of the novel's basis in reality. They do not, of course, suffice for an interpretation: that would require more than factual circumstances alone.

PART TWO

SUMMONSES TO INTERPRETATION

8

On Kafka's Novels*

Martin Walser
Translated by Allan Blunden

The Writer – his Life and his Work

Franz Kafka is a writer who has assimilated his experience so thoroughly that we have no need of biographical information in order to understand his work. For he has already completed the task of transmuting reality *before* he comes to write his fiction, through the systematic impoverishment – indeed the destruction – of his real-life social self, sacrificed in order that he can create in its place a personality wholly devoted to writing. This literary *persona* – '*poetica personalità*', in Croce's phrase – determines the form of Kafka's work; so we need to look briefly at the way it evolved.

As Kafka's social self becomes impoverished, so his literary *persona* grows and develops. In his diary he analyses these processes in order to discern the '*pattern* in a life like mine'. The relentless impoverishment of his social self becomes necessary because Kafka as a writer is no longer able to cope with life in any other way. But it is precisely this situation which makes writing possible: 'The man who can't cope with life while he's living needs one hand free to try and ward off the despair he feels at his own fate ..., but with the other hand he is able to *record* what he sees beneath the ruins; for he sees more things than other people, and different things. He's dead in his own lifetime, you see, and yet he's the one who really survives. ...'

---

* These excerpts are taken from *Beschreibung einer Form*, Carl Hanser Verlag, Munich 1961, pp. 11–108.

The Mode of Narration

Kafka writes his stories in the third person, and does not appear himself as narrator. (We are referring now to the three novels.) Narration as an aesthetic reality in itself does not form part of the book's actual fabric. Consequently the reader is never addressed directly – an important point, when one considers how freely story-tellers throughout history have availed themselves of this device, which remains the peculiar prerogative of narrative writing. (The drama lacks this facility, with the exception of a few experimental works which have tried introducing the author on to the stage.)

[Kafka] is never present as story-teller: the story is simply *told*. He dispenses with this visible narrator, the 'creative manipulator', who has even been described as the '*sine qua non* of all narrative literature'. What we propose to show is that for Kafka, narration *without* a visible narrator is the *sine qua non*, and that his writing nonetheless remains wholly narrative in character. For him this narrative stance is a necessity, the mode which he found to be best adapted to his own needs. He started writing the early chapters of *The Castle* in the first person, so that to this extent he did 'appear' in the novel in the guise of first-person narrator; but later on, in the course of further work on the book, he replaced this first-person form by the use of a third person – namely, K. Thereafter he makes no further attempt to establish a narrative presence in the work.

The light in Kafka's works grows progressively more dim, and his heroes find themselves further and further removed from their goals. These tendencies inevitably serve to diminish the visible solidity of Kafka's narrative world. The hero sees less; therefore he interprets instead. We as readers are totally dependent on this interpretation, since there is no narrator on hand to tell us more than the hero himself sees – for the simple reason that the story is narrated *through* the hero.

Total congruence of author and medium is called for whenever events are leading up to something that is not to be revealed to the hero until later. There are certain developments that begin and end within the individual works, tensions that underlie the action, circumstances that cannot be made known to the hero until after a certain point in time – 'revelations', in a certain sense. The atmosphere created by a literary work depends very largely on whether we as readers are made aware of these circumstances right from the beginning, so that we observe the unknowing hero groping his way towards a discovery of them; or whether we ourselves share his ignorance and surprise. If Kafka had wanted to hint at events to come he would have had to distance himself from the hero on occasion, and thereby remove us from the hero's perspective as well.

Here we are concerned with K.'s interpretations of the people and things around him. [These explain] the frequent use of conjectural language. In fact its frequency increases from one work to the next, until in *The Castle* it has become strikingly stereotyped in form. These interpretations, which always point in the same direction, are conveyed without any intervention on the part of the narrator. Their menacing implications for K. are borne in upon us in the same moment that they are perceived by K. – because we only learn of them *through* K. The expressive force of these menacing implications derives not least from Kafka's refusal to step outside the particular point of view from which they are perceived. All is uncertain: 'it was not clear whether the contempt in her voice was directed at K. or at her own reply ...'; 'the fact that they knew who K. was did not appear to be a point in his favour. ...' When K. thinks that somebody wants to do him a service, this is his immediate reaction: 'His whole manner did not suggest any special desire to be friendly. It was more like a kind of selfish, anxious, almost pedantically insistent attempt to get K. away from the front of the house' [all these quotations are from four pages in the first chapter of *The Castle*].

These interpretations follow a fixed pattern: they are the manifestations of a kind of compulsion always to react in exactly the same way. At the same time the narrative stance adopted by Kafka finds in them its purest form of expression. By telling the story from a single point of view he shows that K. exists in a particular kind of relationship with his environment, and that this relationship never alters. The figure of K. has been intentionally set up – one might almost say 'constructed' – in such a way that interpretations of this kind become a recurrent feature of the narrative. So absolute is the congruence of author and hero in Kafka's case that he prefers to turn things upside down and make the hero an enigma to himself rather than consent to intervene with any kind of authorial interpretation. It is just possible that K. himself has thoughts about his own extremist interpretations at some stage – and in fact there is one occasion (but only one) when he admits that he may have gone too far (*The Castle*, Chapter 20, in K.'s harangue of Pepi). But then he confirms himself in his original opinion once more and says, 'I don't know if that's a true picture of things, but I do know that it's closer to the truth than the picture you paint.' Kafka does not intervene himself; he allows the serving girl and K. to present their opposing views and leaves it at that. He simply tries to preserve a balance of interpretation.

But when a narrator appears as a character within the story we are at liberty to 'interpret' what he says. This is no less true for Kafka than for any other writer, and we find such an instance in *The Trial*, when the prison chaplain tells the parable 'Before the Law'. Following on from the telling of this story, Joseph K., together with the priest himself, suggests a number of possible interpretations. But – and this is a point that many Kafka commentators tend to overlook – these interpretations remain contained within the novel: they are not addressed to us, the readers, as a source of reliable information, but are offered for our interpretation just like any other part of the text. It is exactly the same when K. discusses the Castle with Olga; his interpretations, or perceptions of meaning, are open to interpretation in their turn, and carry their own meaning for us, the readers.

A further consequence of the narrative technique practised by Kafka is the irreversibility of the narrative process itself. Nothing can be anticipated, because there is no narrator to signify what is to come. Events simply take their course: nothing can retard the process, nothing can accelerate it, and nothing can interrupt it.

The essential results of Kafka's method [of doing without a 'broad' world represented by an independent narrator] are these: the hero's impression becomes increasingly absolute and so, consequently, does the reader's; and this in turn is marked by an increased dominance of unsecured interpretations, usually in the subjunctive mode. The work, then, develops from within itself as a process that is irreversible, linear, without commentary, taking place outside any natural time scale.

The world that is narrated in this manner lacks 'breadth', in the sense of richness and variety. But the narration itself – and hence the world that it encompasses – is intensive in character. Sartre proposes that we should no longer seek to express 'beauty' in terms of 'form' or 'substance', but in terms of 'fullness of being'. 'We should like our books to float in the air,' he writes, 'while our words ... quietly and imperceptibly become sleighs that carry the reader into the midst of a world without witnesses. ...' Such is the situation of Kafka's narrative writing, from which the omniscient narrator – indeed any form of visible narrator – has been finally banished.

Function as Personal Characteristic: Collectives

For Joseph K. it is significant that the defendants who fill the interminable attics in the suburb all appear to belong to the 'upper classes' (*The Trial*,

Chapter 3). What is equally significant is that they now constitute, in their capacity as defendants, a new social grouping, a new class. Like every other class in the structured world of Kafka's fiction, this one has what one might call its characteristic posture: in this case the bent backs and sagging knees that are the result of long periods of waiting in the low-ceilinged attics. As a class they have evolved their own social rules, their own superstitions; they comfort and torment themselves with the formula that waiting is not a waste of time, whereas any form of 'independent action' most certainly is. It is essential to keep oneself continually occupied, for there is another rule which states that 'a man under suspicion is better off moving than at rest, because the man who is at rest may be sitting in the balance without even realizing it, being weighed along with his sins' (*The Trial*, Chapter 8). They even have their social pride: as a defendant Block evidently regards himself as superior to Joseph K. because he crawls up to the lawyer's bed on all fours, while Joseph K. remains quietly sitting down – even though he too is a man on trial.

What these defendants are or were in any other context is of no consequence at all; since the story is told through K., who only sees them as defendants, they possess no other attributes that we know of. They are no longer citizens of the world at large, but functional figures in the artificial world created by Kafka: they have no existence outside their role as defendants. Some are having more luck with their case than others, some submit better petitions than others, and so on; but apart from these minor differences of degree they all appear identical. Kafka has no need of more elaborate characterization; he can achieve his purpose with great economy of means simply by slotting a figure into place within the hierarchy of his structured world. The figure is sufficiently sharply defined by the place he assigns to it. These defendants, viewed as a collective body, have their counterpart in the villagers in *The Castle*. Like the defendants, these villagers only exist essentially in the plural. Just as the defendants abandon themselves unthinkingly to their superstitions and their stereotyped maxims, so 'the people [in the village] are busy creating their own confusion' (*The Castle*, Chapter 15). 'Castle stories' are made up: 'there are people here who positively feed on that kind of thing.' Like the defendants, they use this kind of talk to comfort and 'entertain' each other. K. is conscious that he must become 'indistinguishable' from 'the peasants' if he is to gain a footing in this situation (*The Castle*, Chapter 2). We only ever hear about 'the people', 'the peasants'. They too have their 'superstitions', of course (as in *The Castle*, Chapter 15) [Amalia's secret], and their own well-defined patterns of gesture and behaviour: their collective pushing and shoving, their habit of always reacting as a group, their timid and sly whispering among themselves, their dull-witted, frightened childishness – such are their characteristic ways. K. is able to describe them in a single sentence, compressing their entire existence into a few words: what is more, he can speak of them in the singular, since what is true of one is automatically true of all the rest. He begins with a reference to 'their literally tortured faces' and then continues in the singular: 'it was as if the skull had been beaten flat on top, and the facial features distorted into their present shape by the pain of being beaten. ...' (*The Castle*, Chapter 2). 'How humbled they must be,' thought Joseph K. when he saw the defendants for the first time (*The Trial*, Chapter 3); and exactly the same might have been said of the villagers. Their faceless submission is intended to show K. the power of the Castle: such is the underlying function of this collective body, just as it was the function of the defendants, as a class, to show Joseph K. what the experience of a trial can do to a so-called human being.

Companions

The purpose of the figures we shall now consider is to distract the respective heroes to whom they are assigned, making them lose sight of themselves and their objectives. ...

The 'companions' assigned to the hero in *The Trial* are the three junior bank clerks, Rabensteiner, Kullich and Kaminer. It is through them that the world of the Law Court offices, a chaotic world of attics and passageways, makes its entry into the orderly and well-regulated life of the bank. When Joseph K. first finds out about the proceedings against him and is about to return to the bank, these three companions thrust themselves upon him in order to 'distract' him (*The Trial*, Chapter 1). Through such distraction all the various companion figures seek to make Kafka's heroes lose sight of themselves. The assistants in *The Castle* are given the task of providing K. with 'a bit of entertainment' (Chapter 16). And distraction is likewise the aim of the two vagabonds in *America*.

It is indicative of the functional character of these companions that Kafka's heroes are not free to choose them for themselves. K. in *The Castle* describes his assistants as 'a couple of lads who've wafted down from the Castle' (Chapter 18); he has to be expressly informed that they have not 'drifted' to his side, but have been 'assigned' to him (Chapter 5). And just as these assistants have not simply 'dropped down from the sky', so Blumfeld's 'trainees'* have not been assigned to him at random. There is a very definite point to these assignments, and the companions are put there in order to

* 'Blumfeld, an Elderly Bachelor'; see below, p. 153.

fulfil a distinct function. They come suitably equipped for their task: they are 'insignificant, anaemic young men' (*The Trial*, Chapter 1) or 'silly boys' (*The Castle*, Chapter 13), 'mere lads, full of high spirits and a little silly' (*The Castle*, Chapter 12). One can imagine the kind of tasks to which such companions are suited, just from a brief look at the range of expressive possibilities available to them: Kaminer's 'tedious and vacuous liveliness', the way the assistants 'hop about' and 'fling out their arms' (*The Castle*, Chapter 13), while their flesh 'sometimes gave the impression that it was not really living', and the way they walk 'as though [their limbs were] charged with electricity' (Chapter 16), their 'whimpering' and tapping on the window panes, their whispering, giggling, sighing, staring, smiling and grinning – such are their characteristic gestures.

If it is true that Kafka's figures acquire their identity through their function, then it follows that they must lose that identity as soon as they step outside their functional role *vis-à-vis* the hero. In fact the only time this happens is in *The Castle*, when the assistants are dismissed by K. By their dismissal they are made to step outside their function; and with that their whole being – and the way it expresses itself – undergoes a change. The change is almost instantaneous. K. no longer recognizes one of the assistants: 'he seemed older, wearier, more wrinkled, but fuller in the face, and his walk too was quite different from the brisk step of the assistants, whose limbs twitched at the joints as though charged with electricity. ...' (Chapter 16). In their capacity as assistants Arthur and Jeremias had formed a pair, united by their common mission; but now, after K. has ended their association by dismissing them, their 'youthful spirits are quite gone'. If the office of companion were to be transferred to someone else, that person would undoubtedly have to adopt the same gestures and modes of expression; for without these he could not fulfil his function as a companion within the general economy of Kafka's structured world.

In *The Trial* too – and even in *America* – there are hints to support our view that Kafka's figures acquire their identity through their function. When Joseph K. summons his three companions at the bank to his office, he finds their manner perfectly normal; they have 'become absorbed once more into the general mass of clerks at the bank' (Chapter 1). But as he is walking out to the suburbs on the Sunday morning to attend the first interrogation they reappear once more, and now they behave again as they did at the first meeting in Joseph K.'s lodgings: they 'cut across in front of K.', 'lean inquisitively over the railing' and stare after him (Chapter 2); once again they have become disquieting figures who shadow the hero in his movements.

Women

Here too it is clear that Kafka's figures do not undergo any kind of 'spiritual transformation'. The lives of women [in the novels] contain only superficial change – a change in status, for example, and a corresponding change in the way their presence makes itself felt in the work. Their rank and position within the structured hierarchy of Kafka's world is their one and only important distinguishing characteristic, and one which is reflected in the smallest detail of movement and gesture. This determines K.'s intention toward the 'girl from the Castle'. She too is to be used in his struggle, since 'one must take advantage of anything that offers the slightest hope' (Chapter 13). K. does indeed 'take advantage' of women, using them as tools for his own ends. We are told nothing about these women unless it has a significance in relation to their function. So, for example, Kafka differentiates hardly at all between the outward appearance of Leni and that of the Court usher's wife: one has 'dark, shining eyes' (*The Trial*, Chapter 2), the other has 'big dark eyes' (Chapter 6). But what he does represent in some detail is their functional value, which is measured by the quality of their relations with, for example, the Castle officials. . . .

The landlady of the Brückenhof inn, for instance, is the archetypal ex-mistress of a Castle official (Chapter 6). She shows consideration for K. only on Frieda's account. And she does this only because Frieda, like herself, is a former mistress of Klamm's. ('Did I concern myself with you so long as you were on your own?' she asks K., in Chapter 4.) Everything we learn about this woman is connected with Klamm: thus she is forced to evict K. from her house 'out of respect for Klamm's memory' (Chapter 7). The landlady, then, is another figure who has no characteristics of her own; her whole life revolves around Klamm. Although she tells her story from beginning to end, we learn nothing that is not directly related to Klamm. Her function as a figure in *The Castle* is to represent the power and prestige of the Castle and the extent of its influence in the village.

Enemies

Kafka's heroes have enemies whose hostility is based on their own 'personal' decision. . . . Even in *America* they are wholly committed to that world against which Karl must contend. They are in the service of injustice and of a disorder that has donned the semblance of order. So too are the officials who work for the Castle and the Law Court; but they remain 'impersonal', always acting on instructions, in the pursuit of their duty, in accordance with some law – never as individuals in their own right. In a word, they are mere functionaries.

To that extent the enemies appear to contradict what has just been said about the figures in Kafka's world – namely, that they are purely functionaries. But one feature, common to all these enemies, locates them firmly within that structured world again and vindicates them in their role as figures: their hostility towards the hero is always an absolute hostility. They have no *reason* to adopt a hostile attitude: they simply exist as expressions of hostility in its purest form.

The Anti-World and its Representatives

In order to give an account of the hierarchies in *The Trial* and *The Castle*, we must begin by looking at their lowest ramifications. On one occasion in *America* Kafka gives a description of an official that points forward to the later novels: the 'senior hotel clerks' go about dressed in 'black frock coats and top hats' (Chapter 6). When the two employees of the Court come to take Joseph K. away for execution, they too are wearing frock coats and 'top hats [that are] seemingly irremovable' (*The Trial*, last chapter). The officials and agents of authority who are visibly in evidence generally belong to the lower echelons. The descriptions that are given of these lower-placed officials conform to a more or less fixed pattern. Either they are inordinately slender and agile, like the first warder (*The Trial*, Chapter 1), the Clerk of Inquiries (Chapter 3) and Schwarzer (*The Castle*, Chapter 1), in which case they are stylish, dressed always in tight-fitting clothes and generally theatrical in their manner; or else they are 'fat', like the two executioners and the second warder. The black frock coats and top hats, which made their first appearance in *America*, recur many times thereafter.

The higher the rank of an individual figure, the more sketchy is the description that can be given of him. The senior officials are virtually faceless. There is much uncertainty about their appearance, which actually alters according to their function. The image the villagers have of Klamm, for example, is 'correct only in certain basic traits. ... His appearance when he arrives in the village is said to be quite different from his appearance when he leaves ... he looks different when he's alone, different again when he is talking to people, and when he is up at the Castle he is like a different person altogether – which is hardly surprising, all things considered' (Chapter 16). This sentence shows why it is that whenever we speak of 'characterization' we are only able to list a few isolated traits – the sort of thing that would be labelled 'purely external' in the work of another writer. But let us recall once more Kafka's narrative technique: the story is told through the hero, who sees everything 'only' from the outside. But what he sees, or rather the way he sees it, is all that there is to see; that in itself is sufficient as characterization. The example of Klamm makes the point very clearly: outward change, brought about by a change in function, embodies the whole essence of such a figure. Behind the outward appearance there is – nothing. Only one of these many functions and faces is accessible to K., and that is the one assumed by the official in his direct dealings with K. Above all else the officials display an extraordinary degree of nervous sensibility in their contacts with the various parties and hence with K. This extreme sensibility is not a psychological characteristic in the normal sense, but an expressive device aimed at underlining the total class distinction between the official and the party he is dealing with. The degree of sensitivity shown by the official is determined by his rank, so that each official is necessarily characterized and defined by the position he occupies within the hierarchy. Thus we are told by the secretary Bürgel, in *The Castle*, that the officials 'are people who, by virtue of their work, are endowed with a quite extraordinary subtlety of feeling' (Chapter 18).

If the degree of sensitivity is contingent upon rank, then it follows that an official who occupies a senior position must be even more remote from the parties.* This is why we know so little about these senior officials, and why all kinds of legends and exaggerated stories have grown up around them; and this is also the reason why they exercise such a powerful hold over the parties.

Because these officials are merely steps in the 'infinite hierarchy' (*The Trial*, Chapter 7), they cannot have any opinions of their own, nor can they be depicted as personalities. Everything they say is part of the established stock-in-trade of the hierarchical organization to which they belong. Consequently Kafka's figures have no past: this is a dimension that can properly be attributed only to the organization itself.

Although it is impossible to know exactly where these figures stand within the hierarchy of the structured world, they are always adequately defined by their function in relation to Kafka's heroes. Thus the landlady enlightens K. about Momus in these terms: 'I'm not talking about him as a private person, but as he is when he acts with Klamm's assent ... then he's a tool to be used by Klamm. ...' (*The Castle*, Chapter 9). And it is with this 'tool', this mere creature, that K. has to conduct his business! As we have noted many times before, these tools of the authorities have their own very specific and characteristic patterns of gesture and movement. Thus the 'enemies' are agile, quick and given to unexpected moves; the 'companions' are clumsy, and apt to dash about restlessly in all directions; the defendants and villagers are recognizable by their stoop, and by the way they push and shove in a cowed mass, whispering among themselves;

* Because these 'parties' – and Kafka allows the term's legal connotations full play – offend the officials' sensitivity by their very existence. [Ed.]

the emissaries of the organization are theatrical, smooth and stylish, or else fat and greasy; and the officials are defensive, timid, sensitive and suspicious. As we have also indicated before, these patterns of gesture and movement derive from the particular functions which these figures perform. Their physical being is determined by their role *vis-à-vis* the hero, whether it be to confuse him, disturb him, torment him, or simply let him flounder about in the dark. It is quite obvious that no such differences exist between real human beings; and that such a view of man cannot be encompassed by any empirical approach to human existence, in terms of anthropological, biological and psychological factors. Kafka devises new resources of expression to meet his particular needs.

Reification

Kafka shifts the dividing line between the living and the inanimate in a direction that runs totally counter to the laws of nature – and all in the service of his expressive purpose. Thus he can write of a character that he looks 'like a pole that's dangling about', or is 'cut out of tissue paper', so that people can hear him 'rustling' as he walks along. These figures make no sound when they laugh (*The Castle*, Chapters 7 and 15), and instead of coming of their own accord they are 'placed in position' like objects (Chapter 18). . . .

This process of depersonalization goes even further, to the point where some of Kafka's figures manipulate their own limbs and facial features, as if these were not naturally part of themselves but had somehow been presented to them as an afterthought for their use and entertainment. They are themselves surprised, annoyed and amused by all the different things they can do with them. They commend their limbs by 'tapping' them, as though not yet altogether sure of them – as though they might still take on a life of their own.

Everything that is normally contingent upon a personal consciousness capable of perceiving, enquiring and initiating action, or else upon the operation of certain laws of nature, has here taken on an independent existence of its own and become an object to be looked at and observed. When the warder is being beaten he does not cry out like a human being, but like 'some tortured musical instrument', and the cry he utters is a sound 'without pause or modulation' (*The Trial*, Chapter 5). In other words, Kafka has depersonalized both the person and his form of utterance. All the things that normally exist in a state of flux – breathing, light, sound, pleasure, etc. – are arrested and held fast by Kafka, who renders them as tangible *objects*. As he himself says [in a passage omitted from *The Castle*], one must have the strength 'to keep on staring at things without closing one's eyes ... but if one relaxes for a single moment and closes one's eyes, then everything promptly dissolves into darkness.'

Hearings and Examinations

The normal judicial process presupposes the existence of two parties and a third impartial authority, whose task it is to reach a judgment following the hearing. In Kafka's novels one of the two parties is the hero, who is invariably alone (except for one or two minor occasions in *America*). He is defendant or plaintiff (a rigid distinction between the two is not always made), defending counsel and witness, all in one person. The other party is the world of organized disorder – or seeming order – in *America*; the Court in *The Trial*; and the Castle itself, with all its ramifications, in *The Castle*. But the third element is missing: there is no impartial authority to sit in judgment. Judgment has been usurped by those who oppose the hero.

Such is the outcome of all these examinations and hearings: the two K.s wear themselves out precisely because they encounter no real resistance. Their efforts are of no avail because their opponents, being in effect invisible, present them with no targets to hit. Their arguments are nullified by the sheer impenetrability of the mysterious systems that confront them. In the two main novels these hearings and examinations never result in a judgment. True, the two K.s are notified of certain disadvantages in which they have now been placed, but nothing ever happens as a direct result of any negative outcome of such a hearing. It is left to the two heroes to form their own judgments and to pass judgment on themselves. This much is clear already: the opposition attaches no importance to these examinations; they are conducted solely in the interests of the two K.s and the other parties. Up at the Castle they say that the various comings and goings of the parties serve no purpose except to 'leave dirt all over the front-door steps [of the Herrenhof]' (Chapter 17).

Discussions and Enquiries

The two K.s always have to argue their case in person: they need to be physically present the whole time. For them there is no respite from a task that demands all their strength, whereas the opposing order can draw on a limitless fund of set formulas and traditions; the procedures they adopt against the two K.s follow an established pattern that is virtually second nature to them, so that no particular effort is needed on their part. In fact it is not even necessary for the opposing order to encounter the heroes in the person of an agent or representative: it exists, and that is sufficient. The two K.s wear themselves down in their struggle against an order that never actually shows its face. When, for example, K. has those interminable conversations with Olga about whether or not Barnabas is really employed on Castle business, or whether or not Klamm is really Klamm, he is unable to gain any insight at all into the 'inextricable complexity' of the authorities 'up there' (*The Castle*, Chapter 15). The principle of negation is inherent in the very nature of the Castle. Every statement automatically elicits a statement to the contrary, its own suspension.

How Events occur in Kafka's Novels

An episode is invariably set in motion by a *disturbance* of some kind. . . . The disturbance initiates the episode by alarming the opposing order – summoning it to the scene – and thereby setting in motion all that must inevitably follow. In every instance it is the heroes who are responsible for the disturbance. They force the opposing world to concern itself with them; and that is enough to make them guilty in the eyes of that world. The 'burden of proof' for justifying the disturbance is placed firmly on their shoulders. When we use the term 'disturbance', we are of course looking at things from the point of view of the opposing order. The two K.s, however, see things very differently: to them this is no 'disturbance', but the affirmation, no less, of their own existence. The implication is that if they were to back down and cease their disturbance – as the opposing order requires them to do – they would thereby nullify their own existence; but since what they seek is precisely to affirm that existence, they 'disturb' the authorities. The opposing world then proceeds to nullify this disturbance in the manner already indicated: the fact that it thereby nullifies the existence of the two K.s is unintended, in a sense it is a mere by-product of its primary purpose.

The act of nullification is the caesura that marks the end of the episode. This is the characteristic variable of Kafka's prose, its basic formal unit; and the work as a whole is the sum of countless variations on this one formal theme.

Rhythm and Infinity

The Court maintains that it is only drawn towards the guilty: yet it *is* drawn towards Joseph K. It follows, therefore, that any attempt by K. to establish his innocence (and thus in a sense to prevent the trial from really getting under way) must constitute an act against the Court, and a disruption of its order. All the other defendants submit; Joseph K. alone creates a disturbance, and for this reason his efforts must be nullified.

The action of the trial unfolds in three parallel sequences: in the scenes at K.'s lodgings, at the bank and at the premises of the Court. No summary can hope to do more than suggest how some of these strands are developed, because the construction of this novel – unlike that of the earlier *America* – runs on in an unbroken continuity throughout. The three strands are interwoven in complex fashion: one strenuous undertaking [to attain justification] issues into another, just as each act of nullification is followed in due course by another. Lodging-house, Court-room or bank – it really makes no difference where the action is taken up, since the figures in the novel function in exactly the same way wherever they are placed. The pace and rhythm of these episodes is rapid, hard and insistent. There are no pauses, no digressions and no possibilities of escape. The confrontation between the two orders is not interrupted by any long passages of description, in which K., like Karl in *America*, might have been relegated to the role of spectator: on the contrary, K. cannot get away from his case – it is with him wherever he goes. When he walks down the street, people at their windows laugh at him; when he is sitting in his office thinking about his case, the Assistant Manager comes in, laughing out loud; and when he gets home in the evening, he thinks he sees a guard standing outside the house. His whole thinking is a sustained attempt to affirm his own existence – an attempt which is automatically nullified by the episodes incorporated in the action. And of course there are none of those turns for the better which helped to create the long narrative interludes in *America*.

[Having considered the ending of *The Trial*,] let us now ask how *The Castle* might have ended. K.'s goal is to become indistinguishable from the villagers. If he were to achieve this goal, *The Castle* would be a novel in the strict sense of the word. The way that led from his arrival in the village to his final acceptance as a member of the community would be a journey, a progression, whose course would be charted through the gradual unfolding of the action. But it is surely clear all along that K. and the opposing order are so utterly different in kind that any hope of assimilation must be ruled out altogether. The novel does not in fact 'develop' at all. It simply shows us the unfolding of a relationship whose pattern is implicit right from the first page. The more clearly this relationship between the two orders emerges, the more impossible it is for K. to become indistinguishable from the representatives of this opposing order, and the more clearly his position as an outsider is revealed.

Camus sees the conflict between the two opposing orders as a 'living equation'; and the image is a useful one. However, K. is not the 'x' of this equation, as Camus supposes, but a very precise quantity. The two terms of the equation are the Castle (= the quantity that annuls) and K. (= the quantity that affirms); and its value is 'infinite'. The two quantities are incommensurable: the only possible relationship between them is an absurd one. (Camus illustrates the point well by quoting the joke about the madman trying to catch fish in his bath-tub, who carries on fishing even though he knows that 'nothing will come of it'.) Defining the absurd in an essay on 'Philosophical Suicide', Camus writes that the degree of absurdity 'will be progressively greater as the things I am comparing become more disparate'.

If we apply this to Kafka and *The Castle*, then we must conclude that the gulf separating 'eagle' from 'slow-worm'* can never be bridged – not unless K. surrenders his very existence; and this he cannot do, since he has been put into the novel precisely in order to affirm his existence. Such a relationship is the very opposite of an 'ultimate cause': it is an 'absurd' relationship, which abolishes time and the possibility of progress, and exists suspended in a realm of undisturbed infinity, even if this means that in its outward form the work remains necessarily a fragment.

* The landlady at the bridge inn, addressing K. on the subject of Frieda, who had been the mistress of Klamm – 'the eagle' – and is now engaged to be married to K. – 'the slow-worm' (Chapter 4). [Ed.]

9

Endings and Non-endings in Kafka's Fiction*

J.J.White

Some itinerant wise men once came upon a statue which, as most of them could see, had not been completed. Some said it was almost finished, others thought the work only half carried-out; though a few could not even tell whether it was finished or not. When they compared this statue with others by the famous sculptor, many found the unfinished work inferior, simply because it was incomplete. Pointing to torsos from bygone days, some stated that they considered certain kinds of incompleteness better than any final work could possibly be. Others remembered the beautiful figurines which the great artist had also fashioned, and judged that his skills lay in miniature work. And one man, who recalled that the artist came from a distant tribe renowned for its incomplete works, saw in the unfinished statue an embodiment of the infinite sense of longing peculiar to that people.

Attention turned to why the artist (long since dead) had failed to finish the work. Perhaps he had deliberately given up in order to show the problems of completing such a task. Some claimed the fragmentariness was not intentional, that he had simply died before being able to finish; others that he had not decided what final shape the stone should receive. One wise man even suggested that it was because the great man was by nature not interested in perfecting works, for he had left many statues incomplete. However, most of those present proceeded to examine the shape of the nose and ears on the unfinished statue, comparing them with the noses and ears of other statues (which the artist had finished and sold at market), apparently unperturbed by the statue's condition.

*From *On Kafka: Semi-Centenary Perspectives*, ed. Franz Kuna, London 1976, p. 146.

10

Investigations of a Dog and Other Matters
A Literary Discussion Group in an American University

Erich Heller

A small group of university teachers and graduate students met every Wednesday night in order to discuss literary questions, each member having devoted some time during the days before to what in the college syllabus was called 'Introduction to Modern European Fiction'. Only some in the group were teachers of literature; among the others there were a physicist, a theologian, and two teachers who had their homes in the Schools of Music and Speech respectively.

'There are,' said the speaker of the evening, a man of literature, 'no definite methods to be employed in our teaching.' The story to be discussed was 'Investigations of a Dog'.

'So perhaps it is appropriate,' the theologian was quick off the mark, 'to begin by asking a question that has often puzzled me. What did Kafka mean when he said that sometimes he understood the Fall of Man better than anyone?'

'Perhaps,' the speaker of the evening replied, 'it was his way of explaining what, judging by his interpreters, is the persistent problem of so many of his stories and novels. Reading them, we are bound to ask, "What is the guilt of the hero?" – or let's better call him the central character, because he is hardly ever a hero in the heroic sense of the word. He does feel guilty; this much is clear. He is accused, prosecuted, punished, even sentenced to die; yet we never come to know the misdeed that could justify what he feels or what is done to him. Take the story "The Judgment": what is Georg Bendemann's sin if not his futile attempt *to be himself*, to pit himself against his father, the "ultimate authority", as he once referred to him? There is one exception: the soldier in "The Penal Colony" – an exception that, if not exactly confirming the rule, makes it even more disturbing. For in the case of that soldier the discrepancy between offence and punishment, between the soldier's violation of duty and the torture he has to endure, is as monstrous as are the actions of all the secret police agents that were let loose upon the world in the epoch following upon Kafka's death in 1924. Was Kafka's a prophetic vision? Or is the unknown guilt of his guilty men a mundane metaphor for original sin, in fact: for the Fall of Man? Or a combination of that vision and this metaphor? "Guilt is never to be doubted," says the officer in "The Penal Colony" when asked whether the accused had any chance of defending himself.'

At this point an intellectually ambitious young woman with excellent prospects as a literary scholar raised her hand and said that in one of her English classes she had been warned to avoid such questions when dealing with a literary work. A literary work has to be treated *qua* literature. She did say '*qua*'. The question that had just been put was a theological question, a moral question, a question made of stuff quite other than the stuff that renders literature literary.

The teacher of English nodded energetic assent: 'I quite agree. But the trouble is that the dog in this story is ... well, no real dog at all, is he? So that any purely *literary* interpretation will have to follow the line of a fable or allegory – and how can that fail to raise a moral issue?'

'You are quite right,' said the speaker of the evening, 'the dog is very much more reminiscent of *lupus in fabula*, of an animal in a classical fable which, in Dr Johnson's definition, is "a narrative in which beings irrational ... are, for the purpose of moral instruction, feigned to act and speak with human interests and passions". This covers nicely the fables of Aesop and La Fontaine and Lessing, but is it applicable to Kafka?'

'No,' said a teacher in the School of Speech, who was tentatively thinking of having 'The Investigations of a Dog' performed in the semi-dramatic manner practised by the School's Department of Interpretation. 'It is not a fable because there is no "moral instruction" to be found in it. If in its canine way it is about original sin, we, rather late descendants of Adam, cannot reasonably be counselled to avoid it. It is not a fable but a parable.'

'Well,' answered the speaker, 'the philosopher Schopenhauer believes that we all affirm the original misdeed by daily asserting ourselves, in one way or other, and be it only as speakers, as self-willed individuals: original sin by association with Adam. But never mind, if Kafka's story does not teach a moral, it is not a proper parable either. For by the classical canon of genres a parable, although it might have a moral to it, would demand of the dog to behave entirely like a dog. Yet our dog speaks very well, very wittily, very fascinatingly.'

'If it is neither a fable nor a parable, it is simply a story by Franz Kafka. It may be most effective in performance,' said the Professor of Speech.

'Simply?' replied the speaker. 'Is any story of Kafka's "simply" a story? And concerning the moral lesson, read the passage in which the dog narrator relates the "aberation" of "our first fathers" who "had not yet become so doggish as today ... the true Word could still have intervened ...: and the Word was there, was very near at least, on the tip of everybody's tongue, anyone might have hit upon it. And what has become of it today? Today one may pluck out one's very heart and not find it. ..." But our "first fathers", we read, "strayed", having scarcely any notion "that their aberration was to be an endless one, they could still literally see the crossroads, it seemed an easy matter to turn back whenever they pleased, and if they hesitated to turn back it was merely because they wanted to enjoy a dog's life for a little while longer; ... and so they strayed farther." Might this not be enough of a moral lesson? An admonition, perhaps, not to remove ourselves still farther from the reach of the Word?'

'The true Word,' said the Professor of Speech, 'could easily be a Hebrew word. But why go back as far as the Fall? Would it not be enough to think of the unending questioning to which Kafka subjected his Jewishness, to remember his lament that he held in his hand no more than the last piece of fringe of the Jewish prayer shawl, that he was a threefold outsider, a writer, a German writer in the Czech city of Prague and, above all, a Jew to Czechs and Germans alike?'

'Yes, an outsider,' said the literary purist lady, who, despite her initial insistence upon the 'purely literary', had clearly been drawn into the debate. 'When I began to read the "Investigations", I thought I would be reading one of those many outsider stories that have Dostoyevsky's Underground Man as their model and Thomas Mann's Tonio Kröger as an elegantly melancholy German example, more moderate because his outsiderness has only two roots, not three: Toni Kröger is a writer, and, *qua* writer, he feels a traitor to his North-German burgher tradition; and he may well be a born writer, an artist, *because* his North-German burgher father, Consul Kröger, had married a woman from "deep down on the map", from South America. In any case, I couldn't help thinking of Tonio Kröger when I read the beginning of the dog's "investigations", the "investigator" telling us that there was a time when he appeared to have no doubts about belonging to "the canine community", "a dog among dogs"; and yet, "on closer examination", he found in retrospect that "from the very beginning I sensed some discrepancy, some little maladjustment, sometimes causing a slight feeling of discomfort." Indeed, it would happen, so we read, that the mere look of any fellow-dog would suddenly astonish him, as if he had seen such a creature for the first time, and this "would fill me with helpless embarrassment and fear, even with despair". Isn't this a perfect description of what the Underground Man or Tonio Kröger suffers? I don't think Kafka's Jewishness alone could account for this degree of alienation.'

'This may well be,' retorted the speaker of the evening, 'although I should like to exact a penalty for every use of the Hegelian term "alienation". There are less shop-worn words for the kind of inner discomfort that "alienation" vaguely denotes. But it is, I think, indisputable that this narrator dog becomes more and more forcefully aware of some decisive break in his canine tradition, and Kafka may well have been given this "fabulous" idea by his Jewish homelessness; but the sense of otherness, of having left something behind that others take for granted, this compulsion to reflect upon one's human – or canine – situation, this greedy acceptance of the role played by the investigating dog, is the response of all individuals that are intellectually, spiritually more vulnerable than the rest – is their response to the loss.'

'To the loss of what?' interrupted the young physicist, who was anxious to make it quite clear that the discussion was getting beyond him.

'The loss of tradition. It is a loss that we cannot determine "exactly", as we may do with the losses of a commercial enterprise. But it is, for some, even more painful than those "exact" losses. For every tradition, as long as it is intact, is a miniature paradise. No, not because tradition knows no suffering, far from it; but because it does not know the kind of curiosity that the serpent aroused in Eve in order to make her pluck the apple off the Tree of Knowledge. For tradition is, among a thousand other things, the silent and unconsciously wise agreement to curb one's curiosity and not to disturb the sleep of too many unruly dogs. You know what St Augustine answered when somebody enquired of him what God did before he created the world? "He stoked up Hell's fires for the curious," was his answer. And Kafka wrote a brief sketch called "The Test", that ends with the following scene: "He asked me several things, but I couldn't answer, indeed I didn't even understand his questions. So I said: Perhaps you are sorry now that you invited me, so I'd better go, and I was about to get up. But he stretched out his hand over the table and pressed me down. Stay, he said, that was only a test. He who does not answer the questions has passed the test." Perhaps it is the test of a tradition not even to ask them.'

'This is the sheerest obscurantism,' the physicist exclaimed impulsively, 'although our students might well wish on certain occasions that the moral of the story could be applied to college examinations.'

'It would be obscurantism,' replied the speaker of the evening, 'if the plea were for the deliberate suppression of questions. This is not what it is meant to be; not even the anecdote of St Augustine is, in our context, told for such a disreputable purpose. My sole intention was to say something – not very much, I admit – about the nature of a tradition, any tradition. Its principle of coherence is the undisturbed peace in the domain of the unquestionable. Even if it had not been for the assassination of a king, the tradition of the kingdom – mind you, for better *or* for worse – would have been brought into question with the arrival of Hamlet, the insatiable questioner. Of course, Kafka's dog is no prince, but he seems to know the under-Hamlets and sub-Fausts of a civilization that is profoundly inimical to tradition. What are all these restless animals after, our dog would ask, and would be told that "they contribute a great deal to knowledge"; and if he retorted that "most of their contributions are worthless and wearisome", his observation would be shrugged off, and after such encounters he would observe – in his diary, as it were – "Certainly knowledge is progressing, its advance is irresistible, it actually progresses at an accelerating speed, always faster, but what is there to praise in that? It is as if one were to praise someone because with the years he grows older, and in consequence comes nearer and nearer to death with increasing speed." '

'This still does not explain why the story "The Investigations of a Dog" can be read as a comedy version of original sin. And what *is* original sin?' It was, of course, the lady who as yet had not quite overcome her purist leanings who asked the question.

'For Kafka,' the speaker replied, 'it is precisely what it is to the author of Genesis: the inexplicable delight taken in leading a dog's life. But, kidding apart – although the kid will have to be mentioned again in a moment – it is what Schopenhauer called the *principium individuationis*, the principle of individuation, the *Ur-Mythus*, the fundamental myth of existence. Language, in recording the myth, is unavoidably imperfect. For language would not know what to do if it had at its disposal no subjects, no objects, no predicates. This is what made Nietzsche say that we shall not get rid of the notion of God as long as we believe in grammar, that is, as long as we believe that the predicated world has not only a grammatical but a *real* subject: God has created the world. But there was a time without a world and therefore without time – you remember St Augustine's curious enquirer? – a time when there was nothing but God or, if you don't believe in God, plain nothing. The Bible, of course, does believe in God – to the point of claiming him as its author; and in order to make himself understood to human beings, he had to use their language. When he meant to say that everything that was, was nowhere but in him, and therefore nothing was outside him, he had to use names, names like heaven and earth and light and darkness and water and land and grass and trees and whales and cattle and, finally, Adam and Eve, of whom it is said that they were naked and not ashamed and not beguiled the one by the other. Only after they had disobeyed God's will were they ashamed of their nakedness, drawn to each other, driven out of the Garden, and only then did they become the parents of Cain and Abel. Only then were they truly Adam and Eve. Before that they were manners of speaking. For an Adam who does not desire his wife is not Adam, and an Eve that does not desire her man is not Eve. The original sin *is* the act of disobedience committed against God by his first children, but they only *became* his first children by and through their act of disobedience; by discovering and then exercising their own will; by becoming, as language must have it, more human than ever before, just as there was a time, as Kafka's dog puts it – "I cannot put it in any other way," he says – when dogs "had not yet become so doggish as today" and "the true Word could still have intervened". Well, for reasons of its own it didn't, not with the self-will of dogs and not with the self-will of men, and it allowed human history to begin with Cain's murdering Abel.'

'The investigations of Kafka's dog don't seem to promise that there ever will be a time when dogs will again be "less doggish",' said the theologian, ruefully, 'or when there will be no dogs at all, if I follow your interpretation, which certainly differs from that of St Thomas or, of course, Milton. But, after all, the prophet Isaiah prophesied that we shall regain Paradise, where once again "the wolf . . . shall dwell with the lamb, and the leopard shall lie down with the kid. . . ." '

'Did I not say that we shall hear of the kid again? But what sort of a kid is this? No kid whatever. For would it still be a kid if it hobnobbed with the leopard? Would the lamb pasturing next to the wolf still be a lamb? Surely not. For a leopard that is not in the habit of devouring kids is no leopard, any more than the wolf grazing in beatific community with the lamb will persuade us of his wolfhood. Is this "the Bible read as Literature"? Certainly it is read as a work that attempts to describe in language what language, a product of the Fall and, therefore, of individuation, cannot express. Music, perhaps, can. But it is too late and a little too impious to advise Beethoven not to use words – and Schiller's words at that – when, in the last movement of the Ninth Symphony, he celebrates the great, universal, joyous brotherhood of Man and World: "Diesen Kuss der ganzen Welt!" A sequence of musical sounds composed by Beethoven can tell us more of the grand dream in which Cain's misdeed is undone: much more than that inappropriately comprehensive kiss.'

The lady purist no longer felt like voicing any opposition to these blatantly impure speculations. And yet, she seemed puzzled by the wider issue. 'Why should poetry, the art of words, together with all the other arts, aspire to the condition of music? Why indeed – as long as there is music, if not necessarily the kind of music through which Kafka's dog experiences the wondrous suspension of the principle of individuation, the momentary deliverance from the pain of being an "alienated" dog, not quite the dog that other dogs are?'

'Music,' interrupted the Professor of Music, who was, surprisingly, also an avid reader of Kafka, 'plays a remarkable role in Kafka's work, music or at least something like music. There is a moment in *The Trial* when Joseph K., the accused, all of a sudden cannot hear the individual voices of the strange court's officials but merely a din that fills the whole office, a din pierced by a steady high note, like a siren's. Is it a siren that lures the indicted man to his death or does it warn him of the impending catastrophe? Or is the din that drowns the voice of every single official intended to show that each of them denies any individual responsibility for what happens: that it is an inarticulate collective of non-selves which will pass the final judgment on that wretched self? And when, in *The Castle*, all the telephones in the village are connected with all the holders of authority up there, and all of them talk all the time and simultaneously into their telephones; and he who wishes to learn what the authorities think hears nothing but "a humming and singing" sound, and this sound, as we read, is "the only real and reliable thing you will hear", just as if the *principium individuationis*, the individual case, counted for nothing in those upper regions – does this mean that the ultimate information to be given to the applicant is that of a collective, while the individual voices have become incomprehensible? That what counts is something that cannot be counted because it lies beyond any individual who might be held accountable? That in the highest region the individual hardly exists? Or is it simply a satire of modern bureaucracy?'

Even the speaker of the evening had to catch his breath after so much informed and intelligent 'Kafkology' pouring forth from the Professor of Music. 'Excellent,' he said finally. 'But again not "simple". It is both satire *and* the musicology of the end. Yet there is also music, real music, not merely those humming sounds reminiscent of singing. You remember the scene in "The Metamorphosis" when Gregor Samsa, transformed into a repellent insect, nauseated by the food put before him by his compassionate sister, hears her play the violin in the next room? He is astonished – you recall the scene? – that neither his parents nor their lodgers appear to be impressed by her beautiful playing. They are bored. Only he, the degraded Gregor Samsa, feels that the music is "opening before him ... the way to the unknown nourishment he craved", the same kind of nourishment, perhaps, which in a later story – a story from roughly the time of the investigating dog – might have prevented the "Hunger Artist" from starving himself to death: he had to starve, he says, because he couldn't find the food he liked. It was Kafka, the vegetarian, who wrote the haunting story of "A Hunger Artist". But you may be quite sure that he did not think of broccoli but rather of the sound of that fiddle when he made his hunger artist say that if he had ever discovered *his* food, "believe me, I should have made no fuss and eaten my fill like you or anyone else". And now we may read once more the passage in which the mysterious dog musicians play to the investigator dog.'

'I think we have to preface it,' said the speaker of the evening, 'by reminding ourselves that "the concert" was given for the sake of the researcher dog in Kafka's story. He had long lived without knowing what his life was good for; yet he was distinguished from his fellow-dogs by some sense of "discrepancy, some little maladjustment causing a slight feeling of discomfort" that was at the same time "a premonition of great things". And then, literally out of the blue, came "that concert"; and the truth-seeker dog knew that he would have, more radically than hitherto, to ask whether his separate, individual existence could possibly be justified – even if his impulse to question was almost as strong as his disinclination to answer. And he was disinclined to answer because he sensed that his ultimate mission was to attain to the freedom that meant to be free of himself, free of any self, free of original sin, the sin that was Georg Bendemann's unrevealed sin in the story "The Judgment", the sin of self-will and self-assertion. The concert was given by seven dogs – seven: a mystical number. They were naked and not ashamed: "They had flung away all shame, the wretched creatures were doing the very thing which is both most ridiculous and indecent in our eyes: they were walking on their hind legs. Fie on them! They were ... making a show of their nakedness." No wonder the investigator was not even sure he really saw them. He "inwardly greeted them as dogs", but were they not rather ghost dogs from before the Fall, before the Age of Shame? And their terrifying music sounded like an invitation to follow them to the Garden, where the bushes were not yet the hiding-place of those who had reason to be ashamed of their nakedness. And now the investigator dog's description of the music performed by the seven mystery dogs——But please let the Professor of Speech read it aloud. He wants to dramatize the story.'

The Professor of Speech accepted the invitation and read to the group the description of how the music affected the dog:

The music gradually got the upper hand, literally knocked the breath out of me and swept me away from those actual little dogs, and quite against my will, while I howled as if some pain were being inflicted upon me, my mind could attend to nothing but this blast of music which seemed to come from all sides, from the heights, from the deeps, from everywhere, surrounding the listener, over-whelming him, crushing him and over his swooning body still blowing fanfares which were so near that they seemed far away and almost inaudible. ... It robbed me of my wits, whirled me around in its circles as if I myself were one of the musicians instead of being only their victim, cast me hither and thither, no matter how much I begged for mercy. . . .

'I think I was wrong: this is "purely literary" *and* it is about original sin,' said the ex-purist.

And the theologian added, 'Perhaps literature is original sin.'

'I wouldn't go so far', replied the speaker of the evening, 'although there were times when Kafka came close to believing this himself. He once said, "Writing is wonderfully rewarding, but what is it a reward for? . . . For services rendered to the Devil." He truly understood the Fall of Man better than anyone. I suppose we have to thank God that he blessed us all with a lesser degree of understanding. And a little,' the speaker added, 'for the fact that this discussion has come to an end.'

11

Kafka's Parables
Ways Out of the Dead End

Roy Pascal

Many of Kafka's short tales or sketches take the form of the parable. He wrote them throughout his writing life, but few were published in his lifetime, and most appeared only after his death. His models were the biblical stories, especially the oral parables of Jesus, and the rabbinical tradition of illustrative anecdote. We can group his fables with the parables, since many are only parables with animal characters; though normally fables are distinguished from parables by their secular moral message, as opposed to a religious one, this distinction does not hold for Kafka.

A parable transmits a religious truth by means of an illustrative anecdote. Its form is determined by this didactic purpose. The story-line is very simple, so that its meaning is unambiguous. There is no particularization of situation or character, both because incidental issues would distract and because the situation and message are to be made readily applicable to the hearer or reader. Thus the characters are types: the father and the son, the master and the servant, the sower, the good housewife, etc.; likewise, the animals of fables, from Aesop onwards, represent a single characteristic: the wolfish wolf, the wily fox, the innocent lamb. The characters have no past, belong to no specific time or place, but exist only for the purpose of this anecdote.

In most respects Kafka's parables conform to this model. They have the same abstractness, simplicity of structure, and timelessness, and some are as short and bare as the traditional fable or parable. But the absence of the oral element, of listeners waiting for enlightenment, is evident in several ways: some are fairly extensive, and some are told by a character in the first person, a literary rather than an oral form. Above all, they differ from the tradition in the relationship between story and message. They conform to it enough to raise normal expectations: they invite us to follow the incidents of a story with the expectation that the ending will show their coherence, their meaning and the appropriate moral. But with Kafka such an ending is never reached, and the outcome of the story usually accentuates the opaque or disastrous nature of the events and involves us in a baleful riddle. Here are three parables that may stand for many, both in their form and their 'message':

A Little Fable

'Alas,' said the mouse, 'the world is growing smaller every day. At first it was so big that I was afraid, I ran on and was glad when at last I saw walls to left and right of me in the distance, but these long walls are closing in on each other so fast that I have already reached the last room, and there in the corner stands the trap that I am heading for.' 'You have only to change direction,' said the cat, and ate it up.

Give it up

It was very early in the morning, the streets clean and deserted, I was going to the station. As I compared my watch with the clock on a tower I saw that it was much later than I had thought, I had to make great haste, in my alarm at this discovery I became unsure of the way, I was still something of a stranger in this town, luckily there was a policeman at hand, I ran up to him and breathlessly asked him the way. He smiled and said: 'Do you expect to discover the way from me?' 'Yes,' I said, 'since I cannot find it myself.' 'Give it up, give it up,' said he, and he turned away with a great flourish, like a man who wants to be alone with his laughter.

Homecoming

I have come home, I've crossed the threshold and am looking around. It is my father's old farmyard. The puddle in the middle. Old unusable implements, driven into a tangled heap, clutter up the approach to the loft-steps. The cat is crouching on the landing. A ragged cloth, once in fun draped round a pole, stirs in the wind. I've arrived. Who will receive me? Who is waiting behind the kitchen door? Smoke is coming from the chimney, the coffee is being made for supper. Do you feel at ease, do you feel at home? I don't know, I am very uncertain. It is my father's house, but one thing stands coldly beside another as if each were busied with its own affairs, which I partly have forgotten, partly never knew. Of what use can I be to them, what am I to them, even though I be the son of my father, the old farmer. And I don't dare to knock on the kitchen door, I only listen from a distance, I listen from a distance, standing upright, not in such a way as to risk being caught out as an eavesdropper. And because I am listening from a distance I make nothing out, I hear only a faint chime of a clock or perhaps only imagine I can hear it, coming over from childhood. What else is going on in the kitchen is the secret of those sitting there, that they are keeping from me. The longer one hesitates outside the door, the more one becomes a stranger. How would it be if some-one were now to open the door and ask me a question. Shouldn't I myself then be like a man who is intent on keeping his secret.

These are desolate images of suffering, alienation, and despair. In the first, the victim learns that there is a way of salvation, but only at the moment of his annihilation. In the second, the appointed protector of the citizen ridicules the very idea that he might find his way. The third, Kafka's rewriting of the parable of the Prodigal Son, ends not in the openness of confession and forgiveness, but in the cold isolation of selfhood. The effect is all the more shattering since the familiar form leads us to expect a resolution of tensions and confusions. They are parodies of the parable not because they present an anti-moral, but because these models of life-situations resist reduction to abstract formulation or to moral exhortation.

These parables reflect the world of Kafka's great novels, *The Trial* and *The Castle*, which themselves might be called parables. Their heroes, Joseph K. and K., engaged in an obscure search for justification, for a home, can never reach their goal: a dubious law-court or the mirage of a castle. The novels belong to a well-known type: the novel of spiritual search, like *The Pilgrim's Progress* and *Crime and Punishment*, in which the outcome fulfils the suffering and struggle. But they too, like the parables, are parodies, since there is no fulfilment of the heroes' efforts. Their formal similarity to the type has misled many critics into interpreting their endings (or intended endings, for Kafka left both novels incomplete) as expressing the attainment of their goals. But neither in the text of the novels, nor in any statements by Kafka, is there anything to mitigate the despairing exhaustion of failure; Erich Heller's essay on *The Castle* in *The Disinherited Mind* of 1952 should have checked the continuing attempts to force the Kafka novels into a positive Christian or Jewish framework. The parable that the Prison Chaplain tells Joseph K. in *The Trial* is indeed the model for both novels.*

I think the best definition of Kafka's spiritual situation is that given in 1916 by Georg Lukács† for their generation as a whole: 'The abandonment of the world by God is evident in the incongruity of soul and achievement. Human endeavour lacks transcendental co-ordinates.' Lukács found a way out of this dilemma in Marxism; but Kafka remained its victim. His soul could never abate its immortal longings, but they could never be fulfilled and only tormented him, like an uncertain

---

* See Frank Kermode's contribution below, 12. [Ed.]

† In *Die Theorie des Romans*, the last of Lukács's pre-Marxist writings. [Ed.]

gleam through a doorway or a misty outline on a hill. Neither in the novels nor in many of the shorter pieces do we find any mitigation of this bleak despair.

Yet there is something else in other short pieces of Kafka that is not so denuded of hope and comfort. They do not confront the main impact of his despair, but offer a different approach, a different slant, a way, perhaps, of evading it. A way out, perhaps. I have borrowed this term – *Ausweg*, that means 'evasion' as well as 'way out' – from Kafka's 'Report for an Academy'. A captive chimpanzee reports to a learned institution on his progress towards 'an average human standard of culture' and to stardom on the variety stage. He tells how, after his capture, he realized that he could not live without a 'way out' from his narrow cage. Freedom was impossible, so his only way out was to please his guards by imitating human manners, learning how to spit, to smoke, even to drink detestable schnapps, and, bit by bit, to speak and reason clearly. He has no grandiose hopes of these accomplishments; they are only 'ways out' that keep the future open. When he had to choose between the zoo and the variety stage, he chose the latter because it was not a dead end. Modestly proud of his achievement and sophistication, he does not overvalue it: 'in itself it may be nothing, yet it is something inasmuch as it helped me out of the cage. There was no other way, once the possibility of freedom was ruled out.' This wisdom, delivered with a charming mixture of naivety and sober sense, does not seem to have been put into practice by Kafka himself; but the kindly, humorous fable shows that he could, a little ironically, imagine a 'way out' for men too.

Many of the characters in the short pieces bear, like the K. figures, a resemblance to Kafka himself. Again and again we meet the restless seeker, the awkward questioner, the obsessive dialectician. Sometimes, it is true, he is in his tragic mode, like the creature of 'The Burrow', whose safety devices only intensify his insecurity. But the searcher can appear in a different light.

The fictional narrator of 'The Village Schoolmaster' (also known as 'The Giant Mole'), a business-man, tells how he became fascinated by the rumoured appearance of a giant mole and has devoted himself to its study. His main source is a pamphlet written by a village schoolmaster that stoutly contends with the indifference of the public and the scepticism of the scientists. However, the narrator does not completely agree with the schoolmaster and the two quarrel, for each holds to his views all the more firmly since each lacks reliable evidence, and both show an alarming readiness to succumb to the lure of publicity and fame. The gentle, even affectionate amusement at the self-deception of the two protagonists does not conceal their relationship with the tragic heroes of the novels, pursuing with pertinacity and subtlety a goal set by some strange and perhaps dubious inner compulsion.

A comparable tone of satirical amusement pervades the unfinished sketch 'Blumfeld, an Elderly Bachelor'. Blumfeld is a crotchety, irascible and lonely bachelor, living in a state of suspicion of, and aggressive hostility towards, neighbours and colleagues. His barren routine is ruptured, like Joseph K.'s, by a mysterious visitation, but in his case it is an explicit wish-fulfilment. Blumfeld has been wishing for some companion, a pet to welcome him home, but one that would claim no affection or care and not disturb his habits. One day he finds in his home a magical pair of bouncing balls, which dance attendance on him in his rooms and rest quietly when he sleeps. But their tap-tap arouses only his irritation and after a night of great stress he manages to lock them up in a cupboard, returning with satisfaction to his former isolation and not noticing that he has rejected just the sort of companionship he dreamed of. 'The Neighbour' and 'The Little Woman' both allow obsessives to make out their cases. In the first, a business-man describes a new neighbour who, he imagines, is listening through the wall to all his telephone calls and will soon capture all his business. In the second, the narrator tells of the angry dislike he seems to cause a woman he often passes in the street; he describes the harm this irrational distaste causes them both and speculates on possible remedies, rejecting with indignation the only sensible suggestion, that he should take a holiday. In both these stories it is the narrator, professedly normal, sensible and harmless, who is the obsessed inventor of the torture he suffers from. We may suspect this in the novels, but are not allowed to believe it.

The richest and most tender of these humorous sketches is 'Investigations of a Dog' – I like to think of this as Don Quixote's dog, for he has the Don's sincerity and credulousness, his wisdom and folly, his nobility and absurdity. Kafka's dog tells his own story, and with the gravity of tone that belongs to Don Quixote. Misunderstanding the confusing nature of the world, he is led (like a human being) continually to ask the wrong questions and propose absurd answers; yet he has the dignity of the tenacious seeker, forced against his will to question what other dogs accept without thinking, and painfully aware of his isolation. In his youth a magical experience has set him on his deviant course. He sees a troupe of dogs executing an intricate dance, even standing on their hind legs, to the sound of wondrous music that does not come from their mouths. The reader recognizes the brightly lit scene as a circus number accompanied by a hidden band, but our dog finds in it a transcendent mystery. Or again, when he hears the term *Lufthunde* (literally, 'air-dogs'), it is not the reported fact that dogs soar that puzzles his mind, but the reason why, the sense behind it (Kafka is playing on the term *Luftmensch*, 'air-man', commonly used in his day for men who, lacking assets or employment, still made a good living). The dog's most ambitious investigation is a series of experiments to find out how it is that rituals like barking and leaping attract food 'from above'. Since his uncontrollable appetite foils his tests, he decides to fast in complete isolation. Nobly he resists temptations and hallucinations, but when in his weakness he is routed out by a hunting dog, he is so entranced by the music of this dog's voice – magic music that only he can hear – that he abandons his investigation and devotes himself henceforth to the less dangerous study of dog-music.

The grave and the comic are beautifully fused in this charming piece – the conversation of the two dogs is a gem. In it the tragic dilemmas that torment and destroy Kafka's tragic heroes are seen in another light, with tenderness and with a smile, for we see the nobility of the quest even though it is doomed to lead nowhere.

This 'way out' of tender humour works best in the fables, when the object of Kafka's humorous solicitude is an animal. The obsessive preoccupations of the human figures always retain a painful element of enclosedness, of self-centredness, and Kafka seems to have needed the animal fictions if he was to find a serene image of his own obsessiveness. The generous sympathy that attends these humorous sketches indicates a temporary crumbling of that embattled fortress of the self, that defensive lovelessness, that seems to be the instinctive refuge of the heroes of his novels. This positive theme is scarcely made explicit in the novels, though it clearly belongs to the tragedy of both heroes that Joseph K. and K. are not capable of love and use other people only as instruments in their stratagems. But it asserts itself when, in *The Castle*, Frieda, because of this heartlessness, leaves K., and the latter, in a conversation with the new barmaid, confesses that in fact Frieda was more to him than an instrument: that he loved her, and that her love for him, natural and uncalculating, was finer than his own restless scheming. It is the only time that K. emerges from the cloud of his self-centredness, the only time he speaks of another person with love and generosity. He still sticks to his great enterprise, however, and even deludes himself into thinking he might have reached his goal if he had pursued it 'with Frieda's calm and matter-of-factness'. No: love and his tormenting obsession cannot be reconciled. None of Kafka's characters has the spiritual resources of a Raskolnikov or a Prince Myshkin; they are spiritually maimed.

There is still another 'way out' to be found in the shorter tales of a parabolic nature, and this too almost achieves the status of an alternative way. It relates to the concept of authority. The power of the authorities in the novels is all the more unassailable because they are so intangible and inaccessible. Once or twice we are almost led to believe that they exist only in the mind. We could imagine that the cover design for the early story 'Metamorphosis' – a man in a dressing-gown, agitatedly starting up from a sofa in a narrow room, covering his horror-stricken face with his hands, as if aghast at a nightmare – could have been used for the novels too.

The Chinese scholar who, in 'Building the Great Wall of China', gives his thoughts on authority, begins with a discussion of the planning and purpose of the Great Wall. No one knows what authorities planned and carried out the enterprise, and the commonly accepted purpose, defence against hordes from the north, is, the scholar argues, not persuasive, since these hordes held no danger, no reality, for the peoples of the far-flung empire. In this huge empire, he continues, the very idea of the emperor is unclear. His authority holds from the remote past into the future, and the people reject the thought that he might be a mortal like themselves. Living so far from Peking, they cannot imagine a particular emperor, and Peking itself 'is much stranger to us than the next world'. The emperor they obey and believe in is ever-present, everywhere; the imperial edicts governing the building of the Wall have existed from time immemorial. Thus it is the belief that is important, not the specific ruler, and this belief 'is the soil on which we live, the most important means of uniting our people'. The scholar admits that his interpretation creates many problems, but he exhorts his fellows to prudence: 'Try with all your strength to understand the instructions of the leaders, but only to a certain limit, then put a stop to your ruminations.'

To illustrate the significance, even the beneficence, of this man-made belief, the scholar tells a Chinese legend (published separately by Kafka, under the title 'The Emperor's Message'). As the emperor lies dying, he summons his messenger to his bedside and whispers a message he is to take 'to you, a single person, a mean subject, a tiny shadow cowering in the furthest distance from the Imperial sun'. The messenger sets out, thrusting his way through the thronged room. Beyond, there are still other crowded rooms, stairways, courts – 'he will never get through them; and if he did, there would be still more in the great encircling palace, and so forth through millennia.' And were he to burst out of the precincts – 'but never, never can this occur' – there would still be the city to traverse, 'clogged high with its dregs'. 'He will never get through, let alone with the message from a dead man.' This, we recognize, is the typical Kafka theme and logic: the messenger will never get through, and if he were to do so, it would be to no purpose.

But then comes the scholar's unexpected, startling final sentence: 'But you sit at your window and dream it [the message] into being, as evening falls.' The fable ends on an elegiac note; the scholar calls it 'hopeless and hopeful'. The dream is not the nightmare that so often entangles the Kafka characters in horror and *Angst*. Its content is not important; all that matters is that it relates you to the supreme authority, it confirms your identity, gives significance and dignity to your existence. And it is not a mere dream, as opposed to fact. Kafka uses the verb *erträumen*, and the prefix *er* means to bring something to completion, to fruition; so the verb means, you dream it into being, and so dream your worth into existence. For once in Kafka's works the soul does not tantalize with unrealizable objectives or intangible fears, but confirms and encourages. It is the creative dream of mankind, that has enabled man to think and act beyond his material and definable scope, beyond his tangible needs and satisfactions. And this specific function of the dream in Kafka's parable is framed in the story's larger theme, which recognizes that the supreme authority itself is essentially a belief, a subjective, not an objective, reality, the product of a people's need, and beneficent if we so understand it.

The only parallel to this image of an encouraging, hopeful, invigorating dream that I have met is in the strange fragment 'Testimonials' ('Fürsprecher'). Here, an accused man is searching the bewildering corridors of the law-courts for persons who will testify to his character. He can find no one; he is not even sure he is in the right building. This is all 'typical' Kafka and might belong to *The Trial*. But then, as the accused man is tempted to give it all up and retrace his steps, there is again a startling change. He exhorts himself:

Once you have started on a path, stick to it under all circumstances, you can only win! ... And if you fail in the end, that is better than if you fail at the beginning, as you certainly would if you retraced your steps. ... If you find nothing here in the corridors, open the doors, if you find nothing behind these doors, there are higher floors, if you find nothing there, don't worry, hoist yourself up new staircases. As long as you don't stop climbing, the steps will not come to an end, beneath your mounting feet they grow upwards.

What an astonishing image! For once Kafka dismisses bewilderment and despair with a concept of human achievement that itself supplies the guarantee of its worth through the frail permanence of its own persistence. And here is a parable that ends, if not with a moral, at least with a moral exhortation!

What weight should we give these mitigations or alternatives in a general consideration of Kafka? Not much, I suppose. But they are there as possibilities, and may mean more to us than they did to Kafka himself.

12

An Uninterpretable Radiance*

Frank Kermode

There is a famous parable in Kafka's *The Trial*. It is recounted to [Joseph] K. by a priest, and is said to come from the scriptures. A man comes and begs for admittance to the Law, but is kept out by a doorkeeper, the first of a long succession of doorkeepers, of aspect ever more terrible, who will keep the man out should the first one fail to do so. The man, who had assumed that the Law was open to all, is surprised to discover the existence of this arrangement. But he waits outside the door, sitting year after year on his stool, and conversing with the doorkeeper, whom he bribes, though without success. Eventually, when he is old and near death, the man observes an immortal radiance streaming from the door. As he dies, he asks the doorkeeper how it is that he alone has come to this entrance to seek admittance to the Law. The answer is, 'This door was intended only for you. Now I am going to shut it.' The outsider, though someone had 'intended' to let him in, or anyway provided a door for him, remained outside.

K. engages the priest in a discussion concerning the interpretation of this parable. He is continually reproved for his departures from the literal sense, and is offered a number of priestly glosses, all of which seem somehow trivial or absurd, unsatisfying or unfair, as when the doorkeeper is said to be more deserving of pity than the suppliant, since the suppliant was there of his own free will, as the porter was not. Nevertheless it is claimed that the doorkeeper belongs to the Law, and the man does not. K. points out that to assume the integrity of the doorkeeper, or indeed that of

* From *The Genesis of Secrecy: On the Interpretation of Narrative*, pp. 27–8 reprinted by permission of Harvard University Press, Cambridge (Mass.) and London 1979. Copyright © 1979 Frank Kermode.

the Law, as the priest does, involves contradictions. No, replies the priest: 'it is not necessary to accept everything as true, one must only accept it as necessary.' 'A melancholy conclusion,' says K. 'It turns lying into a universal principle.'

'Before the Law' is a good deal longer than any Biblical parable, and reminds us that in principle parable may escape restrictions of length. ... And like Mark's Parable of the Sower, it incorporates very dubious interpretations, which help to make the point that the would-be interpreter cannot get inside, cannot even properly dispose of authoritative interpretations that are more or less obviously wrong. The outsider has what appears to be a reasonable, normal, and just expectation of ready admittance, for the Law, like the Gospel, is meant for everybody, or everybody who wants it. But what he gets is a series of frivolous and mendacious interpretations. The outsider remains outside, dismayed and frustrated. To perceive the radiance of the shrine is not to gain access to it; the Law, or the Kingdom, may, to those within, be powerful and beautiful, but to those outside they are merely terrible; absolutely inexplicable, they torment the inquirer with legalisms. This is a mystery; Mark, and Kafka's doorkeeper, protect it without understanding it, and those outside, like K. and like us, see an uninterpretable radiance and die.

13

The Cunning of a Writer

Joachim Beug

'An exquisitely calculated hell, yet not without its good moments'

When Franz Kafka wrote his rather complicated version of Odysseus' encounter with the Sirens he did so explicitly to prove a point, as he says in the first sentence of the sketch entitled 'The Silence of the Sirens': 'Proof that insufficient, even childish, measures may serve the purpose of salvation.'

Kafka's version begins like Homer's: Odysseus plugged his ears with wax and chained himself to the mast of his ship in order to save himself from the enticing song of the Sirens. It was, however, well known the world over that such measures could not possibly help, for the Sirens' song penetrated everything and inspired passions that neither chains nor mast could contain. But Odysseus did not think of that when he sailed towards the Sirens; he completely trusted his wax and chains and innocently delighted in his little tricks.

The Sirens, however, Kafka says, had an even more terrifying weapon than their song: it was silence. For it is conceivable, even though it never happened, that someone might have saved himself from their song – but never from their silence: 'No one on earth could withstand the devastating hubris inspired by the belief of having by one's own strength overcome the Sirens.' When Odysseus came to the Sirens they did not sing, but because he thought of nothing but his wax and chains 'he did not hear their silence' and thus escaped.

So far the story does indeed prove the point about 'insufficient measures', even if it may not appear to be a very reassuring proof for salvation to depend upon. But Kafka introduces, almost as an afterthought, an argument which thoroughly undermines his own proof:

'There is by the way a time-honoured addition to this story. Odysseus, it is said, was so cunning, was such a fox that even the goddess of fate could not penetrate his inner depth. Perhaps, although human reason cannot grasp this, he really noticed that the Sirens were silent and the fictitious scene above was only held out as a protective shield against them and the gods.'

The writer Franz Kafka himself may be said to have been such a fox. Resourceful as he was in devising measures for his own salvation – through writing – he was even more cunning in undermining his own stratagems. He suspected his suspicions, observed his manoeuvres and wrote down in diaries, notebooks and letters what he observed.

To be sure, his cunning is not controlled, wilful deception employed for specific ends. It differs from Odysseus's traditional ruses in that it is directed inwards, against himself. It seeks to subvert all self-deception and in its course undermines all inner certainties. Thus, what he writes down are not the results of an investigation, but rather notes accompanying an open-ended experiment, an experiment which no one fully controls.

Early on in his diaries he gives a warning – only to himself? – about the reliability of diary entries:

There is a great deal about myself these days that I have not written down, partly because of laziness ... but also partly because of the fear of betraying my self-perception. This fear is justified, for to fix a self-perception definitively in writing would be permissible only if it could be done with the greatest completeness, with all the incidental consequences, as well as with entire truthfulness. For if this does not happen – and in any event I am not capable of it – then what is written down will take on its own intentions and with the overwhelming power of the written word replace what had been only a general feeling, and this in such a way that the true feeling vanishes while the worthlessness of the note is recognized too late.

The dilemma of his self-exploratory writing to be unconditionally truthful and to omit nothing, both of these being necessary and unattainable, appears to have its cause in the process of writing. The transformation of feelings into fixed words, sentences and paragraphs on paper cannot be sufficiently controlled. And this dilemma is not just confined to his personal diary notes: 'The problem of the diary is at the same time the problem of the whole, contains all the impossibilities of the whole. ... It is impossible to say everything and it is impossible not to say everything.' Yet, in spite of these impossibilities, recognized and spelled out so clearly, he continued to write and also keep a diary throughout most of his life, once encouraging himself with the striking argument: 'Hold fast to the diary from today on! Write regularly! Do not surrender. Even though salvation is not coming, I want to be worthy of it at any moment.'

Rereading his own diaries may afford him the reassuring proof that in situations now appearing unbearable he actually 'lived, looked around and wrote down observations'; and once he records: 'leafed through the diary a little. A sort of notion of the organization of such a life.' In a later fragment this distant notion has become more distinct and is expanded into a 'plan of autobiographical investigations':

Not biography but investigation, the search for the smallest possible components. From these then I want to construct myself, as someone whose house is unsafe wants to build next to it a safe one, possibly with the materials of the old one. It is bad, of course, when in the middle of this building work his strength runs out and he now has, instead of one admittedly unsafe but still complete house, one half-destroyed and one half-finished house, and that is nothing. What follows is madness, a Cossack dance, for example, between the two houses, where the Cossack with the heels of his boots scrapes out and throws up the earth until his grave is formed under him.

The diary – and to some extent all of Kafka's self-exploratory prose – may be looked upon as the site of this self-construction and self-demolition, which is carried out with the methodical madness imposed by the imperative to write. In moments of clarity the diary may also serve him as a vantage-point from which to observe the dance. For observe he must – always: 'If I am observed by someone else, I must naturally observe myself too; if I am observed by no one else I have to observe myself all the more closely.' This compulsive self-observation must appear all but incompatible with the first prerequisite of a writer, which, according to Kafka, is 'self-forgetfulness! Not alertness but self-forgetfulness'. But he also knows that there is no reliable vantage-point for the observer of self, that observation interferes with what is observed, and that even with the most suspicious cunning he may not be able to distinguish observation from a stratagem.

There is a fragment in the diary that may suggest that he is in fact the only one excluded from observing what goes on inside him: 'A segment-shaped piece has been cut out of the back of his head. The sun and with it the whole world look in. It does make him nervous, it distracts him from his work, and moreover it irritates him that just he should be excluded from the spectacle.'

Where does this leave the reader of Kafka's letters, notebooks and diaries? Does he not find himself in the role of the uninvited onlooker – or inlooker – the intruder upon private affairs and intimate personal relationships? In a sense he is indeed a reader against the 'will' of the author, for Kafka left clear enough instructions that he wanted all his unpublished papers destroyed. But then perhaps even his last will may have been subverted by his Odysseus-like cunning. In any case, the chosen executor of this will, his friend Max Brod, apparently left him in no doubt that he would never destroy any of Kafka's writings.

Accepting this argument, of course, does not help very far beyond easing one's possible discomfort at prying into personal matters, a feeling that Kafka's letters and diaries rarely, if ever, evoke anyway. But the reader may feel excluded in another, more definitive way when coming upon a diary entry such as this one: 'I don't believe people exist whose inner plight resembles mine; still, it is possible for me to imagine such people – but that the secret raven forever flaps about their heads as it does about mine, even to imagine that is impossible.' The author's sense of being unlike anyone else, which comes across so strongly in this passage, is something each reader will have to confront. At the very least he will be warned not to expect the familiar. But how can the reader hope to be equal to the cunning of this writer? How can he gain a vantage-point from which he may safely judge how to read the text? How can he hope to do better than the 'goddess of fate' in penetrating the inner depth of this fox? These unanswered questions should be kept in mind when reading the following selection of Kafka's own statements about writing.

Felice Bauer, the recipient of over seven hundred letters and twice Kafka's fiancée, once showed a sample of his writing to a graphologist. On reading his diagnosis, Kafka singled out 'artistic interests' as the most misleading of all:

The man in your boarding house should leave graphology alone. I have no literary interests, but am made of literature, I am nothing else, and cannot be anything else. The other day I read the following story in a *History of Devil Worship*: 'There was a cleric with a voice so sweet and so beautiful that all who heard it were filled with joy. One day a priest heard the sweetness of these sounds and said: "This is not the voice of a man, but of the devil." In the presence of all the admirers he exorcised the demon and drove him out, whereupon the corpse (for this body had been animated by the devil instead of a soul) disintegrated and stank.' The relationship between me and literature is similar, very similar to that, except that my literature is not as sweet as that monk's voice. To discover this from my hand-writing, however, one would certainly have to be a very astute graphologist.

Equally emphatically he rejects a phrase that Felice herself found for his preoccupation: 'Not a bent for writing, dearest Felice, not a bent, but my self through and through. A bent can be straightened out or suppressed. But this is what I am.' The price to pay for this 'life as a writer' is rigid, uncompromising aloneness, a radical isolation from the outside world, from other people and – most painfully – from his beloved. Thus he writes to Felice, 'What I need for my writing is seclusion, not "like a hermit", that would not be enough, but like the dead. Writing, in this sense, is a sleep deeper than that of death.' In another of his many disengaging love-letters to Felice he describes their future married life in the following terms:

> But what, dearest Felice, have you to say to the kind of married life in which the husband, at any rate for several months in the year, returns from the office at 2.30 or 3.00, eats, lies down, sleeps until 7.00 or 8.00 p.m., hurriedly has his supper, takes an hour's walk, and then starts writing, and writes till 1.00 or 2.00 a.m.? Could you really stand that? To know nothing about your husband except that he is sitting in his room writing? And to spend the autumn and winter in this way? And by spring be ready to welcome the man, half-dead, at the door of his study, and through spring and summer watch him trying to recover in time for the autumn? Is that a possible sort of life? Maybe, maybe it is possible; nevertheless you must consider it carefully to the very last shadow of a doubt.

It is certainly not a coincidence that the crisis-ridden relationship with Felice Bauer brings out the most poignant portrayals of Kafka's life as a writer. He felt that his work was threatened by her, by the mere thought of marriage. From the point of view of his work she was the greatest enemy and for the sake of self-preservation he had to defend his work against his love. Yet the price he ultimately had to pay for this dubious self-preservation was – for him – the highest conceivable one; in the *Letter* to his father he writes, 'Getting married, founding a family, accepting all the children that are born, supporting them in this uncertain world and possibly even guiding them a little is, I am convinced, the utmost that a man can ever achieve.' The highest human accomplishment – love, marriage and a family – must be sacrificed for the sake of that most uncertain and elusive aim: his writing.

The point would be missed completely, and the edge of this comfortless predicament blunted, if one were to write off as exaggeration what lies in the very nature of Kafka's mind and its exploration of the self: his extremism. Thus when he speaks of 'seclusion, not "like a hermit", ... but like the dead', when he rejects the label 'literary interests' and accepts nothing short of 'identity' between his writing and his being, when he speaks of marriage and family as the *utmost* human achievement, he is concerned with more than just stressing a point. Rather he is reaching out for a truth that is revealed – if at all – only at the extreme boundaries; it is a quest for the absolute which is not supported by firm belief in an absolute.

He has imparted this attitude to Josephine, the mouse singer, artist-heroine of one of his last stories, who also aspires to the highest achievement in her art: 'She reaches for the highest wreath, not because, at the moment, it may be hanging a bit lower, but because it is the highest; if it were within her power, she would hang it even higher.' The only reason given for this – and probably the only reason that can be found – is 'inner consequence'.

The life of one who in this radical sense 'is writing', is sometimes described as a way of dying rather than of living; for not only does writing cut him off from other people and the outside world, but it also stunts the growth of all other human faculties in him. 'Who will confirm the truth or probability of the fact that it is only because of my literary destination that I am otherwise without interests and consequently heartless?' Kafka asks in his diary. And, as if in reply, he notes in a different context:

When it became clear to me that with my constitution writing was the most productive direction for my being to take, everything rushed in that direction and left idle all those abilities which have to do with the joys of sex, eating, drinking, philosophical reflection, and above all music. In all these areas I wasted away. This was necessary because the totality of my powers were so limited that only collectively could they even half-way serve the purpose of my writing.

Again, in this respect also he is like Josephine the singer, who channels all her living energy into her singing, so that anything that does not directly serve her art is denied the possibility of survival. Thus Josephine is so exposed, so abandoned that while she is dwelling in her song 'a cold breath could in passing kill her'.

But even the very real sacrifices Kafka made and the losses he suffered for his writing are for him no reliable consolation, for there is no guarantee that his explanation is a valid one: 'I drew up a detailed list of all that I have sacrificed to writing, as well as of the things that were taken from me for the sake of writing, or rather the loss of which was only bearable with this explanation.' Thus only the loss is absolutely certain, while the explanation may only be hypothetical, and the purpose of his sacrifice remains deeply uncertain.

There is however one elementary certainty: that he must write. This simple imperative appears to be impervious to all doubts that precede or follow from it. It may, indeed, be seen as the ultimate rationale and justification of all the resourcefulness and subversive cunning employed in his self-investigations, as is the case with Josephine the singer, to whom the sole purpose of her being, her art, is so infinitely beyond doubt that she has no qualms whatever about resorting to highly dubious methods when pressing for the kind of conditions she deems necessary for her life as an artist. She feels all the more justified in this because she is convinced that in this world honest methods are bound to fail.

Kafka's certainty that he must write and go on writing remains strikingly unchanged by the vastly conflicting values that he may at different times attribute to writing, and strangely unaffected by the question of ability and achievement: 'Writing as a form of prayer' is an entry in one of his notebooks; in a letter to Max Brod he calls writing 'a sweet and wonderful reward'. But for what? A reward for 'services rendered to the devil'. In a letter written about a year before his death he comes perhaps closest to summing up his relationship to 'writing ... which is for me – in a most cruel way as far as other human beings are concerned (unspeakably cruel – I won't even talk about that) – the most important thing on earth, like his delusion is to a madman (if he lost it he would go "mad") or like pregnancy to a woman.'

What, then, does such a writer write about? He frequently writes about animals; one need only think of his famous beetle, his monkeys, horses, dogs, mice, moles and other unspecified burrow-building creatures. The diary also contains many animal pieces, such as that of the dog that was observed by people on Niklausstrasse and on the bridge as it accompanied an ambulance with loud barks, 'till the dog suddenly leaves off, turns round and proves to be a common strange dog that intended nothing in particular with his pursuit of the vehicle'.

Writing about animals: such a statement is as unsatisfactory as, on the face of it, it is correct, and in a sense it is arbitrary too. But what does Kafka himself say about the themes, the subject-matter of his writing? 'The immense world that I have in my head. But how to free myself and free it without being torn apart. But a thousand times better to be rent apart than to retain it or bury it inside me. That is what I am here for, it is quite clear to me.' The 'immense world' inside his head that needs to be freed, or the representation of his 'dreamlike inner world' – that is how he describes his task. He only indicates the direction of this quest – inwards and downwards: 'Writing has its centre of gravity in the depths.' 'It is necessary to dive down – literally – and to sink down faster than that which is sinking down before you.' More often than not the turmoil inside seems impenetrable: it is 'writing into darkness as into a tunnel'. In one of his rare moments of almost unlimited confidence in his creative powers he may say, 'I can *lift* out of me whatever I want'; and similarly: 'Temporary satisfaction can still be gained from works such as "Country Doctor" ... but happiness only if I can lift the world into the pure, true and immutable.'

If his 'descent to the dark powers, this unchaining of ghosts that are by nature shackled, these questionable embraces of whatever else may go on down below' may rightly be described as 'self-exploratory' and may lead to a clearer 'self-knowledge', such investigations go far beyond what is generally called autobiographical. Their ultimate aim is to raise the world into the 'pure, true and immutable' – alas, an all too elusive aim. And there are reasons for this elusiveness. First, the 'dream-like inner world' lacks clarity and distinction and never ceases to be in tumultuous motion. Kafka once wrote of the 'tempestuous and floundering or morass-like inside that is our self'. Furthermore, it is truly 'immense' and thus never to be surveyed fully. He refers to himself when he describes the 'epitome' of the poor writer: '... what he wants to convey lies in his arms like a heavy sea snake and wherever he gropes, to the right, to the left, there is no end and even what he holds he cannot support.'

The most intractable difficulty seems to be the mysterious and uncontrollable process by which an inner vision may be turned into words: 'When I say something it loses its importance immediately and for ever; when I write it down that also always happens, but sometimes it takes on a new one.' This harsh rejection of speech is striking enough in itself but also, by implication, revealing about the nature of Kafka's writing, which becomes clearer in the following passage from a letter to Felice:

> I totally resent talking. Whatever I may say is wrong in my sense. For me speech robs everything I say of its seriousness and importance. To me it seems impossible that it should be otherwise, since speech is continuously influenced by a thousand external factors and a thousand external constraints. Hence I am silent not only from necessity but also from conviction.

The reasons given for this rejection of speech – external interference that leads to falsification and invalidation of the original idea – imply that Kafka must at all costs keep his writing free of such disturbances; and this, to be sure, means more than a quiet room to work in, important as that may be. A stillness freed of all external interference and constraints is to be created by the written word itself. Again, Josephine, the mouse, and her much disputed art of singing may be called upon to support this point. She also dislikes talking, she is the silent one among the tireless 'chatterboxes' of her mouse folk. 'Is it her singing that delights us or is it not rather the solemn silence that surrounds her meek little voice?' asks the sceptical narrator. And then, more affirmatively, he says, 'Of course it is a kind of piping. Why not? Piping is our people's daily speech. Only many a one pipes his whole life long and does not know it, whereas here piping is set free from the fetters of daily life, and it sets us free too for a little while.' If this 'liberation' is to be seen as the ultimate achievement of Josephine's singing, what about Kafka's writing? For him, language itself, the limitations of words, all too often proved to be the form of external interference that he could neither escape nor overcome:

> It is certain that everything I have conceived in advance, even when I was confident, whether word for word or just casually, but in specific words, appears dry, wrong, inflexible, embarrassing to everybody around me, timid, but above all patchy when I try to write it down at my desk, although I have forgotten nothing

of the original conception. This is naturally related in large part to the fact that I conceive something good away from paper only in a time of exaltation, a time more feared than longed for, much as I do long for it; but then the fullness is so great that I have to give up. Blindly and arbitrarily I snatch handfuls out of the stream, so that when I write it down calmly, my acquisition is nothing in comparison with the fullness in which it lived, is incapable of restoring this fullness – thus it is bad and disturbing because it tempts to no purpose.

The anatomy of his dilemma – that it is impossible to say everything and equally impossible not to say everything – is here analysed with all the clarity of thought which distinguishes Kafka's self-investigations. The stream of inner vision is for the most part submerged, its waters more often than not are murky; and what can be seized and held through efforts at conscious and considered writing is as nothing compared to the inner plenitude. The sea snake in his arms seems endless, both to the right and to the left, and even what he holds he cannot support.

'Talent for patchwork,' Kafka once noted, almost as if latching on to a formula that expressed most concisely not only this dilemma but the very nature of his work: 'If I begin writing again after some time I draw the words as if out of empty air. If I capture one, then I have just this one alone and all the toil must begin anew.' When, in an effort to dispel his fear of writing, he rehearses opening sentences away from his desk, they immediately prove 'unusable, dry, broken off long before their end, and pointing with their prominent breakage into a sad future'. And once in the diary he notes, 'Bitter, bitter, that is the most important word. How do I intend to solder fragments together into a sweeping story?'

The great number of fragments, beginnings and broken-off pieces of stories contained in his diaries and notebooks are evidence enough of this so-called 'talent'; moreover, one also calls to mind that all three novels remained unfinished. Even his completed stories often seemed to him to have unsatisfactory endings, and, what is more, they frequently end in a sentence or paragraph that belies the finality of the conclusion. Thus 'The Judgment' does not end with Georg Bendemann's death – he throws himself from the bridge into the river – nor with his last words – 'Dear parents, I have always loved you' – but with the sentence, 'At this moment an unending stream of traffic was going over the bridge.'

The Great Wall of China of Kafka's story (an unfinished story too) was built in many unconnected sections in different and distant parts of the country. When two such sections had been successfully joined together, the workers would start again in an entirely different area. Thus many gaps came about again in an entirely different area. And there are said to be gaps that may never have been closed. But no one can verify this rumour; the vast expanse of the country and of the Wall does not permit a survey. While the story, rather inconclusively, investigates the reasons for this 'system of partial construction', there is a certain similarity between that vast and ultimately fruitless construction project and Kafka's *oeuvre*. Only, in the latter the gaps are more visible, the broken-off pieces more prominent, and both the aim – completion of the whole – and the energies required for this achievement more firmly denied.

'A finely calculated hell,' Kafka once called his predicament, 'but not without its good moments.' Yes, good moments and, indeed, pleasure, a sweet and devilish pleasure he experienced in his writing. Not only when he was working well, when he felt admitted to the world of his imagination, when he dwelt in his writing, but even at times of the deepest frustration and the clearest understanding of that finely constructed hell, he was able to feel and record pleasure, 'pleasure *and* desperation'. 'The writer is only a construct of sensuality – that is the writer for you!' he said in a letter to Max Brod.

If it is true that Kafka never doubted that he had to write and had to go on writing, he does not often attempt to give reasons for this unshakeable determination. But when he does, his explanations or justifications are tentative, varied, even contradictory: to satisfy his love for Felice, to liberate himself from his overpowering father, to raise himself from 'the underworld', to gain 'salvation or damnation', or simply because he is 'homesick' – 'The longing for a place of refuge necessary for my work is already given in the common old miracle of the rib and the resulting expulsion.' But as he remained certain beyond any doubt that he could never stop writing, the *pleasure* of writing, he felt, 'could be tested to its very core'.

Probing into the depths of that pleasure led him to understand that even writing about death was no exception, was permeated by the same sweet pleasure. And writing death scenes, be it the slow starvation of his hunger artist (in the story of that name), or Joseph K.'s brutal execution, was inseparably entangled with the anticipation of his own death, as the following diary entry shows:

On the way home I told Max that I should lie very contentedly on my deathbed, provided the pain was not too great. I forgot – and later purposely omitted – to add that the best things I have written have their basis in this capacity of mine to meet death with contentment. All these fine and very convincing passages always deal with the fact that someone is dying, that he finds death very hard, that it seems unjust to him, or at least harsh, and the reader is moved by this, or at least he should be. But for me, who believe that I shall be able to lie contentedly on my deathbed, such scenes are secretly a game; indeed, in the death enacted I rejoice in my own death. . . .

But if Kafka thought that through his writing he could induce his own peaceful end, he also realized that he would not succeed in dispelling the real fear of death, however vividly he experienced the vain and sweet pleasure of anticipation and its literary exploitation: 'Sometimes a naive person will wish, "I would like to die and see how everyone mourns me" – this is the scene such a writer is continually staging. He dies (or rather he does not live) and continually mourns for himself. From this springs a terrible fear of death. . . .' His own funeral, he goes on in the same letter, will be a strange one: '. . . the writer, insubstantial as he is, consigning the old corpse, the body that has always been a corpse, to the grave. I am enough of a writer to enjoy the scene with all my senses, or – and it is the same thing – to want to describe it with total self-forgetfulness. . . .'

Josephine the singer ends her career in protest against her people's refusal to exempt her from ordinary daily work. As a last resort, after all her threats and schemes have failed, she disappears. But it is 'curious how mistaken she is in her calculations, the clever creature, so mistaken that one might think she has made no calculations at all but is only being driven on by her destiny, which in our world cannot be anything but a sad one'.

It must remain an open question whether the 'clever' mouse Josephine or the cunning fox Odysseus is the more fitting image for this writer.

14

Kafka and Language

Anthony Thorlby

It is a commonplace of Western literature, during the last hundred years or more, that it has become increasingly preoccupied with itself. More generally still, it can be said of artists of all kinds that they seem to have grown more interested in their medium than in their subject-matter, and in the case of writers this means, of course, in their language: not simply in what used to be called 'style', but in the act of writing and in the phenomenon of words. Of no writer is this more true than of Kafka.

He did not, as a result, gain simply a clearer understanding of what language is. Or rather, he gained an absolutely clear understanding of the fact that its nature is ultimately unintelligible. This paradox, like the paradoxes and parables of which Kafka himself was so fond, only makes sense in metaphysical terms – the terms we use in our efforts to know what knowledge is and to say what words are. Such terms cannot be simply reduplications of those they are intended to explain; they must be transformations of ordinary knowledge, or ordinary language, into another frame of reference. Words lend themselves to just this kind of transformation, passing beyond their original designation of one thing or situation in the world to bring into being other worlds of meaning, which we understand as metaphorical (or 'carried over'). If it were possible to carry over all our language into this larger, purely meaningful dimension, it might be possible to see what can otherwise not be seen: namely, what verbal intelligibility is, and (in the activity of writing) what makes intelligibility intelligible.

Kafka more than once spoke as if the ordinary course of his life had been entirely transformed into writing, and in his work it does appear to have been carried over into this metaphorical hinterland of language: 'My life consists and always has consisted fundamentally of attempts at writing, and mainly of unsuccessful ones.' He felt himself to be a writer, and nothing but a writer, even when he was unable to write and was producing nothing (that he preserved, anyway) or else only fragments. This happened, as he says, a great deal of the time, making him acutely unhappy and, so he believed, ruining his health; on the other hand, not to write made him no less unhappy and did not restore his health. But who shall say whether the writing caused the unhappiness and ill-health, or the ill-health and unhappiness inspired the writing? If anyone could, it must surely be Kafka, who gazed into the dream-like recesses of his mind, where it passes over into bodily sensation, and glimpsed that barely accessible place where thoughts, words, and images arise from physical impressions, from fantasies, and from various degrees of consciousness and well-being. Here 'place' and 'arise' are, of course, no more than a manner of speaking, a metaphor, but in no other way can language make visible its own dark origins. Attempts at defining factually and logically the connection of language with the world do not avoid the risk of carrying the mind beyond the sphere of both fact and logic: on the contrary, such attempts run of their own accord into a still remoter place of sheer abstraction – a place of no-sense or nonsense of which one famous definition by a philosopher contemporary with Kafka will be cited in conclusion.

If paradox and psychosomatic pain constitute understanding, then Kafka understood what writing is, and expressed it in everything he wrote and in his life. It was 'as if' it were only possible to get behind the meanings of words, and know them from some superior point of view, by means of the ghastly process described in the story 'In the Penal Colony' – that is, by having them etched ever more deeply into your back, so that they are known in a sense both from behind and by real contact, until the process kills you. It used to be believed (according to Kafka's story) that then the mind, at the point of death, would realize, with a realization bearing the marks of pure spiritual joy and consummate comprehension, what words *really* say – that is, what their real connection is with one's bodily existence. Did Kafka truly believe that figure of speech, that 'as if'? The story suggests that he did not; one half of himself, in the form of the observer, apparently rejects the horrible fantasy-vision which the other half creates.

This divided, self-destructive pattern characterizes Kafka's fictions generally, as well as his experiences and his reflections on writing; all have a similarly ambiguous, even self-contradictory, quality. 'Writing as a form of prayer,' he notes in his journal, and then describes it in a letter as 'a sweet reward ... the reward for serving the devil'. He goes on writing, on the brink of breakdown, in the face of failure, because he hopes that he will thus achieve 'freedom'. Freedom from what? From the pain, the curse, the 'shame' (as he once called it) of writing. He feared it was 'a shame that would outlive him'. Can literary immortality ever have been conceived more paradoxically or (in an effort to know what it is) have been related to a more dubious frame of reference?

This reference is placed at the close of *The Trial*, but Kafka uses it also in connection with himself in his 'Letter' to his father, a half-literary 'work' of which it is hard to say whether it is a communication or another effort at overcoming writing by writing, at rising to a truth above language. Again, in his journal he draws the same distinction with regard to his writing as the painter in *The Trial* makes with regard to the inscrutable regulations of the 'Law' (which belongs to the same frame of reference as the 'shame'): 'I can get temporary satisfaction from works like "Country Doctor" provided I can still successfully complete pieces of that sort. But [I can get] happiness only if I can raise the world into the realm of the pure, the true, and the unchanging.' This happiness sounds again like the legendary condition of total freedom and innocence described in *The Trial*, of which 'Joseph K.' – all that is left of Kafka in the realm of higher reference: a man who has become a phoneme, the barest component of language – has deprived himself by some unknowable guilt, which ends however in the same deadly sense of shame as that induced by writing. And of just this transformatory, or 'raising', power of language, Kafka remarks on another occasion: 'Metaphors are one of the many things which make me lose faith in writing. The lack of independence of writing, its dependence on the servant girl making up the fire, on the cat warming itself on the stove. ... All these are independent functions of reality, obeying the laws of their own being; only writing is helpless, does not dwell in itself, is pure fun [*Spass*] and despair.'

The last two, contradictory words reveal the permanently divided state of Kafka's mind with regard to language, which provided both the innocent amusement of creatively transforming the world and the despair of reducing to nothing the world's reality and truth. From the beginning he ponders the meaning of his own destiny, a life given over to literature, and only gradually does he come to recognize it. In his fictions he expresses it both purely metaphorically, in fantasies of unforgettable vividness, and also quite analytically, in an almost dull, pedestrian style that tries to render plain and comprehensible his fantastical story. He names here the two voices of literature – of his own literature anyway, perhaps of all literature – 'fun and despair', comedy and tragedy. They are inherent, it seems, in the character of writing.

The brief theoretical reflections on language and writing to be found in

Kafka's letters and journals 'explain' little, however, by comparison with what Kafka criticism has done. Kafka himself had few frames of reference to explain the puzzle of what language is, other than those provided by the metaphorical shifts he discovered through his experience of writing; he explained writing by doing it. Then he could bring together as a total fiction what critical analysis only divides again and explains in other terms. Kafka even appears to have been slow to discover, or surprised at discovering, what the first of his successful stories, 'The Judgment', may have meant; generally he is indifferent to what concerns exegetical critics most – perhaps with good reason. In the last note that he made (12 June 1923) on the subject of language, he remarks that 'every word, turned in the hands of the spirits ... becomes a spear, directed against the speaker. Especially a remark like this.' Kafka is summing up here, as we shall see, his most fundamental insight into language: its metaphorical capacity not only to transform the experience from which it arises in life into something beyond itself, but actually to reverse what was lived as one thing into what is 'thought of' in an infinitely regressing series of reflections (as the passage just quoted goes on to point out). Language presents itself to him as a problem to be overcome. How can he solve it? The passage itself demonstrates the answer.

The word Kafka uses to describe the sufferer is 'speaker', and it occurs to him probably because of the painful disease of the throat with which he was afflicted. This sets his thought in motion, but the thought then flies on the wings of metaphor to a quite different, unexpected conclusion. The note rises to the metaphorical level of the spear, into which he has metamorphosed his pain. Against that pain, that twisting of words against the speaker, he says, there is no appeal, no chance of defence, no *Trost* [consolation]. But, he concludes, 'More than *Trost* is: you too have weapons.' Kafka does not say what these weapons are (in being mentioned, they would be turned against him). But by remaining in the realm of metaphor, rather than of 'remarks' and mere talk, which he tends to regard as a lesser use of words, he affirms his grasp of the weapons of language, a grasp he demonstrates though he does not explain it. He answers weapon with weapon, metaphor with metaphor; he turns language against itself. Like the 'figure in the carpet' in Henry James's story of that name, the all-explaining motif or idea is never spoken; it does not lie outside the story, but is inseparable from the weaving of it.

In other words, the secret of what a lifetime's writing is (which we imagine, as we read James's story – or any of Kafka's – will be revealed in some other terms, translated out of the symbolic speech of its fictions and metaphors into a language that speaks plainly of real things in the world) actually remains completely in the sphere of literature, becoming identical

The building in Bílkova Street where Kafka moved in 1914 – his first attempt to live on his own

Kafka with Ottla, his favourite sister, c. 1915

An art-nouveau building, 'The Golden Pike', where Kaf ka lived in 1915

Max Brod (1884–1968)

Kafka's friend, the Jewish philosophical writer
Felix Weltsch (1884–1964)

The Old Synagogue, built in 1270

ABOVE LEFT The writer and poet Johannes Urzidil (1896–1970), who knew Kafka and wrote on him in his New York exile

ABOVE RIGHT Kafka's friend, the blind writer Oskar Baum (1883–1941)

A view of Prague Jewish cemetery, the oldest in Europe

The Workers' Accident Insurance
Offices, where Kafka worked from 1908
to 1922

King Charles IV's Bridge, connecting
the old and new parts of the city

LEFT Kafka and Felice Bauer, a photograph taken at the time of their second engagement in July 1917

RIGHT Kafka in the Old Town Square, Prague, *c.* 1920

BELOW Marienbad, which the couple visited in the summer of 1916

The John Hus monument and Týn Church on the Old Town Square

with the writing (and reading) of the text. James writes more realistically, leaving threads trailing on the ground of commonplace reality, as it were, while Kafka is more successful in gathering them all up into the fabric of his story. From whatever 'real' impulse in his life his stories sprang, whether from an inner need or an outer situation (and in his personal writings we find traces of both), he is more successful in transforming it entirely into the language of metaphor – indeed, into a self-contained metaphorical world.

The title of Kafka's best known story, which might be more appropriately translated as 'The Transformation' than as 'The Metamorphosis', points to this mysterious capacity of words to transform the stuff of existence into something else. Letters, sketches and journal entries supply many details to show, for instance, how much Kafka himself felt like the untranslatably metamorphosed creature in his story, preferring the solitude of his room to a wedding, often fantasizing about not having to hold a job which stood in the way of his writing, watching his family through a crack in the door, loving his youngest sister, and being inwardly destroyed by his father, before whom his art was a compulsive but futile gesture of self-justification, so that when he could produce nothing he 'lay already on the floor, good for nothing but to be swept up and thrown out' – which is what finally happens to Gregor Samsa, the central figure of the story. Details of a similar kind connect the novel *The Trial* with Kafka's protracted love affair with, and attempts at engagement to, Felice Bauer. A disastrous meeting with her family did actually strike him in the juridical light suggested by that title. The proceedings between them, conducted for the most part through the medium of writing, by correspondence, do often seem to be as endless, one-sidedly obscure, and self-destructive as the legal process in the novel: which is itself as much like a mental or verbal process as any credibly legal one, and quite unlike the course of any recognizable love story. We have the impression that the legal metaphor is being carried over into still more distant spheres of meaning, where it refers only to the verbal process of its own transformations. The German title of the book, as well as much of the vocabulary used in it, make various meanings possible: *Der Prozess* has the senses equally of 'legal trial', 'physical process' and 'proceedings'.

Confronted with what to an English eye look like puns, it may be tempting to dismiss this accidental feature of language as trivial. Much more is involved, however, than the fact that one sound may have different meanings, or even that a word may have more than one dictionary definition: a word also has an infinite variety of possible senses with regard to its use in sentences and in the context of paragraphs or situations. Simplifying, we might say that Kafka sometimes takes a metaphor 'literally'* – for instance, that of 'transformation' (metamorphosis) or of '*Prozess*' (trial or physical process) – as one way of exploring this mysterious potential of words. But we are likely to distract attention from his insight into this potential if, by referring to the literal use of metaphor, we try to see what the image or expression 'really' means – that is, try to translate his stories back into the circumstances from which they may have sprung in his life, or into what they could theoretically indicate in the life of our time. For to do that would presuppose that there is a necessary connection between any fact of existence – be it an object, event, or experience – and the language used to express it. Kafka's fundamental insight, which he discovered not by philosophical reflection but through his slow, painful struggle to write exclusively in his own way, was that there is no such connection. There may be an inevitability in the use of words once a sentence, an image, or a story has been embarked upon, but there is absolutely no way of establishing whether the words are the right words in any other sense: whether, in fact, they are true.

Kafka formulated this insight when he put these words into the mouth of the prison chaplain in *The Trial*: 'One does not have to accept everything as true, one must only accept it as necessary.' The circumstances surrounding even this sentence, however, are illuminating – if darkness can be said to illumine. The sentence is spoken in one context, about sentences originally spoken in another one. The speaker of the sentence has been telling a story and wishes to justify (against the charge that they are 'untrue') the 'necessity' of statements made within the story by one of its characters, and by implication to justify the story itself. The story (the famous parable 'Before the Law', which Kafka had composed separately) he placed in the context of his novel, *The Trial*, thus enabling one pair of characters – in the novel – to discuss the meaning of what another pair of characters – in the parable – have said and done. But this clearly cannot put an end to the question of whether the right words have been used in either set of circumstances or whether they can be shown to be false. The hero of the second story (the novel) has no hesitation in replying, 'A melancholy conclusion. It turns lying into a universal principle.' Then comes the moment when the author must step outside the two frameworks of discussion he has set up and pronounce on them from the viewpoint of a third. Kafka writes (of the novel's hero), 'K. said that with finality, but it was not his final judgment.' In an earlier draft Kafka had put the matter rather more fully: 'When he had said that, he faltered. It came home to him that he had been talking about a legend and judging

---

* This word reverses its sense in the context of Kafka's writing. It appears to return the reader to a world where words keep their feet on the ground of reality – and Kafka's fiction *has* this pedestrian realism. But the ground (and the feet) are nothing but figures of speech.

it, and yet that he knew nothing about its source and origin and that he was equally in the dark about the interpretations.' Both versions (the draft and the posthumously published text) end literally 'in the dark'. The phrase is a metaphor, of course, but in the larger perspective of the novel (which is not identical with that either of the parable or of the hero's point of view) Kafka solves the problem of what would otherwise be an infinite regression of contexts by taking the metaphor literally – that is to say, by representing his hero as lost in the obscurity of an unlit cathedral. His interlocutor, the prison chaplain, tells him how to leave – if he wants to: a finely ironical ending to the chapter, since the chaplain evidently knows his way around well enough in this religious obscurity, having a very little light to guide him. The chaplain's remark about truth and necessity is often misinterpreted as being Kafka's own view, whereas it is a view limited to the context in which it is made; the chaplain can offer the hero a perspective on a legend of his own making. But the hero, of course, wants more than that; he wants to know the meaning of his case – not in a parable, but absolutely. He wants to step outside the framework of his own story – of language – altogether, and to establish his total innocence and freedom. If Kafka has a view of his own, it is that this desire is impossible of satisfaction and ends in self-destruction. At least, that is what the story 'says'.

Are we, then, reduced to telling stories about our human state on earth? (But who says this would 'reduce' us? It might be 'fun' – or despair.) If we are, should we rest content with this condition of our existence and not try to see over the edge of our own horizons: is this the final meaning of Kafka's work – its utterly ambiguous message? The ambiguity would lie in the fact that in his own writing, to which he gave his life as totally and tragically as any of his heroes and which he could not exist without, he does strive precisely to see over the edge: in order to show us that the whole enterprise is quite vain (and *therefore* fit, at best, to be destroyed or forgotten, as he apparently wished?). Kafka's most revealing aphorism must then surely be one of that collection he placed under the title 'Er' ('He') – attributing them to a *persona* who utters aphorisms (which, however short, are still a form of writing), and thus to be distinguished from the simple 'I' of Kafka the man – a being whom Kafka the writer often, in letters and stories, imagines to be dead or dying, killed by the 'wound' which opened, so he said, with the first successful story written in his own manner, 'The Judgment', and who seemed to him later to have the tuberculosis that did actually cause his death as its inevitable consequence: 'He has found the Archimedean point,* but has used it against himself; evidently this is the condition that has enabled him to find it.' If 'he' is a

* A firm point of leverage, or fulcrum, outside the world, which it would then be possible to move.

writer, a man of words, then this aphorism tells us that language does carry us beyond the limits of our world, but, from its extra-worldly vantage-point, condemns, excludes, destroys us in some way. It attends the funeral of lived experience, the funeral of our personal self: an image Kafka once used in a letter to Max Brod to describe the 'naive wish' of every writer.*

Kafka's observations concerning language and writing often have this aphoristic and paradoxical quality, which, when developed at greater length, lends his stories a myth-like character. Myth is a form of narration appropriate for the telling of things that transcend the limits of possible knowledge, for it ventures where no human being could go, beyond the horizons of human existence, among gods and fabulous creatures; and it is told by a voice that is no man's voice, but that of some collective wisdom, inherited from a time before it was considered that every statement must be some individual's statement and confined to his perspective. Freud speculated on the possibility that the illness of an entire community, perhaps of humanity itself, might take the same form in which case no one would recognize the religious myths that provided everyone's explanation and escape as being in reality the 'universal obsessional neurosis' which they so plainly were for Freud, the modern rational observer of the psyche. Kafka's speculations went much further than this, to encompass the dilemma of the observer as well. He knew, like Nietzsche, that mythical assumptions about the world are built into the structure of language, so that we mythologize merely by using it, even though we may not realize this. ('I am afraid we are not rid of God because we still have faith in grammar.') Kafka did not have the same polemical intention of getting rid of God as Freud or Nietzsche, though he may have shared the latter's hope for an aesthetic redemption of the world, which Nietzsche believed could only be accomplished by the most ruthless attack upon religious myths of redemption. Kafka embarks upon stories that are pure myth, full of creatures and situations and sequences of events that we recognize as belonging to the myth-making level of our minds, the level of dreams, reverie, or childhood memory, which Freud too acknowledged as the home of myth. From this level flows his narrative, as though a wound had been opened into the depths of his being; the events of the story arrive and pass with a kind of unexplained, matter-of-fact necessity, 'lending' – or should one say 'borrowing from'? – Kafka's style an air of blank matter-of-factness, even when the most inconceivable mythical and metaphorical transformations are going forward. This is most noticeable in passages where no identifiable narrator speaks, or conversations occur between beings who belong to this imaginative underworld and take its dream sequence for granted.

* See previous contribution, pp 129f. [Ed.]

But in many of Kafka's stories the presence of a narrator is clearly and continuously noticeable; he can be heard, telling either his own story or someone else's, without there being, however, any significant change in the dispassionate, almost colourless, unexceptional style of narration. The narrators seem to lack both personal character and personal feeling, even when the story they are telling is their own. It is as if they have only one motive, one *raison d'être*, and that is to know, record in words, and reduce to pure intellectual clarity and order the events they relate and, in their own terms, comprehend. And this they both totally succeed and totally fail to do. For they are the voice of language itself, the epitome of sense, syntax, grammar, and thought, spirits of rational enquiry; yet what they have to convey is essentially mythic material, the sheer fact and flow of existence, which has no necessary connection with their own standards and laws. They are confronted with an alien world, the non-verbal process of existence, by comparison with which their own linguistic sphere is as frozen as the landscape of *The Castle*, as tortuous as the proceedings of *The Trial*. Yet paradoxically it is they who import the frigidity, the torture, and all the other metaphorical suggestions of meaning into the basically non-verbal, inconceivable 'happening' – no word, by definition, will serve, except to start another myth – that brings an individual consciousness into being, to love, strive, suffer and die: a happening which is particularly liable to metamorphosis and mythification. The paradox of man's linguistic striving to grasp such happenings is this: that the higher it ascends, and the more enlightened, 'pure, true, and unchanging' it becomes, the darker and more inscrutable becomes the mythic ground beneath.

What, then, of man's desire, of Kafka's personal desire, to believe in the 'happiness' of the metaphors and myths that language gives rise to, myths of truth and innocence and salvation, salvation for himself and even for his entire race? Is that a delusion? It was a doubt which Kafka shared with many of his generation: that man, through his language, merely fabricates lies to console his spirit. The writer's task must then be to free his narrative, his reader, and himself from such delusions: that was Kafka's hope and the hope of many of his contemporaries. He must surmount the paradox of his position, the paradox inherent in language itself – namely, that in speaking of the world, he cannot help making of it something other than it is. And to accomplish this, Kafka had, as it were, to work continually against himself, against the natural mythological aspiration of language towards ever 'higher' meanings, ever more absolute comprehension. He had – to quote from another of his parables – to build the mine-shaft, not the tower of Babel; the tower of Babel, intended (let it be recalled) to link earth with heaven, would have been an acceptable construction, Kafka also wrote, provided no one ever tried to ascend it. By showing the nothingness of linguistic constructions, he hoped to make instead the incommunicable substantiality of existence manifest. This mindless reality, at the opposite pole from language, he idealized with a passion that only a man whose life had become metamorphosed into literature could feel with such intensity; in Kafka this feeling borders on the mystical.

The ambiguous character of Kafka's conception of his task, and indeed of his use of language and of his way of telling a story (for with him it is a matter not of a theoretical idea but of a compulsive practice), is nowhere more plain than in his last two stories. 'Josephine, the Singer' and the unfinished tale, 'The Burrow', are both obviously about art, and, for all their transformation into the semblance of animal fables, about Kafka's own art. To use the jargon of much later linguistic theory, which Kafka so often anticipates, he both constructs and intellectually deconstructs his stories at the same time. Their mythic substratum has unmistakable power, doubtless springing from personal sources in the first place, for they express the feelings of a dying man as he looks back over a lifetime consumed by literature, at the cost of not living in the real world and of isolation from his people. Beyond that, through the medium of the basic imagery and metaphor, the power which Josephine possesses of unifying her people, especially in times of peril, recalls the role which the songs, psalms and epics of ancient peoples played; and there is indeed a perennial sense in which language not only unites but makes a people, giving individual men a feeling of belonging together, a spirit of community, which is more immediate and profounder than the merely utilitarian advantages which language as a tool of practical communication can provide. But the narrator, who scarcely seems to belong to Josephine's people, so well does he understand her and her singing, dissipates by his solemn humour the illusions and foolishness which flourish in that mythic atmosphere. Even her singing is not, by any absolute standard, really singing at all; but then, there are no absolute standards by which that can be judged for certain – only the still undeniable psychological effect of her singing, and legends of ancient times when singing truly was song. Since then the situation has become 'mousey-all-too-mousey', to parody a Nietzschean phrase that reminds us of the similarly destructive/creative attitude towards the fabrications of language in both Kafka and Nietzsche.

The same ambivalent attitude is expressed still more subtly in 'The Burrow', where the story is told by the burrowing creature itself, and any comparable stylistic distance between the narrator and his subject-matter (or the mythic ground of the story), would appear to be impossible. Yet the deconstruction of that ground is effected still more radically, and with tragic pathos rather than humour, by virtue of its being due to the workings not of a narrator's external comments but of the protagonist's expression of his own predicament – namely, by the force of linguistic utterance alone. The protagonist-narrator is as completely buried in his own story as he is in his burrow; there he has laboured inwardly to secure a place of personal salvation, yet with every word we see that he has spent his life digging his own grave. The metaphoric transformation of writing into an activity 'like' burrowing with one's head through the ground carries a myriad implications which Kafka imbues with both positive and negative significance. Something is actually constructed after all, by writing and by thinking in words; the German title of the story makes this meaning stand out quite plainly: *Der Bau* means firstly something built, a structure. But what kind of structure do words make in the solid ground of physical existence? They are signs, no more, and do not carry within themselves the substance of the things they say. Quite the contrary: they signify their absence, the replacement of the mysterious wholeness of the world, of which the bustling life above ground and the deadly, but no less necessary, inescapable presences and processes below the surface are but two aspects – the replacement of all that by an insubstantial nothing, a noise that in the end can only announce our doom, a labyrinthine void, something exactly 'like' a burrow.

The preoccupation of modern art with itself, with which we began this discussion, and of Kafka's writing with its own processes and the medium of language, through which we have followed it, certainly does not reduce the importance of his fictions but explains rather why they have come to be acknowledged as occupying a 'place' of central importance for many aspects of Western civilization. The fact that the most diverse crises of modern times, whether social, political, psychological, or religious in their own terms, can also be seen reflected in Kafka's work, albeit in purely symbolic and metamorphosed form, suggests that all of them intersect at some common point. For all their various and separate dimensions of theory and fact, they meet when they take the uncertain step 'over' into the metaphor of meaning. Doubtless that meeting-point has always been crucial to philosophy, religion, and art; but increasingly, in the hundred years or so at whose centre Kafka stands, it has been approached through intense scrutiny of the phenomena of expression themselves, and with ever more radical doubts and assumptions about what it is that these phenomena generally express. The similarity in this respect of Nietzsche's thinking to Kafka's, or again of Freud's, has already been hinted at, though their theories are nowhere mentioned in his fiction. It would have been equally possible to find comparable areas of enquiry in the work (say) of Saussure or the Prague Linguistic Circle, which was to form in Kafka's native city, though not quite in his lifetime; in Kierkegaard's writings, some of which Kafka read; or in those of many modern philosophers which he could not know, from Husserl to Merleau-Ponty. One may be cited in conclusion, one who came from the same cultural ambience as Kafka and who concluded in 1921, as a result of his first research into the question of language, that further enquiry was impossible. Wittgenstein gave up philosophy for thirteen years – recalling Kafka's wish that his own writings should not be preserved or his publications reprinted – after he had thought his way to the following paragraphs; it was a way he had pursued with the utmost intellectual concern for what language can say clearly and incontrovertibly:

My sentences* serve as elucidations in the following way: anyone who understands me eventually recognizes them as nonsensical, when he has used them – as steps – to climb up beyond them. (He must, so to speak, throw away the ladder after he has climbed up it.)

He must transcend these propositions,* and then he will see the world aright.

---

* The word that Wittgenstein uses is *Sätze*, which means either 'sentences' or 'propositions'.

15

Freud and the Magic of Kafka's Writing

Walter H. Sokel

To call Franz Kafka 'the Dante of the Freudian age' would not be without justification. The statement implies this analogy: as Dante had given poetic expression to the world view developed conceptually in scholastic philosophy, Kafka presented in fictional terms the image of man as conceived by Freud. Like all such sweeping statements that seek to pinpoint an extremely complex relationship, the analogy would call for far-reaching and profound qualifications. As I shall briefly point out, at least one half of it would have to be negated from the start. Yet let us look further into the possibility of its validation.

Historically, Kafka's writing career coincided with the appearance of the fundamental texts which established psychoanalysis. In 1895 Freud and Breuer had published the pioneering *Studies in Hysteria*, which was followed in 1900 by Freud's *Interpretation of Dreams*, and, the year after, *The Psychopathology of Everyday Life*. In 1905 followed the case history, *Dora, Three Essays on the Theory of Sexuality*, and *Jokes and their Relation to the Unconscious*. It was the publication of these works that laid the foundations of Freud's fame and that quickly spread his notoriety. In Kafka's most formative decade as a writer, the influence of Freud radiated through the intellectual avant-garde of Central Europe and, in his native Prague, Kafka could not escape it. Freud was discussed and lectured on in the literary salon of Frau Berta Fanta, which Kafka frequented. He became personally acquainted with and was greatly attracted to the psychoanalytic thinker and reformer Otto Gross, whom the avant-garde of Kafka's day hailed as a martyr to the Oedipal family institution. Kafka frequently referred to psychoanalysis in general, and in his correspondence showed himself familiar with psychoanalytic concepts and literature. He was very interested in a book in which the psychoanalyst Wilhelm Stekel had referred to his 'The Metamorphosis', and Kafka's immersion in the thought, if not the actual writings, of Freud could not be more tellingly confirmed than by the tone of stating the obvious with which Kafka lists Freud among the associations that came to him in reading over 'The Judgment', the evening after it was written. 'Thoughts of Freud, naturally,' Kafka observed.

Kafka shared with psychoanalysis the genetic approach to human existence. He agreed with Freud in attributing overwhelming importance to early childhood experience and upbringing and, like Freud, accused the Central European variant of the late Victorian middle-class family of twisting and crippling human life. This statement of Freud's, from one of his essays of 1908, seems to have been echoed by Kafka whenever he viewed his own life in relation to his father:

> Those who succumb to nervous illness are precisely the offspring of fathers, who, having been born of rough but vigorous families, living in simple healthy country conditions, had successfully established themselves in the metropolis, and in a short space of time had brought their children to a high level of culture.
> [IX, 182]*

Kafka's long autobiographical letter to his father of November 1919 reads like an elaboration of Freud's sentence. This letter is a remarkable document, not least because of its cultural-historical significance as one of the most consistent applications of Freud's theory of the Oedipus complex to one particular life. In his letter, which represents Kafka's basic autobiography, he employs the perspective of the Oedipus complex with so pure and radical a consistency that the French 'anti-Oedipal' psychiatrists Deleuze and Guattari have been persuaded to see it as a deliberate caricature of Freud's fundamental doctrine, 'a magnifying of Oedipus to the point of the absurd'.

Analogies which centre on the Oedipus complex, or on the masochistic component underlying the themes of Kafka's life and *oeuvre*, seem all too obvious for comfort. They tend to obscure the equally, or even more important, fundamental differences between the founder of psychoanalysis and the creator of the 'Kafkaesque' mode of perceiving and presenting human life. Despite the many striking thematic parallels, Kafka was by no means a Freudian or a follower of any psychoanalytic persuasion. The most important difference lies in Kafka's categorical rejection of psychoanalysis as a means of therapy. In sharp contrast to Freud, Kafka saw emotional illness not as something remediable and extrinsic to human existence. What Freudian psychoanalysis diagnosed as 'neurosis' was for

* See note on p. 158.

Kafka a spiritual or existential anguish, inseparable from the whole being of the one who suffered it. 'There is only one illness,' Kafka said in one of his letters, 'and medicine hunts it blindly like a beast through unending forests.' The illness of which he speaks is neither psychological nor physical; it is individual existence itself. Kafka rejected the irreligious humanism that lies at the basis of Freud's psychoanalysis. He completely and resolutely despaired of Freud's rationalistic faith in the curative power of scientific knowledge. Since Kafka could not accept its therapeutic hopes, he had to dismiss the very *raison d'être* of psychoanalysis. For him, sensuous life as such was the disease for which there was only a single cure – death. Kafka's violent condemnation of sexuality – 'coitus is the punishment for the happiness of being together' – makes him a radical opponent of the naturalism firmly believed in by Freud. Physical life, propagated by what Freud called 'Eros' and aided by intelligence, always remained Freud's supreme value, even when, in his later stages, he saw a well-nigh tragic dilemma for man in the ineradicable conflict between the life-affirming instinct of Eros and the equally powerful death instinct, which manifests itself in self-destruction and aggression. Kafka's anti-naturalistic abhorrence of the flesh and all its works – 'the sensuous world is only the evil in the spiritual one,' he noted – could be viewed by Freud as nothing but a symptom of a severe neurosis. For Kafka, on the other hand, neurosis, such as the *Angst* which for ever haunted him, was a 'fact of faith', an 'anchoring of man in distress', 'preformed in his being and subsequently continuing to shape it. ... And here,' he added with melancholy resignation, 'one tries to cure?'

In an informative essay, 'Kafka and Psychoanalysis', Hartmut Binder has argued that the basic opposition of Kafka to Freud, as it emerges from passages such as the one just quoted, resides in the Freudian restriction of neurosis to the individual case and family situation. According to Binder, Kafka, in contrast to Freud, sees 'forces at work [in neurosis] which far transcend the individual's experience'. For Kafka, the therapeutic process of psychoanalysis fails to grasp the roots of illness 'in the suprapersonal anthropological dimension'. Binder overlooks the presence of the anthropological dimension in Freud's theory. The Oedipal family situation is seen by Freud, even in his early work, and progressively more sharply as his theory develops, in anthropological terms. It is viewed by him and his followers as the foundation of human society and civilization, and it is held to have worked its traumatic effects on all mankind. Kafka himself acknowledges the anthropological side of Freud, when he remarks that psychoanalysis views neurosis as the foundation of all religion. The main point of difference thus does not lie in the absence of a collectivist angle in Freud, but rather in the existential direction which Kafka's view of neurosis takes in contrast to the socio-cultural view of Freud. For Kafka, *Ángst*, like religion, is man's desperate attempt to find a resting-place in his 'distress', his frantic search for the 'anchor' in his 'thrownness' (to use Martin Heidegger's peculiarly apt term here), for a refuge 'in any maternal soil' that promises stability. Freud sees man capable of overcoming his original *Angst* by the strengthening of his ego in the face of super-ego and Id – a process of maturing which is both socializing and individuating. For Kafka, as for the existentialists, *Angst* constitutes the very 'essence' of the person, the forming element that 'continues to shape him' as long as he lives. For Freud, man would prosper and be properly himself if freed from his neurosis; while, for Kafka, without his illness he would not exist. Since individuated life itself is the illness from which man suffers, Kafka is able to call 'the therapeutic part of psychoanalysis' 'a helpless error'.

Having said all this, we should recall that the case against too close a Kafka-Freud connection must not be overstated. It does justice only to one side of Kafka, and not necessarily the dominant one. Among the strongest 'Freudian' components óf Kafka is his ambivalence, and one of the main critical tasks is to follow the various ramifications of this ambivalence. Kafka's avowed pessimism about the sensory world is counterbalanced by professions of fervent belief in the blessings and joys of physical fitness, practical energy, and vitality, which link him to turn-of-the-century vitalism, to Thomas Mann's nostalgia for the *Bürger*, and also to Freud's struggle in the cause of mental and emotional health. It is by no means clear whether Kafka's 'reluctant pessimism' was usually meant to be extended to the human condition, or whether it was not mainly restricted to himself and those he considered similarly afflicted. His preoccupation with the kind of education that would protect a future generation from falling victim to his own plight speaks against his exclusive immersion in mystic spirituality. There are similarities between Kafka's views on education, as they emerge in his letters to his sister Elli, and Freud's essay 'Civilized Sexual Morality and Modern Nervous Illness'.* Here, for all their differences, Kafka seems to share with Freud the general outlook of enlightened humanism.

Because of a deep split between Kafka's nature and his contrasting allegiances to pure spirit on the one hand, and Freud's concept of eros, on the other, Kafka's opinions can never provide a consistent world view. If we restrict ourselves to his opinions, all we can say is that he was close to Freud at the naturalistic or vitalistic pole of his being, and radically opposed to him at the spiritualist or mystical pole. However, if we proceed to examine the striking analogies between the working of the human mind, as expounded by Freud, and certain structural peculiarities of Kafka's

* Parts of that letter are quoted on pp. 160–1 below. [Ed.]

148

fictional world, we shall arrive at an aspect of Kafka which is not only compatible with Freud's thought, but almost incomprehensible without it. Let us recall that Kafka, after writing the work of his 'break-through', mentioned 'thoughts of Freud' as *'naturally'* occurring to him in connection with it. That is, he found a 'natural' link to Freud in the form and theme (he does not distinguish between them) of what he considered to be his best and most authentic writing. Kafka's own awareness of this connection emerges as a factor of crucial significance for the case, which this essay will attempt to argue, for a close kinship between the structure of the human mind, as conceived by Freud, and the principles of Kafka's creative method.

I shall concentrate on the structural role of the magic or fantastic element in Kafka's work and its relationship to two key concepts of Freudian psychoanalysis – repression and projection. Such a focusing might help to illuminate not only the relationship of Kafka's writing to the psychoanalytic view of man, but also to clarify the function of one of the most striking features of Kafka's work. By 'fantastic' I understand those narrated events in which the reader finds startling and puzzling deviations from his normal expectations, unexplained violations of what he would consider possible in the empirical world. Among very many examples are the unexplained metamorphosis of a human being into an animal, the apparently self-propelled movements of inanimate objects, the miraculous condensation or expansion of spatial distance. The fantastic is the other side of the magic. In magic, to use Freud's words, we encounter 'omnipotence of thought' or will, and its victory over the laws of nature. In the fantastic, the same seems to hold true, but the thought or will to which we could ascribe this victory over empirical experience is not perceived. At the very beginning of his writing career, the twenty-year-old Kafka, in a letter to his friend Oskar Pollak, called his own writing 'magic'. In his first extant work, 'Description of a Struggle', the first-person narrator performs acts of magic, altering features and dimensions of the landscape at will. The 'magic omnipotence of thought' here exhibited is transformed in Kafka's mature work into the fantastic, in which events defying the laws of nature happen, or seem to happen, without, and even contrary to, any discernible will. This important shift from the magic to the fantastic in Kafka's work corresponds to the difference between conscious and unconscious wishes in Freudian thought. Magic, with which Kafka equated his writing, remained its hallmark in a figurative sense, too. What we have come to call 'Kafkaesque' designates the peculiarly unsettling effects that radiate from the unexplained mysteries in his fiction and make for its special place in literature.

The most systematic attempt to explain the fantastic in Kafka, or at least in one of his most famous works, 'The Metamorphosis' of November/ December 1912, was undertaken by Tzvetan Todorov within the framework of a general treatise on the fantastic in literature. Todorov (not unlike Jentsch, in his definition of the central concept of 'the uncanny' in Freud's essay on 'The Uncanny', 1919) sees the fantastic as the effect produced on the reader by uncertainty as to the appropriateness of a natural or a supernatural understanding of the events depicted. What distinguishes Kafka from traditional authors of the fantastic genre is the reversal of direction, in his work, of the movement between natural and supernatural. In the traditional fantastic, text and reader move from a natural to a supernatural ambience. In Kafka's tale (Todorov argues) the opposite occurs. The story moves from the supernatural – the mysterious metamorphosis of the travelling salesman Gregor Samsa into a verminous insect – to the acceptance, by himself and his family, of this mystery as 'natural'. Its final 'naturalization' appears as 'the banality of evil', the brutal callousness of the petty bourgeois family in which the miracle dies, while the trivial round of everyday life triumphs.

Todorov's reading, certainly persuasive on one level, ignores a counter-movement, from the natural to the supernatural, which clearly emerges when we take Gregor's reflections on his past life into account. Gregor recalls how badly he had wished to quit his job and tell his hated boss his true opinion of him, which would make the exploiter tumble from his high seat. However, consideration for his family, whose debt to the firm had to be paid off first, had forced Gregor to silence his own rebellious wish. Instead he had, in his sleep, managed to get transformed into an insect. His metamorphosis, at a gruesome price, fulfilled at least part of the wish he had not dared to carry out himself. It freed him from his job and obligations as the breadwinner of his family. The sequence of events in the story thus initially describes the opposite of the movement discerned by Todorov. It shows a natural desire preceding and leading to the supernatural event. In this respect it is not Todorov, but Freud, who will help to illuminate the function of the fantastic in Kafka's work.

The connecting link between Freud's theories and Kafka's tale is Freud's concept of repression, which he declared to be 'the cornerstone . . . of the psychoanalytic theory of the neuroses' (XIX, 196). Repression results from the rejection by the ego of a wish the ego finds incompatible with its need for parental and societal approval. The rejected wish, if strong enough, does not simply go away. It is pushed back into the unconscious. Freud carefully distinguishes between unconscious and preconscious systems of the mind. The preconscious is the locus of thoughts eventually admissable to consciousness, while the unconscious is the lower depth of the self, where all forbidden wishes gather and fester and from where they constantly seek to re-emerge into consciousness. The mind is then split between a consciousness which refuses to know and an unconscious in which the repressed seeks to gain expression and fulfilment. The ego, through its preconscious censor, constantly beats back the efforts of the unconscious to re-enter the light of consciousness. If a forbidden wish happens to be particularly powerful, the ego is forced to yield, up to a point. What then results is a compromise. The wish is allowed to slip into consciousness, but only in unrecognizable disguise. Our dreams are such compromises. Sleep weakens the ego sufficiently to permit the forbidden wish to slip past the censor, but the ego is still strong enough to force a disguise on it. What is allowed to appear to consciousness, the 'manifest content' of the dream, is a product of concessions made by both sides. Analogous compromises appear in waking life as parapraxes – malfunctioning of the self, such as slips of the tongue, forgetfulness in regard to appointments, duties, or words, and 'accidental' injuries – and as neuroses. Like the dream, neurosis arises in instances in which both the repressed wish and the repressing ego are particularly strong. Their conflict results in a pathological condition. That part of the neurotic compromise that is allowed to emerge into consciousness is the neurotic symptom. It is analogous to the manifest content of a dream.

These characteristics of the psychic compromise are found again as structural and functional features of the apparently supernatural event narrated in Kafka's 'The Metamorphosis'. Gregor's metamorphosis is preceded by his inhibition of a wish. For the time being, Gregor has repressed his desire to walk out of his job. At the time when his transformation takes place, in his sleep, he is not conscious of this desire. No connection between his former wish and the strange event is made explicit. However, by choosing to narrate Gregor's wish in the casual context of his musing and reminiscing, the author creates an implicit link. It places the reader in the role of the Freudian analyst, whose hermeneutic task it is to be aware 'that even the apparently most obscure and arbitrary mental phenomena invariably have a meaning and a causation' (XIX, 197). As the Lacanian sequel to Freudian psychoanalysis has made explicit, the patient's life and associations, communicated to the analyst and 'read' by him, form as much of a 'text' to be interpreted as do literary texts. The parallelism of hermeneutic tasks between analyst and textual critic must not be overlooked simply because of a difference in 'texts' – lives as against words – and ultimate purpose. Both have to discern patterns in a multiplicity of signals, and both ultimately depend on communications with which they are confronted. The distinction between lives and texts is not as absolute as the New Critics wanted to make us believe.

If we consider the function of the metamorphosis in the total context of all phenomena narrated in the text, we find that it fulfils the function which a neurotic symptom, particularly hysterical illness, fulfils in the total context of a life communicated to the psychoanalyst. Its function is to fulfil a rejected wish in a disguise which makes it unrecognizable as such a fulfilment. It appears as a calamitous malfunctioning, a gigantic 'parapraxis' of Gregor's body, as an inexplicable blow of 'outrageous fortune', which relieves its victim of all responsibility for the fulfilment of his wish, and punishes him for it into the bargain. In contrast to his previous, openly acknowledged desire, its present 'unintended' fulfilment is divorced from Gregor's ego. On the contrary, his ego seeks to demonstrate by most strenuous efforts that he is eager to continue to support his family, and is prevented only by his 'unfortunate' situation from doing so. Gregor's metamorphosis is a divorce of bodily behaviour from conscious intention. It seems to exemplify the concept of the 'compromise', which is crucial to the psychoanalytic theory of the neurotic symptom. Freud writes,

A symptom is not merely the expression of a realized unconscious wish; a wish from the preconscious which is fulfilled by the same symptom must also be present. So that the symptom will have *at least* two determinants, one arising from each of the systems involved in the conflict.

(v, 569)

The metamorphosis, in Kafka's mature version of the theme, functions exactly like a symptom as here described by Freud. It is the synthesis of two opposed tendencies. While it fulfils the rebellious wish of the repressed unconscious and liberates Gregor from his hated job and obligations to his family, it also satisfies the preconscious ego's craving to appear innocent, to exhibit good-will, and ultimately to atone for what it has allowed to occur. Gregor has realized his wish for freedom unconsciously, literally in his sleep. But the shape in which his unconscious wish-fulfilment appears literally embodies the disapproval with which his consciousness views his own act. From the perspective of his conscious, or pre-conscious, ego, which is the perspective the reader shares, Gregor's unconscious revolt appears not only unfortunate, but in a most reprehensible guise. Upon waking up, Gregor appears to himself unrecognizable. The product of his unconscious emerges as an object of supreme disgust, alien to himself, a 'colossal' specimen of what is most parasitic and contemptible – 'vermin'.

The fantastic in Kafka's tale thus behaves like the uncanny as seen by Freud. It is a 'return of the repressed'. The unconscious re-emerges in unrecognizable disguise to haunt the conscious ego. It is the ego's humiliation and punishment. In the split self, of which the metamorphosis provides such a clear and drastic example, the wish fulfilment of one part of the self acts as the humiliation and punishment of the other. Kafka's work narrates as an individual's fate what Freud describes as a general problem of wish fulfilment in a divided self:

No doubt a wish fulfilment must bring pleasure, but the question then arises 'To whom?' To the person who has the wish, of course. But, as we know, a dreamer's relation to his wishes is a quite peculiar one. He repudiates them and censors them – he has no liking for them, in short. So that their fulfilment will give him no pleasure, but just the opposite. ... Thus a dreamer in his relation to his dream-wishes can only be compared to an amalgamation of two separate people who are linked by some important common element ... if two people are not at one with each other, the fulfilment of a wish of one of them may bring nothing but unpleasure to the other.

v, 580, Footnote 1

We find an analogous structure in 'Blumfeld, an Elderly Bachelor', another example of a miraculous occurrence narrated in Kafka's *oeuvre* – the strange story of the two small celluloid balls* that follow the 'hero' wherever he goes until, ashamed of these unwanted companions, he succeeds in interesting two children in them who, he hopes, will take them away. As in 'The Metamorphosis', Kafka suggests that the fantastic is the return of a repressed wish in unrecognizable disguise. Aware of the monotony and unrelieved isolation of his bachelor's life 'in secret', which no one observes, Blumfeld thinks of acquiring a young dog as a 'companion'. But the ego, appearing in Blumfeld in its most narcissistic form, brushes this desire aside. Such 'companionship' would involve cares and responsibilities which would impose too great a strain on Blumfeld's self-centred addiction to absolutely unmolested privacy and comfort. Therefore, Blumfeld dismisses his wish. But immediately, as if in direct answer to it, he perceives a 'noise which paws produce when pattering one after the other over a floor'. These 'paws' turn out to be the two celluloid balls that, virtually inseparable from him, will provide him with the companionship for which one part of his self longed, while the other denied it.

This is the place to introduce into the discussion a second structural principle, closely related to repression and equally vital to both Freud and Kafka. This is the concept of projection, which holds that what appears as external fate, accident, illness, or the behaviour of the outside world towards us, may sometimes be a projection of our own unconscious will and thus be of our own doing. Such a dominance of the inner over the external world occurs in our dreams, in which all phenomena express only the dreamer's mind and will. Schopenhauer pointed this out long before

* For a fuller account of this story see above, p. 116. [Ed.]

Freud, in a remarkable passage about dreams of frustration: 'That which creates the obstacles and frustrates our lively desire ... is after all only our own will; operating, however, from a region that lies far beyond the image-producing consciousness ... and, therefore, appears as inexorable fate.' Schopenhauer goes on to suggest that human life itself may behave analogously to dreams. What appears to befall us from outside may be the fulfilment of our unconscious wish. What Schopenhauer arrived at by philosophical speculation, Freud extended and systematized by what was, at least to his view, scientific observation and reasoning. He established the sway of the psychic and inward over the physical and external world basically in three areas.

1. In his early studies of hysteria, he discovered that there were illnesses in which the body obeyed the unconscious mind. The relationship between body and mind thus was not always a one-way street, with the body swaying the mind (as in the view of nineteenth-century materialist science), but that in certain, not infrequent, cases the reverse held true.

2. In the many instances of parapraxis of 'the psychopathology of everyday life' he showed that accidents and failures ascribed to chance may often be the result of the individual's inner conflicts.

3. He added to the stature of dreams by demonstrating for them a significance which they had not appeared to possess in the view of science prior to him. What is more, he sought to prove dreams to be the product of deep-seated inner forces, and essentially independent of stimuli from the sleeper's physical environment or from somatic sources in which science had hitherto seen the main cause of and explanation for dreams.

In the light of Freud's theories, much of what used to be ascribed to the material world external to the individual was now seen as a projection of his inner life. Reversing the centuries-old direction of natural science, Freud reclaimed much lost ground for the human 'soul'. Ultimately, of course, Freud also saw the psyche as subject to the physico-chemical universe. However, before the ultimate explanation was reached, there was an area where the opposite chain of command prevailed, where the physical world merely appeared to be the cause of what turned out to be the work of the (unconscious) mind of man. This area harboured psychosomatic illnesses, parapraxes, dreams, and neuroses and psychoses in all their forms.

It is this dominance of the inner over the external world which makes the insights of Freudian psychoanalysis touch so intimately on the nature of Kafka's narratives. The fantastic in Kafka is a projection or prolongation of psychic tendencies in the protagonist, a fact which is clearly hinted at by the texts. In Blumfeld's case, we have already seen how the mysterious appearance of the balls in his flat is the oblique fulfilment of his rejected wish for 'companionship'. It is the function of Kafka's 'miracles' to make the external world of his fiction conform to the unacknowledged wishes of his characters. This, of course, is precisely the method of dreams, as seen by Freud. Kafka indicates in subtle ways that Blumfeld's bouncing 'companions' are the embodiment of an inner need. As we have seen, his very first perception of them reminds him of a 'pattering of paws'. The narrator thus provides a very obvious link to Blumfeld's wish for a dog. Furthermore, the time sequence, in which the noise is heard immediately after Blumfeld has dismissed his desire for a 'droll' and playful young creature, strongly suggests that the miraculous toys are the extension of, and the answer to, his repressed longing for escape from his solitary and routinized adulthood into companionship, playfulness, and youth. The balls are heard before they are seen; they are sounds before they appear as objects. The perception of the miracle thus proceeds from what Herder called the 'inner sense', in contrast to the distancing and objectifying sense of sight. Hearing makes the distinction between subjective and objective reality more difficult to discern. Even when Blumfeld finally sees the balls, they seem to try to stay behind him, thereby reducing his chances to scrutinize and examine them. Furthermore, they behave in exact conformity with Blumfeld's movements, as though they were a part of him, and, what is most crucial, the text gives no evidence that the balls are ever perceived by anyone except Blumfeld. The possibility of a hallucination thus remains open.

But even where such a possibility is excluded, as in 'The Metamorphosis', where the miraculous is an objective fact of the fictional world, Kafka hints at a connection with those nocturnal hallucinations which we call dreams. Although it is explicitly stated that the metamorphosis is no dream, the text also tells us that Gregor was transformed in a night of 'unquiet dreams'. His vermin shape thus emerges from among his dreams, as though one of them had been projected into external reality and become part of it.

In 'Blumfeld', the relationship of the miraculous to the protagonist's psychic conflict is even more explicit. During the night, after Blumfeld has managed to keep the balls temporarily quiet under his bed, he frequently awakens from his 'dreamless' but 'unquiet' sleep, with the 'delusion' that someone is knocking on his door:

> He knows quite well that no one is knocking; who would knock at night and at his lonely bachelor's door? Yet although he knows this for certain, he is startled again and again and each time glances in suspense at the door, his mouth open, eyes wide, a strand of hair trembling over his damp forehead.

It is his own perception, and not an objectively external sound, that

Blumfeld 'hears', as he himself lets us know in no uncertain terms. Thus it is clear that what he hears is a message from himself to himself – the message of his desire for a companion, which his egotism had repressed. He perceived his own desire for the other as the other's attempt to come to him – a constellation of psychological factors expressed much more subtly in Kafka's last fragment, 'The Burrow'. The 'suspense' with which Blumfeld stares at the door, and the symptoms of extreme excitement which the narrator describes, clearly reveal the ambivalence between longing and fear with which the Kafka protagonist always experiences his relationship to 'the other'.

One of the most common disguises used by the preconscious censor, according to Freud (in *The Interpretation of Dreams*, 362) is the 'reversal, or turning a thing into its opposite'. The dreamer's own thought or wish is projected into and perceived as someone else's behaviour towards him. For instance, a death wish directed at one's father may be disguised as the father's assault upon the son, a fact which sheds interesting light upon Kafka's 'The Judgment' and its forerunner, 'The Urban World'.* The 'knocking' on Blumfeld's door is a striking example of such a reversal. Blumfeld perceives his own wish for the open door, for breaking out of his solitude, which was evident in his initial wish for a dog, as someone else's attempt to come to him. Here the narrator makes this 'reversal' obvious, and it is even clear to the protagonist. In other works, such as *The Trial* and 'The Burrow', the disguise is much more difficult to detect.

As in a Freudian slip of the tongue, it is the words of Blumfeld's thought that betray what his consciousness conceals. When Blumfeld, in his narrated monologue, names the activity of the balls, he comes up with the verb *locken* – 'to entice' or 'to tempt'. By this choice of word, the narrator makes Blumfeld inadvertently admit that the balls embody a 'lure', a temptation for him. Like the knock on his door, they are a message to him from a part of himself that the 'elderly bachelor' has tried to deny. The fact that they are two, perfectly attuned to each other, demonstrates a lesson in that 'companionship' and 'loyalty' that Blumfeld, feeling these qualities painfully lacking in his life, had hoped to get from a puppy. By clinging to him and to each other, the celluloid balls seem to make light of his principle of self-sufficiency and wear away his narcissism. They behave as the projection of his own longing for 'the other', and they encounter the same resistance from the official part of his divided self which had made him suppress his original wish for a dog.

Kafka presents the perplexing element in his work as the projection of unacknowledged forces in his protagonists. To take a famous example, the

* The unfinished story of another father-son relationship; see Kafka's diary entry after 21 February 1911. [Ed.]

mysterious court of Joseph K.'s trial is rung in by Joseph K.'s own hand. In response to his ringing for his breakfast, the 'stranger' appears, who turns out to be Franz, one of the warders arresting Joseph K. (Franz and Joseph K. are, of course, transparent allusions to Franz Kafka's divided self.) Joseph K.'s intention had been to call the maid; the result of his act is his arrest. Joseph K.'s ringing constitutes a parapraxis, a *Fehlleistung*. It reveals the same kind of self-alienation that we find at the beginning of 'The Metamorphosis'. Gregor Samsa fails to 'recognize' the part of himself that has emerged from his unconscious, and Joseph K.'s wish for punishment appears to his consciousness as a 'stranger'. This stranger tells him that he and his fellow-warder are 'closer to [him] than any other people in the world'. As an analysis of *The Trial* would bear out, Joseph K. does not recognize, either literally or figuratively, what is 'closest' to him – namely, his twin needs for exculpation and punishment. He is ashamed of these needs, and tries to keep their expression, his trial, hidden from the world. Appropriately, 'shame' is the last noun of the novel: 'It was as if the shame of it must outlive him'. Yet shame is evident in Joseph K. even before the plot begins. At the very opening of the novel, before 'the stranger' appears, Joseph K. notes that he is being watched from a window across the street. He feels annoyed and bothered by it, as though something secretly shameful were connected with him. That resistance to scrutiny, that need to hide, which is shame, precedes the reason for it. The emotion comes before its motivation. In a sense, it generates it.

This is the method of dreams. It characterizes the beginnings of Kafka's writing, and he remained faithful to it to the end. In his first work, 'Description of a Struggle', the sad fate of a character, the Fat Man, profoundly upsets the first-person narrator. However, long before the Fat Man appears on the scene, an unexplained moaning has disturbed the narrator's sleep all night. The Fat Man and his tragic misfortune function as the materialization of that sadness which the narrator has heard in himself. The miraculous contraction and expansion of distance in Kafka's work likewise confirm and extend what the protagonist expresses by words, thoughts, or behaviour. Like the dreamer in his dream, Kafka's protagonist is the secret source of the mysteries that assail him.

The convergences of Kafka's and Freud's views of the working of the mind – explicitly and systematically analysed by Freud, implicitly shown by Kafka – are numerous, profound, and amazing. Here I have not been able to do justice to more than a small number of them. The significance of these convergences for Kafka's art can become fully clear only from an exploration of the most fundamental difference between Kafka and Freud:

their contrasting attitudes toward the ego. Such an exploration, however, would go beyond the limits of this paper.

Note

Quotations from Freud are from the 'Standard Edition', ed. James Strachey; the volume number is indicated by the Roman numeral following the quotation. *The Interpretation of Dreams* was translated and edited by James Strachey, New York, 1965. The quotation from Schopenhauer is my own translation of a passage from *Sämtliche Werke*, edited by Arthur Hübscher, Leipzig 1938, I, p. 230. The quoted remarks of Kafka about illness and psychoanalysis (pages 146–7) are my translations of two passages from (1) *Briefe*, 1902–24, edited by Max Brod, New York 1958, p. 320; (2) *Briefe an Milena*, edited by Willy Haas, New York 1952, p. 246. The quotation from Hartmut Binder is my translation of a passage in *Motiv und Gestaltung bei Franz Kafka*, Bonn 1966, p. 103.

16

Kafka and the Muirs

Joyce Crick

Once upon a time – in the summer of 1921, to be exact – a pair of newly-married lovers ran away from Scotland – or, to be more accurate, from Guilford Street, London, WC1 – to Prague in the very middle of Europe. Which is a happier start to a new life's tale than pausing on a frozen bridge, or waking up one morning to find oneself arrested. They were Edwin and Willa Muir, escaping, on the strength of a reviewing commission from Van Wyck Brooks of *The Freeman*, to write, learn new languages, explore and grow.

To English-speaking readers, their names have ever since then been inextricably linked with the works of Franz Kafka. It may be illuminating to ask what part they played in the making of Franz Kafka's world – his posthumous world, that is – what they did for his English reputation, and what picture of Kafka English-speaking readers carry away from their translations.

There were from the start affinities between Muir and Kafka which make of the translating a deeply congruent part of Muir's own creative life. His formative experiences – the loss of religious transcendence, the failure of secular remedies, the closeness to dream and archetype, the tidy, weary office hours, the vision of horror – all have their equivalents in Kafka's world, including two peculiarly Scottish cradle gifts: the Calvinist conscience and a problematic relationship to a national culture and language. Moreover, their shared awareness of an absent metaphysical dimension is congruent with certain affinities in their mode of writing. The novels of the one and the poems of the other point beyond the immediate,

ization; they provoke the reader into the effort towards interpretation. In this respect, Kafka is more radical than Muir: where Muir's fable is elusive, Kafka's general order is unreachable; where Muir's poems often evade interpretation, Kafka's novels are so constructed as to frustrate it. Muir did not learn the negative allegorical mode from Kafka, but he was quick to recognize it in him, and Kafka may have reinforced it in Muir's own works. Certainly he admitted very early to that elusive thing, 'influence'. But to pursue these affinities would be to tell the tale of Kafka in Edwin Muir's world, and that is another story. What they did not share were Muir's fortunate gifts of a childhood out of time and out of Europe, a place in the memory which he came to call Eden, and a loving companion throughout his life.

The Prague the Muirs ran off to in 1921 was the capital of the new state of Czechoslovakia, not of the old Austro-Hungarian province, and very conscious of its newness. They found the gulf between the German and the Czech communities after the war deep and bitter: 'We never got a hint that Kafka and his friends had even existed in the city,' recalled Willa. 'An invisible but unyielding barrier cut off German-speakers from Czech-speakers, and it was only the Czech-speakers that we came to know.' Could they have got to know Kafka or Kafka's works in the early 1920s anyway? Kafka's publications were not unknown. The performer Ludwig Hardt actually held some public readings from them at the Mozarteum during that autumn and winter, and they were reported in the German press. Kafka himself was in Prague intermittently during their nine months' stay there: ill on leave from his office, partly working on *The Castle*, in the throes of his affair with Milena. Writing in his diary that bitter autumn, 'I do not envy a particular married couple; I only envy all married couples,' what could he have said to this pair? Noting of his own work, 'this entire literature is an onslaught on the frontiers,' what could he say to a late beginner tentatively writing his first poems? To a high-spirited classics scholar briskly learning Czech? Only two years older than Muir, he was nearing his end as they were beginning.

And as yet they had no German. But that was soon to be remedied. They moved on to Dresden, from winter into spring; there 'the German language, compared with Czech, was generous with clues to its meaning.' They were happy there. Willa recalled 'a glow of joyous feeling'; Edwin wrote that he 'seemed at last to recover from the long illness that had seized me when, at fourteen, I came to Glasgow'. They 'were learning German and reading German poetry', and moved, after a chance meeting with Willa's old friend A. S. Neill, to join his experimental school at the garden city of Hellerau. ('You should send young Felix there,' Kafka had written the previous year to his sister Elli Hermann, of his ten-year-old nephew: 'It will save him from the mean, lukewarm, squinnying spirit so strong in well-off Prague Jews.' Other letters of his from this time indicate considerable acquaintance with the school and community.) Willa taught at Neill's school, Edwin explored German poetry. 'Edwin and I soon became fluent in German since every word we learned was on active service.' They lived in a closed garden, innocent of the social and economic problems besetting Germany. But history soon intruded on the idyll: inflation came in 1923 and with it deep disruption. Hard times soon struck their patron at *The Freeman* too, and Van Wyck Brooks could no longer renew Edwin's reviewing commission. They were broke and took refuge with Neill in Austria. But their American friends continued helpful. A cable arrived from Ben Huebsch of New York, asking them if they would translate three of Gerhart Hauptmann's plays into blank verse. They would. And that is how their career as translators began.

Willa's classics training ensured competence and accuracy: 'Edwin's interpretations tended to be wild and gay.' 'I should not care today to be faced with these translations,' she adds. But they had hit upon an activity which, however irksome it might sometimes become, was to ensure them a livelihood for the next fifteen years or so, and enable them to conduct a life on their own terms. Best sellers (Lion Feuchtwanger), minor classics (Hans Carossa), major novelists (Hermann Broch) all came their way. In most of this work, Willa played the greater part. She was the better linguist, translated on her own, and was able to free Edwin for the outburst of his own creativity during the coming decade. She established a reputation which called forth a tribute from the Rhein-Verlag – she was 'the best translator from the German' – which Hermann Broch was happy to pass on. After their return to England in 1924 they remained in touch with German and Austrian letters, and Edwin was among the first to greet Max Brod's initiative in causing Kafka's three unfinished novels to be published posthumously: *The Trial* in 1925, *The Castle* in 1926, and *America* in 1927, followed by the collection of shorter fragments and aphorisms, *The Great Wall of China*, in 1931. They had reached the stage where their reputation was secure enough for Edwin to make his own suggestions for translations. He urged *Das Schloss* on Secker and Warburg, and so, in 1930, Kafka's last novel became his first to be published in English. It is worth recalling Muir's comments, fresh from the task of translating it. In a letter to his friend Sydney Schiff he is introducing an unknown author with great enthusiasm and some puzzlement: 'strange in atmosphere ... a purely metaphysical and mystical dramatic novel; the ordinary moral judgments do not come in at all; everything happens on a mysterious spiritual plane; and yet in a curious way everything is given solidly and concretely.' There are certain tentative insights in this rather muffled prose which he formulates more sharply later, but which in essence remain with him throughout his lifetime preoccupation with Kafka: above all, the sense of a duality of levels – 'metaphysical' and 'solid' – which was to crystallize into 'religious allegory', the formula that was to give a generation of readers the terms in which to understand and misunderstand Kafka's novels. Muir's use of the term 'dramatic novel' does not register that absence of a guiding narrative voice which, fifty years later, is one of our first assumptions in reading Kafka; it is rather a derivative from his earlier, far more crisply and confidently formulated category in *The Structure of the Novel* (1928): the dramatic novel, in Muir's scheme, is the novel of fate, apprehended under the category of time but allowing imaginative glimpses of the universal totality, of a scale and stature comparable with poetic drama. This puts *The Castle* in the company of *Wuthering Heights* and *Crime and Punishment*. And atmosphere? Kafka's stories (Muir writes in his *Autobiography*) 'continued themselves into our dreams, unfolding into slow serpentine nightmares, immovably reasonable'.

For a generation, the English and American reading public's view of Kafka was determined by the choice of *The Castle* as the first of his works to be translated. True, it was followed in 1933 by the collection of shorter pieces *The Great Wall of China*, which in Muir's view 'gives a more clear and general notion of Kafka's intentions as an artist and thinker'. But these were followed and overwhelmed by the translations of the other two novels, *The Trial* in 1937 and *America* in 1938. (There were, incidentally, two changes of publisher; alas, the books had not sold well.) The English view was determined too not only by the preponderance of the novels, but by the nature of the Muirs' rendering of the texts, by the interpretations offered in Edwin's 'Introductory Notes', and by the fact that the texts were largely based on Max Brod's unrevised 'readers'' versions.

Let us look first at the nature of the translations, and then at Edwin Muir's commentaries in the wider context of his poetry and critical preoccupations.

As to the translations of Kafka, a computer might manage to distinguish between the contributions of husband and wife – Willa has left control-passages which she translated alone – but it would have a hard time of it. Accepting the German Academy's first bestowal of their Translator's Prize, a fitting crown, Willa recounted once again what their procedure with Kafka had been. Each read the text separately, carefully, 'to make ourselves familiar with its innermost nature'. Then, quite arbitrarily, they tore the book in two and each translated a half. Then each worked over the other's version – he with his finer sense of style, she with her greater accuracy and flair – until a seamless web emerged. The activity, as she put it, was 'more a matter of living experience than the object of analysis'. Edwin was more cautious. He recognized translation as 'a secondary art', was acutely aware of the possibility of violation, especially in the virtually insoluble problem of rendering German word order into English: 'The word order of Kafka is naked and infallible ... only in that order could he have said what he had to say. Yet the firm order has to be disarranged, the original edifice of the sequence dismantled and put up again. ... No other modern writer has made the words run more easily and naturally than Kafka. ... So our main problem was to write an English prose as natural in the English way as he was in his own way.' Willa amplifies more generally: 'Thought flows into moulds that are quite different from one's native speech. The very shape of thought has to be changed in translation and that seems to me more difficult than rendering words and idioms into their equivalents.'

Two general principles of translation emerge from this living experience: the aim for a rightness, within the terms of the English language, that would make the work they produced read as 'literature' rather than as translation; and the aim for 'naturalness' as the style of thought unfolds. In Kafka's case this meant addressing problems of syntax rather than of vocabulary and idiom.

The first aim will take us far afield. One may quite simply say 'they succeeded' and leave it at that. That these texts exist as literature in English is witnessed by their countless readers who have no German. But Hans Hennecke, no mean translator himself, pays a subtler tribute to the transparent quality of their language, which reads not as English translation but as *translatable* English, when he points out how easily their English can be turned back into German, and into Kafka's German at that. This quality is not confined to their style as translators. As far as Edwin, at least, is concerned, it is a characteristic of his own mature prose. Pages of his *Scott and Scotland* (1936), for example, spring not simply from the problem of Schiller's *On Naive and Sentimental Poetry*, but from its very diction, too; also, many of the analytic passages in his autobiographical novel *Poor Tom* (1932) will translate into Hermann Broch's German. Is it a matter of empathy? Of the subtle openness of a writer who found his own voice late? It extends from diction to questions of idiom: that reflexive 'continued themselves' quoted on page 162, for example, is more idiomatic in German than in English.

The ultimate determinants for this curious characteristic, I think, are to be found in Muir's peculiar development as a self-taught late beginner, from a culture whose use of English as a literary language was problematic.

His childhood vernacular had been Orkney, 'a mixture of Norse, Scots and Irish ... the second person singular was in full working order ... it still keeps some of the quality of a chant ... a splendid voice for telling stories in ... the syntactical feeling is much stronger than in ordinary urban or educated speech.' He speaks of 'traditional inversions which give such an exact value to the order of words in a sentence'. But it was a long way to travel from the creative language of pastoral to a medium of high literary culture, and one beset with the dangers of insecurity and pedantry. Poets 'wrote in an English laboriously learned from grammar books'. And 'the islands produce a terrible number of professors.' Willa too experienced language as problematic. The little girl's domestic Shetland vernacular was mocked on the mainland, but her response was one of confident adaptability: 'I learned to speak broad Montrose.' And she speculated later that there lay the origin of her own considerable linguistic gifts. But Edwin did not acquire a new language so readily. At first he only lost his old one. When he made his literary début, his style was both idiosyncratic and derivative. He made for the sharp rhythms and sophisticated generalities of aphorisms after the manner of Nietzsche.

Later, as a mature writer, in the teeth of Hugh MacDiarmid's reactionary, revolutionary – and creative – use of Lallans, Muir opted for English. He did not have the hostility of the borderer towards English, and he lacked the perversity of genius. But the main reason for his choice was that he read Scottish history differently. Scottish poetry had been driven from Eden by Knox's Calvinism; poetry was replaced by arid polemic until the vacuum was filled by the uneasy linguistic compromises of Burns and Scott. His *Scott and Scotland* is his own lament for the makars. Scottish literature had passed the point of no return. The conclusion he drew from this situation was to reaffirm English. This, and his translating Kafka, were essentiat acts of his poetic personality.

Much has been written about the problematic linguistic and cultural situation Kafka lived in: his German was that of a narrow linguistic group in a predominantly Czech-speaking town. 'Prager Deutsch' was narrow in vocabulary, uncertain in idiom, with no roots in a living local language, a papery German, coloured by pidgin-Czech and traces of Yiddish. Kafka developed a purified and clarified literary language out of this poverty-stricken and confused medium: correct, sober, expressive, flexible. He had a shrewd insight into the uses of literature to small nations, and an ironic envy of the latter. He had no equivalent, in his linguistic experience, to Orkney speech, but once Muir had lost the language of Eden, the conditions of their search for a literary language were not dissimilar: members of a fringe culture, broaching the language of a major literature, their immediate vernacular narrow and uncertain.

After derivative beginnings (Kafka destroyed his), they both developed, Kafka supremely, towards a sobriety and clarity which strike one as interchangeable; hence what emerges from Muir's renderings reads 'naturally' as 'literature' and not as 'translation'.

But let us return to the Muirs' translating workshop, for a discussion of translation cries out for instances. They had aimed for 'naturalness', and had seen word order as a greater problem than idiom. But in concentrating on rendering both the ease and the complexity of Kafka's syntax – in which they were supremely successful – their eyes were less alert to Kafka's frequently 'unnatural' use of idiom. *Pace* Willa, it *does* present problems, and problems which have to do with Kafka's literary renewal of a tired vernacular. Let us look at a few examples: first, the thunderous condemnation of son by father in 'The Judgment':

Kafka: Ein unschuldiges Kind warst du ja eigentlich, aber noch eigentlicher warst du ein teuflischer Mensch!

The Muirs: An innocent child, yes, that you were, truly, but still more truly have you been a devilish human being!

'Eigentlich' is natural speech. 'Noch eigentlicher' is strange; it is an unidiomatic intensification which expresses precisely that degree of higher reality which Muir discerns in his essays on Kafka – but misses in this translation. Their rendering makes both phrases quite natural. (The inversion, by the way, is gratuitous; is it a residue of Orkney speech?)

Secondly, there is the passage where the strangely metamorphosed commercial traveller gives an elaborate, devious recital of the miseries of his life:

Kafka: Sie wissen auch sehr wohl, dass der Reisende ... so leicht ein Opfer von Klatschereien ... werden kann, gegen die sich zu wehren ihm ganz unmöglich ist, da er von ihnen meistens gar nichts erfährt und nur dann, wenn er erschöpft eine Reise beendet hat, zu Hause die schlimmen, auf ihre Ursachen hin nicht mehr zu durchschauenden Folgen am eigenen Leibe zu spüren bekommt.

The Muirs: And you know very well that the traveller ... can so easily fall victim to gossip ... which he mostly knows nothing about, except when he comes back exhausted from his rounds and only then suffers in person from their evil consequences, which he can no longer trace back to their original causes.

To start with, we must note the achieved ease of the syntax – though the omission of a clause has also eased the complication of Gregor's double-think – and then observe the Muirs' 'natural', unobtrusive rendering of 'am eigenen Leibe': 'in person'. The German phrase 'am eigenen Leibe spüren' is equally unobtrusive, but it has a faded physical reference which 'in person' lacks, and which Kafka exploited to give us a clue as to the nature of the physical transformation. Kafka was taking a dead metaphor literally.

There is, thirdly, that initial alarming speculation in *The Trial*:

Kafka: Jemand musste Josef K. verleumdet haben ...
The Muirs: Someone must have been telling lies about Joseph K. ....

This makes a splendid sudden start, but lacks the covert sense of *legal* offence which introduces the grand metaphor of the novel. On the other hand, two alternatives – 'traduced' (E.M. Butler), 'falsely denounced' (J.P. Stern) – overdo the latent meaning. One returns and sees the virtue of the Muirs' neutral rendering – as well as the virtue of the latest version: 'spreading lies about' (C. Waller, 1977).

The Muirs have a tendency to translate into the word most closely related philologically, so that 'drosselt' becomes 'throttles'; 'Fesselung', 'fettering'; 'Chef', 'chief'; and 'Klienten', 'clients'. But the meanings of such pairs of words are not always equivalent, nor always equivalently idiomatic. Above all, the Muirs' vocabulary is more vivid than Kafka's neutral speech. This may be the lively Willa's contribution. There is no proving it, but certainly the diction of Edwin's poems is as restrained and general as Kafka's; while Willa, translating an extract from Kafka's diaries on her own (the five-finger exercise in sustained metaphor of 24 and 25 December 1910, in which he describes his writing-desk as a baroque *theatrum mundi*) turns a dusty 'Rumpelkammer' into a glorious Scottish 'glory-hole'. (But then the passage is much more deliberately virtuoso than anything Kafka normally wrote, which is probably why he noted 'feeble' at the end.) The flimsy 'leichtgebautes Haus', where Georg Bendemann lives, is ruinously 'ramshackle' in English. The pallid 'schwaches Grün' he looks out onto becomes a warm and springlike 'tender green'. Ronald Gray has noted how the Muirs' image of Kafka's hero as modern pilgrim has subtly and consistently affected their rendering of *The Trial*: Joseph K. is a much more decent fellow than Josef K. And there is one occasion when one of them is splendidly, impatiently wrong. In his 'Introductory Note' to *America*, Edwin has cause to quote that important aphorism which he and Willa had previously translated quite soberly and rightly in *The Great Wall of China* as 'There is a goal, but no way; what we call the way is only wavering.' But here Edwin puts: 'What we call the way is only shilly-shallying.' I would like to think that that was slipped in by a brilliant lady with a penchant for music-hall songs, who had no fundamental doubts about either goal or way.

Translation is a matter of swings and roundabouts. These examples indicate that the Muirs have overlooked certain problems of idiom, mainly in their care for the syntax. They opted for the natural surface rather than for the unnatural undercurrent. One begs their forgiveness for this niggling. 'Mach's einer nach und breche nicht den Hals.' Those who have followed them and rethought such instances as I have quoted above – Malcolm Pasley, Ernst Kaiser, Eithne Wilkins and many others – have elsewhere relied to a great extent on the Muirs' first versions. The Muirs' Kafka has become historical.

But they laboured under disadvantages. Having learned their German quickly and on 'active service', they accumulated literary and sub-literary references only at random. For instance, Willa had to ask Hermann Broch what the famous Götz-quotation was. (He replied, gentle English reader, very charmingly, that his typewriter was too delicate to tell her.)

Moreover, the Muirs' use of Max Brod's first German texts has in the long run been to their disadvantage. Brod's first service to his dead friend had been to produce for the general reader as coherent and complete a text as possible. His editorial hand was more devoted than scholarly, and his first editions have needed such frequent updating – in the light not only of Kafka's drafts and fragments, which Brod appended to later editions, but also of countless professional editorial emendations – that retranslation has become desirable. *The Castle* the Muirs could only translate from Brod's first, imperfect edition. *The Trial* and *America* were both rendered into English after the publication of Brod's second, fuller editions of 1935, and so the Muirs certainly had the opportunity to use the extensive drafts and fragments that Brod printed in these. But apart from including the final available paragraphs of *America*, it seems they chose not to do so. Their version of *The Trial* takes over Brod's four-line 'completion' of Chapter 8, which was present in that position only in the first edition (1925). Later publications contain Brod's note, 'This chapter was not completed.' Their position *vis-à-vis* the English-speaking public was much the same as, if less tendentious than, Brod's towards the German-speaking reader. In introducing a new, difficult writer of whose greatness they were convinced, it was as well at that stage not to blind the reader with editorial apparatus, nor to confuse him with still greater fragmentation.

There remains the question of Edwin's 'Introductory Notes' to *The Castle*, *The Great Wall of China* and *America*. Here too his position was not unlike Brod's, in that he wished to familiarize a public with something rich and strange. He also wrote, over the same span of time, a number of articles on Kafka which have very much the same character as the forewords: they are extended introductions, not so much critical as expository and empathetic. Lacking a clear line of argument, they are difficult to summarize, and lend themselves better to collage. I propose to deal with 'Introductory Notes' and articles together, for they cover similar ground in material, interpretation, even formulation, expanding here, contracting there, stressing different aspects, attempting afresh the same enigmatic encounter, shifting marginally but not fundamentally in judgment.*

But first a Word Against Introductions. However strange Kafka was fifty years ago, however well-meant the efforts to make him accessible, these 'Introductory Notes', in focusing on certain aspects, inevitably cloud, obscure, deflect from others. The innocent eye of the reader may be a fallacy, but in Kafka's case it scarcely had a chance. And new readings of Kafka became possible only after critics had taken issue with the Muir canon. Here too Muir's position is similar to Brod's. Indeed, his own view is in many respects shaped by the fact that Brod was there before him. Brod was so prompt with a specific interpretation that he diverted attention too soon from the *openness* of Kafka's symbolism, that very characteristic which Michael Schmidt calls Kafkaesque in Muir's poetry. Elements in Brod's now familiar interpretation, particularly as found in the 'Nachwort' to the 1926 edition of *The Castle*, determined Muir's view of Kafka: above all, of Kafka as a metaphysical writer preoccupied with the incommensurability of the human and the divine dimensions. Neither Brod nor Muir have a sense of Kafka's scepticism; rather they insist upon his last-ditch faith. Brod understands the castle as the unattainable abode of divine grace, K.'s pursuit as the search for integration into human society. He invokes the names of Abraham, Kierkegaard, Pascal to make the strange gulf bridgeable.

All this is familiar to the English-speaking reader because it forms the basis of Muir's interpretation too: '*The Trial* and *The Castle* may best be defined as metaphysical or religious novels. Their subject-matter is not the life and manners of any locality or country, it is rather human life where it is touched by the powers which all religions have acknowledged, by divine law and divine grace.' For a familiar resting-point, Muir does not look to Kierkegaard but to Bunyan, and utters his fateful formulation: 'Perhaps the best way to approach *The Castle* is to regard it as a sort of modern *Pilgrim's Progress*, a religious allegory; the desire of the hero in both cases is to work out his salvation. ...' Having made his comparison, Muir is quick to make his contrast: 'If anyone wanted to estimate how immensely more difficult it is for a religious genius to see his way in an age of scepticism than in an age of faith, a comparison of *The Pilgrim's Progress*

---

* In chronological order, these are 'Introductory Note' to *The Castle*, London, Secker and Warburg, 1930; 'A Note on Franz Kafka', *The Bookman*, New York, LXXII, no. 3, Nov. 1930; 'Introductory Note' to *The Great Wall of China*, London, Secker and Warburg, 1933; 'Franz Kafka', *Life and Letters*, London, June 1934; 'Introductory Note' to *America*, London, Routledge and Kegan Paul, 1938; 'Franz Kafka', in *A Franz Kafka Miscellany*, New York, Twice a Year Press, 1940.

with *The Castle* might give him a fair measure of it' ('Introductory Note' to *The Castle*).

But despite this – illuminating – emphasis on difference, the mere discovery of a familiar comparable example and the reassuring label of a definite genre have made of this interpretation a highly influential Reader's Aid. This formulation, more than anything else Muir wrote on Kafka, has affected the common reader's view – some would say, disastrously so. Michael Hamburger credits it with the making of the political allegories by the young left-wing novelists of the 1930s, such as Edward Upward's *Journey to the Frontier* or Rex Warner's *The Aerodrome*. But a kind of allegorical writing is generally characteristic of the period. For all their differences, Muir and the young men of the left were concerned with the relationship of part to whole, of the individual to the general, be it of party member to ideology, of individual dreamer to the collective unconscious, or of convert to mother church. If these relations are expressed in the process of an ongoing narrative, the result is a kind of allegory. Day Lewis used Kafka's aphorism of the point of no return as the motto for his *Magnetic Mountain*; Auden's early verse is full of quests and battles and desert landscapes. Muir's formulation is characteristic of the decade; it crystallized a tendency rather than made it. The 1930s were ready to read Kafka as allegory.

Erich Heller's objection to the phrase 'religious allegory' (in *The Disinherited Mind* of 1952, generously reviewed by Muir) goes deeper He takes as his starting-point the epoch-making shift in theological symbolization that came with the Reformation. The old sacramental symbolization understood the bread and the wine to be consubstantial with its referent, the body and blood of Christ. The new symbolization dissociated the physical from the spiritual and understood the former as only representative of what it itself was not. The pattern, and something of the metaphysical charge, of this distinction is maintained when Goethe and Coleridge make their distinctions between Symbol and Allegory. To Coleridge, the literary Symbol 'partakes of the reality which it renders intelligible', and 'may be working unconsciously in the writer's mind during [its] construction'; 'it presumes no disjunction of the faculties, but simple predominance.' Whereas Allegory 'is but a translation of abstract notions into a picture-language which is itself nothing but an abstraction from objects of the senses', and 'it cannot be other than spoken consciously.' Goethe's posthumously assembled *Maxims and Reflections* make a similar distinction: 'the Symbol turns phenomenon into idea, idea into image in such a way that the idea remains infinitely effective and unattainable – and unutterable even when uttered in all languages.' 'Allegory turns phenomenon into concept, concept into image, but in such a way that the concept may be grasped and understood in the image and, limited yet complete in the image, may be given verbal expression through it.' In this view the Symbol still has a last breath of sacramental authority and is infinitely richer than Allegory. Heller argues urgently and persuasively that Kafka's negative figurations belong – alas – to the former.

But once applied empirically, the distinction is too rigorous. Allegory is rarely met with in its purity; it is better thought of as mode rather than as genre. Heller recognizes the difficulty in his own discussion of *The Castle*. All interpretation allegorizes, said Northrop Frye, and this was never more true than of Kafka's novels. However, if we look at how Muir actually uses the term, we will find that he gives full weight to the predominance of the creative imagination and constantly draws together image and interpretation: 'The virtue of a *good* allegory [my italics] is that it expresses in its own created forms something more exact than any interpretation of it could ... [Kafka's] allegory is not a mere recapitulation. ...' ('Introductory Note' to *The Castle*). And: '*Pure* allegory would not have expressed his conception of life or his idea of man's moral problems' (*Miscellany*). And again: 'An allegory has not justified itself if it contains nothing more than its interpretation, and the logic of Kafka's narrative is so close that it builds up a whole particularized system of spiritual relations with such an autonomous life of its own that it illuminates the symbol rather than is illuminated by it ... his allegory is not a mere recreation of conceptions already settled, and the entities he describes seem therefore newly discovered, as if they had never existed before' (*Bookman*).

What Muir is describing here by the term 'good allegory' is an extended symbolism in Coleridge's sense. And he rightly uses the term 'allegory' because he is dealing not with a single image, but with a process, with a sustained and continuous narrative. Heller's objection turns out to be quixotic. But he is right to dispute Muir's central assertion that for Kafka, as for Bunyan, 'the goal and the road indubitably exist and that the necessity to find them is urgent'. He answers with Kafka's own aphorism: 'There is a goal, but no way; what we call the way is only – wavering.'

For Muir the purposefulness of Kafka's religious quest remained almost an article of his own faith. Each of his essays voices the same burden. And to the end of his life, Dora Dymant recalled, he worried at the question, 'But Kafka did believe, then?'. Not that her replies gave him much reassurance. His poem 'The Law' crystallizes the problem of negative theology which he read in Kafka's works. No groping here. It is achieved and absolute, and is his finest comment on the Kafka problem.

O you my Law
Which I serve not,
O you my Good
Which I prize not,
O you my Truth
Which I seek not:

Where grace is beyond desert
Thanks must be thanklessness;
Where duty is past performance
Disservice is only service;
Where truth is unsearchable
All seeking is straying.

If I could know ingratitude's
Bounds I should know gratitude;
And disservice done
Would show me the law of service;
And the wanderer at last
Learns his long error.

If I could hold complete
The reverse side of the pattern,
The wrong side of Heaven,
O then I should know in not knowing
My truth in my error.

The above collage has been drawn from the writings of the 1930s, the dark decade when the Muirs were translating Kafka's three novels and collection of posthumous pieces. The war came, and there was to be no more literary mediation from the German. Not until the war was over did they resume their old connection and bring out the major short pieces, *In the Penal Colony* (London, Secker and Warburg, and New York, Schochen, 1948). Apart from short extracts from Kafka's diaries, from Willa's pen, that was the end of their translating Kafka. Other translators took over as diaries, letters, further posthumous pieces reached the publishers. The late forties and early fifties saw the second Kafka wave in England and America. After the long interval, in 1947 Muir wrote one last expository essay on Kafka, first published in Czech and then in English in his *Essays on Literature and Society* (1949). He had in the meantime returned to post-war Prague as head of the British Council there, and this completion of the circle of his life enabled him to introduce, or reintroduce, Kafka to the Czechs. It is the most coherent and elegant and all-of-a-piece of his Kafka articles. The material is familiar, but the tone no longer tentative; the universal situation, the incommensurability of man and God, the allegorizing interpretation – 'the image of a road comes to mind' – are all there, but with far greater openness to the tenor of the allegory: 'justice, grace, truth, final reconciliation, father, God'. Muir had drawn attention before to Kafka's imaginative invention, but this essay stresses Kafka's art so much more that it alters the nature of the appreciation: 'The value of what he says does not depend on the truth of his metaphysical structure, any more than the value of what Dante says depends on his theology.' That sounds like a contribution to Eliot's discussion of poetry and belief. It also sounds like a farewell. Here, rather than in earlier writings, we may locate the discriminations of the poet with one foot in Eden, confronting the frustrations of the one he had called a religious genius in an age of scepticism. Muir actually rejects his old term 'allegory' – but since he had never meant allegory in the narrow sense in the first place, this amounts to less of a change in his evaluation than does the redoubled importance he ascribes to the autonomy of Kafka's imagined world.

'TO FRANZ KAFKA'

If we, the proximate damned, presumptive blest,
Were called one day to some high consultation
With the authentic ones, the worst and best
Picked from all time, how mean would be our station.
Oh we could never bear the standing shame,
Equivocal ignominy of non-election;
We who will hardly answer to our name,
And on the road direct ignore direction.

But you, dear Franz, sad champion of the drab
And half, would watch the tell-tale shames drift in
(As if they were troves of treasure) not aloof,
But with a famishing passion quick to grab
Meaning, and read on all the leaves of sin
Eternity's secret script, the saving proof.

The sonnet form compels a more condensed statement than is normal in Muir. The diction has his usual generality, but reveals more specific references than just the lowly tribute from the mean to the great. As in reading Kafka, more and more possibilities offer themselves, including a tribute to the major poet from the minor, from this Scottish, sometime-Calvinist poet, who had once repudiated 'the frustrate and the half' of his culture. The opening categories, the damned and blest, are certainly Calvinist, but they also resound with the religious Kafka-interpretation of those 'Introductory Notes' of the pre-war years. Who, indeed, are We? – the inauthentic and half-hearted, uncertain of their destiny, neither damned nor blest, exposed to shame (which might outlive them?), perverse and foolish, who go to such great lengths not to heed the advice given them on their way. They are we; they are the K.s, with whom Muir, in his humility, identifies. Earlier poems of his had dealt with evasions of the true path as devious as those of any K.: '... even at my dearest cost / I'd save me from the true knowledge and the real power.'

But the sestet turns, and discerns what alternative Kafka himself (and long and intimate acquaintance makes it right that Muir should address him as 'dear Franz') could bring to the accumulation of shames and sin: not dismissal, not repudiation of the drab and half, but taking their part. Using metaphors drawn from Kafka's own works (hunger, script) Muir still holds to his old interpretation, suggesting that the salvation which baffled the wayward K.s was to be found in their creator's hungry pursuit of meaning. Can we, in that word 'proof' – proof as demonstration, proof as all-but-final version – even hear a reassurance of the possession of that paradoxical knowledge which Muir himself could only express in 'The Law' as a wish and a speculation?

> If I could hold complete
> The reverse side of the pattern,
> The wrong side of Heaven,
> O then I should know in not knowing
> My truth in my error.

Note on Sources

Biographical material on the Muirs is drawn variously from: Edwin Muir, *The Story and the Fable*, London 1940; *An Autobiography*, London 1954; *Selected Letters*, ed. P.H. Butter, London 1974; Willa Muir, *Belonging*, London 1968; P.H. Butter, *The Life of Edwin Muir*, Edinburgh 1966.

Poems are quoted from Edwin Muir, *Collected Poems*, London 1960.

Quotations from Kafka are from *Briefe 1902–1924*, Frankfurt a. Main 1958; *Tagebücher 1910–1923*, Frankfurt a. Main 1954.

The Muirs' translations are quoted from the first editions: *The Castle*, London 1930; *The Great Wall of China*, London 1933; *The Trial*, London 1937; *America*, London 1938; *In the Penal Colony*, London 1948. Extracts from Kafka's diaries are from translations by Willa Muir, *Orion*, I, London 1945.

The observations on 'Prager Deutsch' on p. 164 derive from sources assembled in Klaus Wagenbach's *Franz Kafka: eine Biographie seiner Jugend*, (Berne 1958), pp. 80–98.

Other sources are: Hermann Broch, *Briefe, Gesammelte Werke*, VIII, Zürich 1966; R.A. Brower, ed., *On Translation*, New York ... 1966; Ronald Gray, 'But Kafka wrote in German', in *The Kafka Debate*, ed. Angel Flores, New York 1977; Dieter Jakob, 'Das Kafka-Bild in England', *OGS*, V, 1970; Michael Hamburger, 'Kafka in England', in *Zwischen den Sprachen*, Frankfurt a. Main 1966; Erich Heller, *Kafka*, London 1974; Hans Hennecke, 'Rede auf die Preisträger Edwin und Willa Muir', *Jahrbuch der deutschen Akademie für Sprache und Dichtung*, Hamburg 1959; Elgin Mellown, 'The Development of a Criticism', *Comp. Lit.*, XVI, 1964; Michael Schmidt, *Fifty Modern British Poets*, London 1979.

17
Challenges and Protests

Commentary by J.P. Stern

Walter Benjamin *(Translation by Harry Zohn)**

Kafka criticism by the German ideological left begins as a protest against Max Brod's appropriation of his friend's writings, first in his novel, 'Zauberreich der Liebe' ('Magic Realm of Love', 1928), then in his Kafka biography of 1937. Without committing himself to the precise (Jewish? Judaeo-Christian?) nature of Kafka's spirituality, Brod sees the man and his work (the two are not clearly separated) as a prophet, a 'homo religiosus' of messianic significance. In a chapter of his biography entitled 'Religious Developments' Brod claims that the proof of this religiousness lies not in an affirmation of faith but in something very like its opposite: 'What, in its essential truthfulness, ultimately proves and purifies [Kafka's] faith is that its rudiments have been wrested from the jaws of radical scepticism – this is what makes them strong and infinitely valuable.' (It should be added that the quotations Brod adduces may be used more readily to prove a very different point – that Kafka's 'truthfulness' leads him to a 'radical scepticism' from which no faith can come. Certainly Kafka affirms the existence of a 'spiritual world', but one which is debased and ceases to be spiritual as soon as man enters it.)

Brod's peculiar ex-nihilo-fideism ('The greater the doubt – the firmer the faith') is very much more than the eccentric opinion of a minor novelist. In one form or another it is the central ideological belief of the inter-war era. The form it takes in Walter Benjamin's view of Kafka (as self-centred and self-revealing as everything else he wrote) is something like this. The consistency of the truth about the world has been lost (even a physicist like Sir Arthur Eddington sees that!); the more truthfully Kafka recognizes this situation and

* From *Illuminations* by Walter Benjamin, translated by Harry Zohn, Collins/Fontana Books, London 1973, pp. 145–8.

reconstructs it in his narratives, the closer he comes to the truth about the world (which has been lost), the greater his work and (because it is work in the face of a lost truth) the greater its failure. In a letter to his friend Gerhard Scholem, dated 12 June 1938, Benjamin writes:

Kafka's work is an ellipse with foci that are far apart and are determined, on the one hand, by mystical experience (in particular, the experience of tradition) and, on the other, by the experience of the modern big-city dweller. In speaking of the experience of the big-city dweller, I have a variety of things in mind. On the one hand, I think of the modern citizen who knows that he is at the mercy of a vast machinery of officialdom whose functioning is directed by authorities that remain nebulous to the executive organs, let alone to the people they deal with. (It is known that one level of meaning in the novels, particularly in *The Trial*, is encompassed by this.) When I refer to the modern big-city dweller, I am speaking also of the contemporary of today's physicists. If one reads the following passage from Eddington's *The Nature of the Physical World*,* one can virtually hear Kafka speak.

I am standing on the threshold about to enter a room. It is a complicated business. In the first place I must shove against an atmosphere pressing with a force of fourteen pounds on every square inch of my body. I must make sure of landing on a plank travelling at twenty miles a second round the sun – a fraction of a second too early or too late, the plank would be miles away. I must do this whilst hanging from a round planet head outward into space, and with a wind of aether blowing at no one knows how many miles a second through every interstice of my body. The plank has no solidity of substance. To step on it is like stepping on a swarm of flies. Shall I not slip through? No, if I make the venture one of the flies hits me and gives a boost up again; I fall again and am knocked upwards by another fly; and so on. I may hope that the net result will be that I remain about steady; but if unfortunately I should slip through the floor or be boosted too violently up to the ceiling, the occurrence would be, not a violation of the laws of Nature, but a rare coincidence. . . .

Verily, it is easier for a camel to pass through the eye of a needle than for a scientific man to pass through a door. And whether the door be barn door or church door it might be wiser that he should consent to be an ordinary man and walk in rather than wait till all the difficulties involved in a really scientific ingress are resolved.

In all of literature I know no passage which has the Kafka stamp to the same extent. Without any effort one could match almost every passage of this physical perplexity with sentences from Kafka's prose pieces, and there is much to indicate that in so doing many of the most 'incomprehensible' passages would be accommodated. Therefore, if one

* Quoted by Benjamin in German translation. [Ed.]

says – as I have just said – that there was a tremendous tension between those of Kafka's experiences that correspond to present-day physics and his mystical ones, only a half-truth is stated. What is actually and in a very literal sense wildly incredible in Kafka is that this most recent world of experience was conveyed to him precisely by this mystical tradition. This, of course, could not have happened without devastating processes ... within this tradition. The long and the short of it is that apparently an appeal had to be made to the forces of this tradition if an individual (by the name of Franz Kafka) was to be confronted with that reality of ours which realizes itself theoretically, for example, in modern physics, and practically in the technology of modern warfare. What I mean to say is that this reality can virtually no longer be experienced by an *individual*, and that Kafka's world, frequently of such playfulness and interlaced with angels, is the exact complement of his era which is preparing to do away with the inhabitants of this planet on a considerable scale. The experience which corresponds to that of Kafka, the private individual, will probably not become accessible to the masses until such time as they are being done away with.

Kafka lives in a *complementary* world. (In this he is closely related to Klee, whose work in painting is just as essentially *solitary* as Kafka's work is in literature.) Kafka offered the complement without being aware of what surrounded him. If one says that he perceived what was to come without perceiving what exists in the present, one should add that he perceived it essentially as an *individual* affected by it. His gestures of terror are given scope by the marvellous *margin* which the catastrophe will not grant us. But his experience was based solely on the tradition to which Kafka surrendered; there was no far-sightedness or 'prophetic vision', Kafka listened to tradition, and he who listens hard does not see.

The main reason why this listening demands such effort is that only the most indistinct sounds reach the listener. There is no doctrine that one could absorb, no knowledge that one could preserve. The things that want to be caught as they rush by are not meant for anyone's ears. This implies a state of affairs which negatively characterizes Kafka's works with great precision. (Here a negative characterization probably is altogether more fruitful than a positive one.) Kafka's work presents a sickness of tradition. Wisdom has sometimes been defined as the epic side of truth. Such a definition stamps wisdom as inherent in tradition; it is truth in its haggadic consistency.

It is this consistency of truth that has been lost. Kafka was far from being the first to face this situation. Many had accommodated themselves to it, clinging to truth or whatever they happened to regard as truth and, with a more or less heavy heart, foregoing its transmissibility. Kafka's real

177

genius was that he tried something entirely new: he sacrificed truth for the sake of clinging to its transmissibility, its haggadic element. Kafka's writings are by their nature parables. But it is their misery and their beauty that they had to become *more* than parables. They do not modestly lie at the feet of the doctrine, as the Haggadah lies at the feet of the Halakah. Though apparently reduced to submission, they unexpectedly raise a mighty paw against it.

This is why, in regard to Kafka, we can no longer speak of wisdom. Only the products of its decay remain. There are two: one is the rumour about the true things (a sort of theological whispered intelligence dealing with matters discredited and obsolete); the other product of this diathesis is folly – which, to be sure, has utterly squandered the substance of wisdom, but preserves its attractiveness and assurance, which rumour invariably lacks. Folly lies at the heart of Kafka's favourites – from Don Quixote via the assistants to the animals. (Being an animal presumably meant to him only to have given up human form and human wisdom from a kind of shame – as shame may keep a gentleman who finds himself in a disreputable tavern from wiping his glass clean.) This much Kafka was absolutely sure of: first, that someone must be a fool if he is to help; second, that only a fool's help is real help. The only uncertain thing is whether such help can still do a human being any good. It is more likely to help the angels (compare the passage about the angels who get something to do) who could do without help. Thus, as Kafka puts it, there is an infinite amount of hope, but not for us. This statement really contains Kafka's hope; it is the source of his radiant serenity. . . .

I transmit to you this somewhat dangerously compressed image – in the manner of perspective reduction. . . . To do justice to the figure of Kafka in its purity and its peculiar beauty one must never lose sight of one thing: it is the purity and beauty of a failure. The circumstances of this failure are manifold. One is tempted to say: once he was certain of eventual failure, everything worked out for him *en route* as in a dream. There is nothing more memorable than the fervour with which Kafka emphasized his failure. His friendship with Brod is to me primarily a question mark which he chose to put in the margin of his life.

Bertolt Brecht (*Translations by J. P. Stern*)

The writers of the ideological left – they have little more in common than Marxist learnings of various shades, and an almost entire lack of political power – reject all discussion of Kafka's spirituality or religiousness: Bertolt Brecht especially is infuriated by Benjamin's talk of Kafka's 'mysticism'. They read the writings as an extended description of the world seen as the hell capitalism has made of it – a description, not an explanation. (There is of course only one explanation, given by Marxism-Leninism.) Those who reject the work (mainly the party officials of the Stalin-dominated International) do so because, being 'merely' a description, the work fails to supply the appropriate didactic message of how to change the world.

Brecht's remarks on Kafka* are better than that – how much better? They are based on the premise that Kafka's work belongs to 'bourgeois literature' :

I myself, generally speaking, prefer modern Czechoslovak† literature to all other bourgeois literatures; I am thinking of names such as Hašek, Kafka and Besruč [*sic*]. Some of this is easy to read, immediately accessible, some requires study, Kafka most of all.

Brecht's remarks are largely condemnatory, and yet every now and then it seems as if the condemnation were imposed on a suppressed note of appreciation, as though an artistic achievement of a very high order were taken for granted; Kafka is certainly not to be associated with his bourgeois admirers:

All reasons for claiming [Kafka] as one of their own must be vigorously denied to the vermin [of capitalism] on either side of the divide between journalism and literature – with means which in their effectiveness were perhaps available only to earlier, barbaric ages. In case of need I would not hesitate for an instant to bring about total extermination.

Kafka's interpretation of the story of the sirens –

But the sirens have one weapon more terrible than their song, and that is their silence. It may never have happened but it is perhaps not unthinkable that some may have escaped their song, but no one has ever escaped their silence –

strikes Brecht as not realistic enough:

I should prefer to believe that the loud voices heard by the oarsmen were cursing that damned prudent provincial with all their might, and that our hero was writhing about (as we are assured by witnesses he did) because he was simply feeling embarrassed.

---

* These and most of the subsequent remarks are quoted from W. Mittenzwei, 'Brecht und Kafka', in *Franz Kafka aus Prager Sicht* (German version of the proceedings of the Liblice Conference of 1963, ed. Eduard Goldstücker), Prague 1963, pp. 119–29.

†The word *böhmisch* ('Bohemian') having been appropriated by the Sudeten Germans for their nationalistic ends, Brecht resorts to calling Kafka a 'Czechoslovak' writer. Petr Bezruč's *Silesian Songs* were known to Brecht in Rudolf Fuchs's German translation, and Jaroslav Hašek's *The Good Soldier Švejk* was first performed, in an adaptation by Max Brod and G. Reiner, in Berlin in 1929.

In his conversations with Walter Benjamin in 1933, Brecht describes Kafka as:

a prophetic writer with but a single theme ... a theme which, in its most general terms, may be described as astonishment. It is the astonishment of a person who is aware that enormous upheavals in all relationships are imminent, and is yet incapable of adjusting to the new order ...

and whereas the K.s are surprised by everything that comes their way, Hašek's Josef Švejk is surprised by nothing, for to him everything seems possible.

He [Kafka] was unable to represent any process whatever in our sense without distorting it. In other words, everything he describes makes statements about something other than itself. The inconsolable seriousness and the despair in the gaze of the writer is his response to the permanent visionary presence of the distorted things.

It is inconceivable that this remark was made by someone insensitive to the very special quality of Kafka's prose, and yet Brecht can write, presumably at much the same time:

It is possible to read works full of mistakes with profit, too, if they also contain something else – it is not mistrust that destroys reading, but lack of mistrust.

And in the early 1950s, in the introduction to an article that remained unfinished:

I see I have mentioned many flaws in these few sentences which I intended as homage, and indeed I am far from setting it [Kafka's work] up as exemplary. ... We find in him strange disguises prefiguring many things that were, at the time when his books appeared, plain to very few people. The fascist dictatorship was, so to speak, in the very bones of the bourgeois democracies, and Kafka described with wonderful imaginative power the future concentration camps, the future instability of the law, the future absolutism of the state *apparat*, the paralysed, inadequately motivated, floundering lives of the many individual people; everything appeared as in a nightmare and with the confusion and inadequacy of nightmare; and at the same time as the intellect clouded over, the language became more lucid. ... Now we are come [as in Dante] before the gate of that country where all that suffer are defenceless – the country that has forfeited the heritage of intelligence.

In a note written in 1955, a year before his death, Brecht, as though still conducting his argument with Kafka, comes back to his favourite theme:

In an age when science is capable of transforming Nature to such an extent that the world seems almost habitable, humankind can no longer describe itself as victim, as the object of an unknown but fixed environment. It is hardly possible to conceive the laws of motion from the standpoint of a child's ball.

Georg Lukács (*Translation by Allan Blunden and J.P. Stern*)

Seeing that the standard English translation of 'Against a Misunderstood Realism'* leaves out or smoothes over some of the difficulties of Lukács's original text, we have thought it best to offer a new version.

Franz Kafka is the classic example of [the modern individual's] arrest by blind and panic-stricken *Angst* in the face of reality. Kafka's unique position in contemporary literature derives from his ability to give direct and simple expression to this emotional disposition [*Lebensgefühl*] – the form in which he presents the basic content is free from the pseudo-technical, as well as from manneristic and formalistic devices. Here content in its bare immediacy determines its own form – an aspect of the creative process which seems to place Kafka in the family of the great writers of realism. Moreover, subjectively speaking, his membership of that family is all the more indisputable since there are very few writers whose originality and elemental impact in the grasping and representation of the world is so fully developed, who so powerfully express their astonishment in the face of the world's unprecedentedness. Especially today, when experimental or cliché-ridden routine dominates most writers and readers alike, such vehement impetus is bound to leave a powerful impression. What increases its impact is not only the simple sincerity of the feeling that creates such writing, but the corresponding simplicity and matter-of-factness of the world this writing creates. Here lies Kafka's most original achievement. Kierkegaard said, 'The more original a man, the deeper the anguish in him.' Such precisely is the originality with which Kafka formulates his anguish, creating with an irresistible necessity the things and structure of objective reality which that anguish is supposed to evoke and which are supposed to correspond to it. The artistic reasons for Kafka's uniqueness lie not in his invention of new formal means of expression, but in evidence, at once insinuating and provoking deep indignation, which is provided by the object-world he creates and his characters' reactions to that world. 'It is not the monstrous that is shocking,' writes Theodor W. Adorno, 'but its matter-of-factness.'

* *Wider den missverstandenen Realismus*, Hamburg 1957, pp. 86–8.

The world of modern capitalism, seen as a form of hell on earth, and the helplessness of all human endeavour in the face of the power wielded by that world: such is the stuff of which Kafka's fiction is made. As always in art, in its simplicity and sincerity his style is the result of a complex interplay between many contradictory tendencies. Let us consider a single aspect of his work here. Kafka was writing at a time when the objective social reality that gave rise to his fear still had a long way to go – historically speaking – before it would emerge in its final, concrete form. The world he portrays and demonizes is not yet the world of fascism – which, when it comes, really *is* demonic in the fullest sense – but the old Habsburg monarchy, which Kafka's so-called 'visionary' fear imbues with a ghostly solidity. The indefinable character of this fear finds appropriate artistic expression in the milieu he creates: a timeless world beyond the reach of history, intellectually and spiritually indeterminate, yet steeped in the atmosphere and local colour of Prague. Thus Kafka profits from his historical situation in two ways: on the one hand the concrete particulars of his fictional world, deeply rooted as they are in the soil of Imperial Habsburg Austria, are imbued with a palpable sense of the here and now, a semblance of social reality; on the other hand the ultimately indeterminate quality of this social reality is rendered with the authentic naivety of one who merely surmises, who really does not *know*. Consequently [Kafka's rendering of that social reality] is able to evolve more naturally into some 'eternal' *condition humaine* than later portrayals of the demonic and terrifying social reality, from which certain existing social factors have had to be artificially excluded (cunningly concealed by the use of formalist stylistic devices) in order to make the representation of human existence as governed by some sort of timeless destiny possible at all. This produces a much more powerful immediate impact and has far greater suggestive force: but it does not alter the fact that the concrete particulars of Kafka's world, too, are ultimately in the service of an allegorical purpose. For these wonderfully expressive details point always to some reality presented as transcendent – they point to that very 'essence' of the imperialistic epoch which Kafka has anticipated with remarkable intuition, reconstituting it in his work as an essentially timeless mode of being. These details do not serve, as they do in realism, as focal points, as distillations of the changes and conflicts in the life to which they belong; in the final analysis they are merely the cryptic symbols of some incomprehensible Beyond. The more telling they are in terms of their immediate evocative power, the more unfathomable this gulf becomes, and the more obtrusive the allegorical discrepancy between being and meaning.

Günther Anders

Günther Anders's contribution to this debate was initiated outside the German-speaking countries (where Kafka was banned). It must be seen against the background of post-war French existentialism – more specifically, in the light of the question, What did Kafka mean to the men and women in the maquis?

The test to which they subjected his writings may seem barbarous to us, but it undoubtedly determined the reception of his work, not only for its many readers, but also for the theatrical producers and film-makers of the post-war era. The maquis, after all, represented what the thirties had been searching for – here was 'reality' at last. If 'The Trial' and 'The Castle' did nothing to strengthen resistance against the German occupation, did they not actually weaken it? 'Faut-il brûler Kafka?' Well – no, says Günther Anders, but ——

The case he argues in 'Kafka – pro und contra' (German edition 1946, English translation 1953) is almost entirely 'the case for the prosecution'. By nature of his literary gift (Anders writes), Kafka is precluded from drawing the world without distorting it. The focus of his stories is on the weak, but he seems unable to portray the weak without siding with the strong. The only two motives of action and inaction he recognizes are fear and guilt – identifying guilt as the necessary effect of isolation and weakness, he ends up by equating might with right. Freedom, in his stories, is presented as a deprivation, and service, to whatever master or cause, as the only source of meaning available to his characters. His notion of beauty is Medusa-like and belongs to the aesthetics of terror. To speak of him as a modern 'homo religiosus' is to misinterpret his undoubted seriousness and sincerity – what prevents him from proclaiming his atheism is no more than embarrassment, a weak feeling of being ashamed.

'Faut-il brûler Anders?' His indictment is somewhat subtler than this brief summary suggests. But even though it is an exaggeration and a distortion, it nevertheless reveals actual traits and tendencies in what Kafka wrote. Underlying Anders's critical argument is a literal-mindedness which places fiction, private letters and diaries all in the same moral and ideological category as it would a party programme, 'ukaz' or religious tract. Given the pressures of the age in which Anders wrote, it is an honourable attitude, but it is one that makes literature impossible. The plea for the defence (one may recall, among many, the case of Andrey Sinyavsky, on trial before a Moscow judge for writing a 'subversive' novel) is that literature is only possible in that narrow area of freedom and integrity which Western convention accords to metaphors and fictions and other products of the human mind – an area in which words are disconnected from their immediate pragmatic function.

Here is the conclusion of Anders's book:*

* Trans. A. Steer and A.K. Thorlby, Bodley Head, London 1960.

183

The Summing Up

He is like a man skiing on loose stones; by his somersaults and bruises he wants to prove to those who pretend the stones are snow that they are nothing but stones.

Like a man sitting before an empty plate and obstinately scooping up mouthfuls with his spoon in order to show those who think the plate is full that it is in fact empty.

Like a man who translates the cracks in slate-rocks as if they were hieroglyphics; by the very absurdity of his translation he wants to prove to those who always talk about the meaning of rock-formations that the cracks are really nothing but cracks.

The character of the age in which he lived is divided and confusing. On the one hand, in almost all its pursuits, in technology, economics, politics, and science it had long ceased to look for a 'meaning'; with the 'death of God' it had also lost the conception of Providence, indeed of any meaningful purpose; it had even ceased to trust in the concept of Progress, that last short-lived, optimistic substitute for Providence and for all other lost concepts of a meaningful world. On the other hand, this period was intellectually and spiritually not able to bear, not 'up to', the meaninglessness of its own activities: it carried along with it the potsherds of long-shattered religions, the remnants of metaphysical and moral vocabularies, as ornaments and amulets.

Kafka took the potsherds seriously. He glued them together into lenses which gave him a meaningful vision of the meaningless world. If his account still contains much that is illogical, modish, or absurd, he is not to blame.

But those who saw him skiing on the stones thought they saw fresh snow forming beneath his skis. And so did he.

Those who saw him eating from an empty plate thought that his eating proved the existence of the soup or was somehow likely to conjure it up. So did he.

Those who listened to his translations were fascinated by the profundity of the texts from which he made them. So was he.

Those who looked with him through the lenses saw in the distortion a world whose existence they had not suspected. So did he.

So did he: this is his guilt. He himself was not equal to his own monstrously ironic adventure.

His guilt is reflected in many ways. Perhaps a balance sheet of his achievements might be presented like this:

He is a realist of the dehumanized world: but also its exalter.

He is a moralist: but does not enquire after the good or evil of a world which he respects in all its ignominy.

He wants to arrive in the world: but he reaches it by way of disaster.

He demands a paradise: but his only concern is how to get into it, not how to create it.

He is frightened by the overwhelming power of the dehumanized world of things: but he passes on his terror through the images of his creation.

He distorts the truth in order to isolate it clearly for our better understanding: but he isolates and immobilizes our understanding as well – he paralyses us.

He discusses rights: but does not even know if he has the right to do so.

He is an atheist: but makes of atheism a theology.

He is a philosopher: but an agnostic.

He is a sceptic: but one who is sceptical of his own scepticism.

Whatever *is*, is to him, if not reasonable, at least justified: to him might is right. And those who have no rights are guilty.

His philosophy is that of the ineffectual conformist who sees himself with the eyes of the authority he has courted in vain.

Kafka the man, with his personal integrity, his warmth and freedom from false pathos, remains untouched by this indictment. And there are many witnesses – direct and indirect – to testify to his friendliness of heart. It reaches us through all the paralysing entanglements of his prose, though alas only as a word of consolation from the prisoner in the neighbouring cell.

Guilty, then?

His work is not of today, but of the day before yesterday. He could not have foreseen the historical situation in which it would be made use of. His allusions to the world of terror and conformity, a world of which we now are the contemporary witnesses, were not then allusions to anything which existed.

But, you will say, it is *today* that he exercises his influence. What counts is not the motive but the effect. Should we therefore destroy his works?

No.

In a situation in which literature is capable of doing great harm, the source of the danger lies deeper. More decisive changes have to take place than can be effected by mere literary rejections. It is not Kafka's works that must be destroyed, but their dangerous fascination. The severest treatment which we should inflict on Kafka would be perhaps to understand him so well that his appeal is destroyed.

Let us therefore define as clearly as possible the position he holds, and explain the nihilism that is implicitly and explicitly expressed by his writings, so that anyone who appeals to Kafka to justify his own attitude towards the world, or anyone who imitates him, thereby stands condemned. From great warnings we should be able to learn, and they should help us to teach others. The picture he has drawn of the world as it should not be, and of attitudes which should not be ours, will be of use to us if it becomes imprinted on our minds as a warning. It is a picture drawn by a good man, who finally came to doubt the value of his work, and even pleaded for its destruction. His work could never be of use either to himself or to others as positive counsel; but as a warning it may be truly helpful to us after all.

Karel Kosík (*Translation by J.P. Stern*)

In 1963, the Czech philosopher Karel Kosík published his 'Dialectics of Concreteness', a book which, in the Prague Spring of 1968, was read by many as a philosophical foundation document of the new 'socialism with a human face'. The book presents an interesting combination of existentialism and Marxism. Kosík's aim is to define the individual's 'concrete' and 'dialectical' understanding of a given historical situation or 'totality' and hence to safeguard his capacity to influence and modify that totality; and Kosík contrasts this active and critical understanding with the concept of 'pseudo-concreteness', which he attacks as a merely utilitarian grasp of the everyday world in the world's own conformist, 'fetishistic' and falsely abstract terms. This false consciousness – compounded of mystification, defective understanding, practical considerations and fear – determines our attitude to the everyday, and in Georg Büchner's 'Danton's Death' (1835), Brecht's epic theatre and Kafka's stories Kosík finds illustrations of it. Here is one strand of Kafka's work which could be presented by Kosík as relevant to alienation in Western capitalist society, while being understood by his readers as a protest against alienation in the Marxist totalitarian state:

We have characterized the everyday as a world in whose regular rhythm man moves mechanically, instinctively, and with a feeling of familiarity. Consciousness of the absurd arises when man reflects on the meaning of the everyday and fails to find that meaning: 'It is so terribly boring, having always first to pull on a shirt and then a pair of trousers over it,' says Danton, 'having to crawl into bed at night and out again in the morning, and always to be putting one leg before the other – one simply can't imagine how this might ever change. That's very sad, and to think that millions of people have been doing it and millions of people will go on doing it. ...'

To be himself, man must perform various tasks in life automatically. The more perfectly automatized such activities are and the less they involve consciousness and reflection, the better they serve man. The more complicated human life becomes, the more contacts man enters into and the more functions he fulfils, the wider must be the *necessary* sphere in which human tasks, habits and processes are automatized. The process by which the everyday of human life becomes automatic and mechanical is an *historical* process; and this is why the frontiers between the possible and the necessary sphere of automatization on the one hand, and the sphere which in the interest of man may not be automatized on the other, are liable to historical change. With the increasing complexity of civilization, man must subject further and wider spheres of his activities to automatization in order to free space and time for genuinely human problems. The inability to automatize certain life-tasks prevents people from living. . . .

The everyday familiar world is not a world we know and recognize. In order that this world may be presented in its reality, it must be torn out of its fetishistic intimacy and revealed in its alienated brutality. The naive, uncritical experiencing of daily life as man's natural environment has this in common with the critical attitude of philosophical nihilism: that both regard a certain historical form of the everyday as the natural and unalterable basis of all human community. The alienation of the everyday is projected in man's consciousness now as an uncritical attitude, now as the feeling of absurdity. In order for man to perceive the truth of the alienated everyday, he must achieve distance from it and rid it of its familiarity – he must 'do violence' to it. In what kind of society and in what kind of world do people have to 'become' vermin and dogs and apes, so that their real likeness should find adequate expression? In what 'violent' metaphors and similes must man and his world be presented, so that people should *see* their own faces and *recognize* their own world? It seems to us that one of the chief principles of modern art, poetry and drama, of the plastic arts and film, is this 'violence' done to the everyday – is the destruction of pseudo-concreteness. (The theory and practice of the 'epic theatre', founded on the principle of alienation, is only one of the ways in which art destroys pseudo-concreteness. Brecht's connections with the intellectual atmosphere of the twenties and with its protest against alienation are obvious. The work of Franz Kafka too may be understood as an artistic destruction of pseudo-concreteness.)

PART THREE

FICTIONS AND SEMI-FICTIONS

18

A Normal Enough Dog:
Kafka and the Office

Roy Fuller

After gaining his doctorate in jurisprudence, Franz Kafka worked temporarily for an insurance company and then in 1908 joined the legal department of the *Arbeiter-Unfall-Versicherungs-Anstalt für das Königreich Böhmen in Prag*, usually referred to in English translation as the Workmen's Accident Insurance Institution, and which hereafter is abbreviated to 'the WAII'. It was government-sponsored and may be thought of as a sort of Friendly Society, though no precise English equivalent existed or exists. From Gustav Janouch's *Conversations with Kafka* and other biographical writings (and indeed from Kafka's own *Diaries*) the impression is given of clean but institutional corridors, shared offices, and agreeable superiors with absorbing hobbies – an ambience perhaps not utterly unlike that of the Board of Trade in the late nineteenth century when Cosmo Monkhouse, Edmund Gosse, Austin Dobson and, for all I know, other *littérateurs* were on the staff. Apart from his periods of illness during the First World War, and the last few years of his life, Kafka went on working for the WAII and this has inevitably been felt to be of especial biographical interest and significance.

The importance attached to this side of Kafka's diurnal life comes partly from the notion that writers, particularly poetic writers, are unfitted by nature for work of an ordinary kind. This idea took thorough hold after the rise of Romanticism, when some artists showed their dissatisfaction with society through their life-styles as well as in their artistic work. No one presumably thought it odd (or even now so thinks) that Milton was secretary to the Council of State, yet much of the attention focused on the American poet Wallace Stevens arose out of his long and prosperous career as a lawyer with an American insurance company. There is also the question whether in some dissimilar occupation one can successfully moonlight as a writer – I mean, looking at the matter from the point of view of having reasonable time and energy for the moonlighting occupation.

Max Brod has been principally responsible for the idea (held, I suppose, by many interested in Kafka) of the malevolent influence of the WAII. The point was put, I think not too extravagantly, by a blurb writer on the jacket of the first volume of Kafka's *Diaries* when the English translation was published in 1948. Brod's thesis, says the blurb, is 'that it was not so much the son's difficult relationship with his austere father – to which most modern psychologists would attribute Franz Kafka's fatal neurosis – but rather the evil of his being caught up in the daily round of office life and having to work day in day out to the point of exhaustion in a dissatisfying and uninteresting job, that led to his illness and death.' In his biography, Brod rarely passes up an opportunity of reviling Kafka's occupation: 'the pestilential necessity he found himself under of earning his daily bread' is one phrase, likely to be even more virulent in the original German; another is 'damned to scribbling legal documents' – 'scribbling' being an inaccurate cliché. Much of Brod's feeling here came out of his own experience rather than Kafka's. Chapter III of Brod's biography, called 'To Earn One's Living or Live One's Life', starts with a remarkable page or two on the topic in question, from which the following passage is taken:

... when it came to the point of choosing a profession, Franz postulated his job should have nothing to do with literature. That he would have regarded as a debasing of literary creation. Bread-winning and the art of writing must be kept absolutely apart, a 'mixture' of the two, such as journalism, for example, represents, Kafka rejected – although at the same time he never laid down dogmas, but merely withdrew, as it were, with a smile on the explanation that 'I just can't do it.' He influenced me and my choice of a profession for years with these views of his and, like himself, out of respect for Art, I went through agonies, in the most hideous, prosaic, dry, profession of the law and I didn't find the road to theatrical and musical criticism until years later. Today I regard Kafka's severity on this point as a noble error, and regret the hundreds of joyless hours I let slip by in a mood almost of despair, wasting God's high creation, time, in offices just like those in which Kafka now set out on his martyr's way.

Brod's talent proved to be capable of standing up to a life in Grub Street. Perhaps we might fairly say that to prosper there, or even to survive, has usually indicated, in Brod's time and ours, the second-rate – the likeness of the voluntary work to that Grub Street is willing to pay for. In the case of Kafka there was a gap about as wide as could be. Moreover, his fear – conviction – of not succeeding in a commercial sense was paralleled by fear of artistic unsuccess. The latter was by no means merely the neurotic inability to finish a fiction or the equally neurotic compulsion to start it over and over again in almost the same phrases (perhaps peculiar to Kafka), but a genuine self-questioning of ability which exists with especial acuteness in the area between talent and genius. One must not forget, too, that for Kafka literary hackwork would surely have presented problems as severe as those in his chosen literary work, so for him it would not have been a softer option.

Brod's claim that the diaries sustain his thesis that Kafka's job was Kafka's downfall is arguable. Certainly passages of complaint by the diarist can be found. For instance: 'it is a horrible double life from which there is probably no escape but insanity' (19 February 1911). But this is preceded by the following not wholly unambiguous condemnation: 'When I wanted to get out of bed this morning I simply folded up. This has a very simple cause, I am completely overworked. Not by the office but my other work. The office has an innocent share in it only to the extent that, if I did not have to go there, I could live calmly for my own work and should not have to waste these six hours a day which have tormented me to a degree that you cannot imagine. . . .'

Also, the unexplained intrusion of 'you' puts the entry at a remove from reportage – a remove, found so often in the diaries, varying from the closeness to reality of a species of unposted letter to the fantasy of apparently more or less free invention. Sometimes, too, it is the office that makes the entry 'creative' (inclining to the inspiration Wallace Stevens used to find in his daily walks to work), as in this entry for 24 January 1914:

> Recently, when I got out of the elevator at my usual hour, it occurred to me that my life, whose days more and more repeat themselves down to the smallest detail, resembles that punishment in which each pupil must according to his offence write down the same meaningless (in repetition, at least) sentence ten times, a hundred times or even oftener; except that in my case the punishment is given me with only this limitation: 'as many times as you can stand it'.

The office work itself must quite often have given analagous opportunities for creativeness. Brod's biography quotes a passage from the WAII's annual report for 1909 (or 1910: Brod is unclear), a passage written by Kafka. It concerns the prevention of accidents from machines, and compares cutters on square spindles with those on cylindrical spindles. A few sentences are sufficient to show the closeness of this to a characteristic effect of Kafka's fiction:

Although an extremely cautious operator could take care not to allow any joint of his finger to project from the timber when guiding it over the cutter head, the main danger defied all caution. The hand of even the most cautious operator was bound to be drawn into the cutter space if it slipped, particularly when, as often happened, the timber was hurled back (by the cutter block) while the operator was pressing the article to be planed against the table with one hand and feeding it to the cutter spindle with the other. This lifting and recoiling of the timber could not be anticipated nor prevented as it may have been due to gnarls or knots in the timber, to an insufficiently high cutting-speed, to warped cutters, or to uneven pressure of the operator's hands on the article.

The point must not be pressed too hard, but the style here (characteristic in any case of the lawyer who has had to master temporarily and expound the details of some unfamiliar life or process and which may be seen, for example, in written judgments of the English High Courts) Kafka plainly carried over into his imaginative work. One need only instance the phrase somewhat over-violent for the context ('hurled back'); the technical process apparently clearly described but remaining enigmatic; the presentation of the recalcitrance of the material world; the constant alternatives in happenings or causes. These things are allied to but rather different from 'the semi-ironical use of legal and official jargon' which, Malcolm Pasley notes (in his preface to Volume I of the translated *Shorter Works*), became 'an integral part of his literary style'.

The pages in Brod's biography already referred to emphasize Kafka's lack of 'push' (the English word found by the translator seems remarkably apt). Brod is speaking of favours Kafka might have squeezed out of his father, such as a few years of study abroad, but the missing quality would also have operated adversely in the literary rat-race, as Kafka would have been aware. Of course, it may have affected his career in the WAII, but as a professionally qualified man in an essentially non-commercial organization he would be able to soldier on with a protected status. In fact he was promoted a number of times over the years, and the impression one gets is always of an efficient and respected employee.

Apropos of the burdens of the double occupation, Brod says that in the WAII the office day ended at two o'clock, enabling Kafka to sleep in the afternoon, readying himself for the evening's literary work. Though the working day may have begun as early as 8 am, there seems no question that the WAII post resembled the bobbies' jobs Gosse and Co. had in the English Civil Service before the First World War.

Brod thought that without a job Kafka would have written better. His causal argument is crude. We may prefer to withhold final judgment, as Wallace Stevens, in one of his letters (to Thomas McGreevy, 17 February 1930), did about his own case:

If Beethoven could look back on what he had accomplished and say that it was a collection of crumbs compared to what he had hoped to accomplish, where should I ever find a figure of speech adequate to size up the little that I have done compared to that which I had once hoped to do? Of course, I have had a happy and well-kept life. But I have not even begun to touch the spheres within spheres that might have been possible if, instead of devoting the principal amount of my time to making a living, I had devoted it to thought and poetry. Certainly it is as true as it ever was that whatever means most to one should receive all of one's time and that has not been true in my case. But, then, if I had been more determined about it, I might now be looking back not with a mere sense of regret but at some actual devastation. To be cheerful about it, I am now in the happy position of being able to say that I don't know what would have happened if I had had more time. This is very much better than to have had all the time in the world and have found onself inadequate.

As for Wallace Stevens, it can be argued that perhaps the main material cause of his becoming a 'modern' poet (fairly suddenly, I suppose round about 1912) was his getting a safe, semi-institutional job with the Hartford Accident and Indemnity Company: it solved, *inter alia*, the twin problems of the long hours and other ardours of private legal practice and of the burden of pleasing artistically a reasonably large public. One rather suspects that Stevens found his job at bottom 'easy', as did Kafka (see the letter to his parents drafted by Kafka and quoted by Brod in his chapter on Kafka's 'engagement').* As I have said in another connection, there is no really satisfactory material mode of life for the poet (and Kafka can be ranked as such), so speculations such as Brod's are idle in the last analysis. Finally, while on this topic, one must point out that for a man often seedy, who died at forty, quantitatively Kafka wrote an amazing amount, despite all difficulties; and that, after all, is a large part of the business of being a writer. Deliberately to use the word 'seedy' is not to try to underplay the trials of Kafka's health, certainly not the appalling later stages of his tuberculosis. But, like his job, his health was more a counterpart than an enemy to his creative life. Kafka's struggle was not just with his job, his illnesses, bourgeois customs, but with existence itself – the inevitable result of the coming into being of his body: 'I write this very decidedly out of despair over my body and over a future with this body' is an early diary entry.

It may be asked why Kafka had to take a job at all.† With a little more of the push hoped for by Brod, could he not have secured an allowance from his well-to-do father? The answer is that the mores of the family would not have allowed it; that Kafka himself always contemplated a financially

* 'My work at the office is wearisome and often intolerable, but fundamentally easy. In this easy way I earn more money than I need.' (Chapter 5.) [Ed.]

† See also Kafka's letter to Ottla, excerpts from which are quoted above, p. 27. [Ed.]

independent existence, involving ultimately and above all his own dwelling, separate from his mother and father. One says 'the answer', but of course these perfectly commonplace and comprehensible middle-class inhibitions and desires are almost insanely intensified in Kafka's life, just as his long engagement can be said to be a caricature of the long engagements not rare in the lower to middle middle-class society of my youth, and which perhaps still linger in provincial pockets. 'Almost insanely intensified' is a phrase that must not be misunderstood: no really esoteric considerations are involved. Kafka himself put the business beautifully, as well reported by the young Janouch in his *Conversations with Kafka*:

Kafka said ... 'the poet is always much smaller and weaker than the social average. Therefore he feels the burden of earthly existence much more intensely and strongly than other men. For him personally his song is only a scream. Art for the artist is only suffering, through which he releases himself for further suffering. He is not a giant, but only a more or less brightly plumaged bird in the cage of his existence.'

'You too?' I asked.

'I am a quite impossible bird,' said Franz Kafka. 'I am a jackdaw – a *kavka*. The coal merchant in the close of Tein Cathedral has one. Have you seen it?'

'Yes, it flies about outside his shop.'

'Yes, my relative is better off than I am. It is true, of course, that its wings have been clipped. As for me, this was not in any case necessary, as my wings are atrophied. For this reason there are no heights and distances for me. I hop about bewildered among my fellow men. They regard me with deep suspicion. And indeed I am a dangerous bird, a thief, a jackdaw. But that is only an illusion. In fact, I lack all feeling for shining objects. For that reason I do not even have glossy black plumage. I am grey, like ash. A jackdaw who longs to disappear between the stones. But this is only joking, so that you will not notice how badly things are going with me today.'

Herbert Tauber, in his pioneering *Franz Kafka: An Interpretation of his Works* (first published in Switzerland in 1941), constantly emphasizes Kafka's preoccupation with the 'world of phenomena' – everyday reality. The preoccupation is in both the autobiographical material and (with the qualification about naturalism I shall make later) the fiction. I have remembered for over thirty years, for instance, the start of the diary entry for 26 September 1911: 'The artist Kubin recommends Regulin as a laxative, a powdered seaweed that swells up in the bowels, shakes them up, is thus effective mechanically in contrast to the unhealthy chemical effect of other laxatives which just tear through the excrement and leave it hanging on the walls of the bowels.'

This is immediately followed by a brief description of a conversation with Knut Hamsun who, while it was going on, 'put one foot on the table, took a large pair of paper shears from the table and trimmed the frayed edges of his trousers'. This taste for the bizarre commonplace must have great appeal for the poet, who (like Kafka) loves the world of phenomena but uses it for rather more than its own sake. It must also prompt the reflection that there are advantages in a life, however disagreeable, that constantly pits such a writer against the varieties of the everyday – such as are displayed by office life in a large organization. I must not claim that his years with the WAII kept Kafka's responses supple, but the purely literary (and solitary) life has drawbacks for the poet, whose temperament and methods he to a degree shared. Of course, it can be said that Kafka is always at pains to exclude from his fiction the naturalistic (distinguishing that term from the realistic), but that does not mean his imaginative writings could ever have done without refreshment from a fair chunk of the actual.

I shall close this discussion of what constituted for Kafka a substantial and important proportion of his relatively short adult life by referring to my novel, *Image of a Society*, published in 1956. Wanting to depict a writer who worked as a lawyer in a large organization, Kafka's case came irresistibly to mind (and I welcomed it as being different from my own). I had to transfer the chap from pre-First World War Prague to post-Second World War 'Saddleford', but the process brought out the sordid and ludicrous elements in such a life (and I did not attempt to underplay them) which the passage of time and the abstracting process of literary biography (and, indeed, Kafka's fiction itself) have tended to remove from Kafka's real life, despite such reminders as Regulin. There is a striking little episode in *Conversations with Kafka*. Janouch is walking with Kafka from the office: as they near the family warehouse, Kafka's father emerges in overcoat and top-hat and says in a loud voice, 'Franz. Go home. The air is damp.' Nothing more. Through the youthful Janouch's eyes the encounter is almost alarming but we must suspect that the everyday reality had elements of Chaplin as well as Caligari. My lawyer/writer in *Image of a Society* is compelled by family pressures to play three-handed solo whist with his father and mother, a dish of Liquorice Allsorts on the table, before contriving to escape to visit his fiancée.

Kafka's sexuality was as realistic as everything else about him: one thinks immediately of items like the brief but vividly particularized descriptions of girls in the diaries ('The upper front teeth of Miss K ... slant towards each other ... like legs which are quickly crossed at the knees'). Yet it is not difficult to account for such things as the long engagement to Felice Bauer. Again one goes to the diaries for a revealing peep-hole on the relationship; there he writes of 'the quite hostile grimace she made in the entrance hall of her house when I was not satisfied to kiss her glove but pulled it open and kissed her hand'. In *Image of a Society* the erotic relationship of the engaged couple has stopped short at a more advanced state of play, and again this admits more freely a farcical strand.

One must not bring Kafka too far down into the commonplace. Philip Witt, the Kafka counterpart in *Image of a Society*, necessarily suffered from lack of genius, compared with his original. Nevertheless, when it came to demonstrating practically how the art arose out of the life, I hoped I was showing some decent blooms as well as the compost. Philip Witt meets and is attracted by the wife of an office colleague, to whom he thus initially writes:

Dear Mrs Blackledge,

The innocent would start by imagining your surprise: the bold would assume that you felt no surprise. But I can think of nothing except addressing the envelope and sending its contents to the house of a man I call by his Christian name but to whom I would never send a letter. Writing a letter is easy even for the guilty, timid man: and he can often quite quickly bring himself to post it. But this letter implies the serious but absurd trappings of espionage: an envelope addressed on an untraceable typewriter or with the left hand, signed with a false name – 'your loving aunt, Ada'. Perhaps – no, I'm sure – you've often had letters in circumstances like these and find all my guilt, procrastination, sense of fate, incomprehensible. After all, you'd say, the envelope wasn't disguised, except in so far as it was in a handwriting you didn't know; and its contents aren't, so far as you know, in code.

A man briefly visits a family under a false name, makes love to the daughter, departs leaving no address. Later he wonders if she had a child and thinks for a few moments quite seriously of all the terrible consequences, of no effect on him, of his action. Or a ghost, with the most frightful effort, removes himself from the place of purgatory where he circles, to visit the living about whom in spite of his death he is still anguished: but none of them see him. How will you think of this letter?

Perhaps you will remember it later in the day, laugh, and go and tear it up.

P.W.

I suppose, having the thing to do again, I would try to bring out the ironically comic side more, though the letter and its reception and consequences have their comic aspects, particularly (as with Kafka) in their implications. What I think is nearer the mark is the style of the letter, very much founded on that of a lawyer's draft, which has to exercise ingenuity so as to cover contingencies, some remote – the square and cylindrical spindles style, referred to before.

Ambiguity in documents – in life itself – is a notable preoccupation of lawyers, which they simultaneously try to detect and cure (and about which they have built up a body of law and practice). This element is sometimes characterized as Kafkaesque. Lawyerlike, too, is the discovery of unintended meanings. Later in my novel I give an entry in Philip Witt's notebook which makes an allegory of society as a whole out of the building society for which the lawyer works, by showing the two classes of members of the society, investors and borrowers – the prosperous and the indigent – served by a third class, the building society's management who, according to their position in the management hierarchy, may themselves be either prosperous or indigent, thus putting in doubt the truth of the service they give:

Imagine a society composed of two classes – the prosperous and the indigent. The classes have come together, drawn by self-interest, the prosperous to reap a profit by lending to the indigent, the indigent to exist by borrowing the wealth of the prosperous. But how were two such classes, their interests in mortal opposition, brought together and induced to persist in a calm and ordered relationship? The answer is that the machinery of the society consists of a third and much smaller class whose interest is merely to serve the interest of the other two classes. It is the third class which ensures that the needs of the indigent answer to the superfluity of the prosperous, that the profits of the prosperous are properly related to the capacity of the indigent, that the multifarious transactions of the whole society do not exceed nor fall much below the society's means. The members of this third class are rewarded according to their relative importance in the machinery: thus, in their private capacity, they may either be members of the prosperous or of the indigent class.

But, you ask, are the two main classes really in equilibrium, does the third class serve them impartially? On a true analysis of the society is it not evident that the interest of the prosperous is paramount, that the machinery of the third class exists to preserve it, and that the members of the third class – even the privately indigent members – are necessarily, by virtue of their task in the society, permeated with the idea that, though while things go well a fair balance between the two other classes can and should be preserved, the protection of the possessions of the prosperous is their paramount duty? For, if those possessions are allowed to pass permanently to the indigent, will not the society ipso facto be destroyed?

Alas, these questions cannot be veraciously answered – at any rate by members of the society. Almost all of the prosperous and most of the indigent believe in the essential fairness of the society. Many of the third class have ceased to visualize the aims of the society, being unable to see beyond their own function as part of its complicated machinery. But one or two of this same class, though dedicating their whole lives to the service of the society, have in fact come to disbelieve in its proposed aims: these, beneath the veneer of their skill and devotion, are neurotic, unstable, and unhappy, but fortunately they do not constitute any serious threat to the continuance of the society.

I have adduced these examples of mine not least to show simply how the ordinary, far from precluding the transcendental, inspires and sustains it.

Kafka's work illustrates the business with greater subtlety and variety. One thinks of *America*, where more often than not it is detail (rather than the turns of the narrative, say, or the hero's reflections, the parable or allegorical element being almost entirely absent) that lends the fiction its fabulous, its bizarre quality – as when (and I open the book at random) Mr Green puts a slice of pigeon into his mouth, 'where his tongue, as Karl chanced to notice, took it in charge with a flourish'. Many observations, giving the book a good deal of its power, have an hallucinatory quality, though (like Shakespeare's imagery) rooted in ordinary, even domestic life – as the telegraphist's head 'bound in a steel band' and, a candle being lit, 'a blue zig-zag pattern' appears on the ceiling. And where the narrative is fantastic, as in the story 'Blumfeld, an Elderly Bachelor', the details make it plausible and are themselves rendered ominous: for example, the description of the floor of the wardrobe when Blumfeld imprisons the bouncing balls and, on his way out afterwards, the look of the charwoman's son: 'The image of his mother, not one feature of the woman has been omitted in this child's face. Bandy-legged, hands in his trouser pockets, he stands there wheezing, for he already has a goitre and can breathe only with difficulty.'

Kafka's greatness in his life and art arises from his joy in the world, despite the weakness in body and character that often made living in that world such an agony. I believe, as I must have made clear, that his role in the WAII, laying on him social tasks and responsibilities ('Let each child have that's in our care / As much neurosis as the child can bear' – Auden's lines come to mind here), deepened his art. He may well have seen this himself. One of his last works, 'Investigations of a Dog', written after the WAII had pensioned him off on account of ill-health – the disease that killed him: with grotesque appropriateness almost an accident arising out of his (writing) work – begins with what is surely a retrospective and revealing glance at his years of office life, as one of the sceptical part of that 'third class' in society:

If I cast my mind back today and recall the time when I was still living in the midst of the dog community, taking part in all its concerns, a dog among dogs, I soon find on closer examination that something was not quite right from the very beginning; there was always a little discrepancy somewhere, a slight discomfort would overtake me in the middle of the most solemn public functions, occasionally even in a gathering of friends; no, it was not occasionally, it was very often; the mere sight of some fellow-dog dear to me, this mere sight caught somehow afresh, would embarrass me, alarm me, fill me with helplessness and even despair. I tried to soothe myself as best I could; friends to whom I confessed my trouble helped me; there was a return of more peaceful times, times in which such surprises were indeed not lacking, but were accepted more calmly, were fitted into the pattern of

Two drawings from
Kafka's diaries

LEFT Photograph from the Matljany Sanatorium, 1921

RIGHT Kafka's friend, the Czech journalist and translator Milena Jesenská, with whom he corresponded from the time of his stay at Meran in 1920 onwards

BELOW Prague: Hradčany Castle

ABOVE Roofs of the Old City

RIGHT St Vitus's Cathedral and its choir on the Castle Hill. Some of its details are reminiscent of the last chapter of *The Trial*.

Kafka's parents, Hermann and Julie

Dora Diamant (Dymant), with whom he lived in Berlin from September 1923 to March 1924

RIGHT The last photograph of Kafka, winter 1923/4

ABOVE A recent plaque on Kafka's house near the Old Town Hall

LEFT *Reading Aloud*, a drawing of Kafka by Friedrich Feigl

my life more calmly; they may have induced a certain sadness and weariness, but apart from that they did not prevent me from holding my own, as an admittedly somewhat cold, reserved, timid and calculating, but all things considered normal enough dog. How indeed, without these intervals for recuperation, could I have attained the age that I enjoy at present, how could I have struggled my way through to the serenity with which I view the terrors of my youth and endure the terrors of age, how could I have got to the stage of drawing the consequences from my admittedly unfortunate, or to put it more cautiously, not very fortunate disposition, and of living accordingly as far as my strength allows? Withdrawn, isolated, occupied solely with my little investigations, amateurish, hopeless investigations which are, however, indispensable to me, and so presumably they do afford some secret hope after all – such is the life I lead; but all the same I still manage to keep my people in view from the distance, news of them sometimes penetrates to me, though it is indeed becoming gradually more infrequent, and occasionally I let them hear from me as well. The others treat me with deference, they cannot understand my way of life but they do not hold it against me, and even young dogs whom I sometimes see passing in the distance, a new generation of whose childhood I have scarcely a vague memory, never refuse me their respectful greeting.

19

'I always wanted you to admire my fasting'

or, Looking at Kafka*

Philip Roth

'I always wanted you to admire my fasting,' said the hunger artist. 'We do admire it,' said the overseer, affably. 'But you shouldn't admire it,' said the hunger artist. 'Well then we don't admire it,' said the overseer, 'but why shouldn't we admire it?' 'Because I have to fast, I can't help it,' said the hunger artist. 'What a fellow you are,' said the overseer, 'and why can't you help it?' 'Because,' said the hunger artist, lifting his head a little and speaking, with his lips pursed, as if for a kiss, right into the overseer's ear, so that no syllable might be lost, 'because I couldn't find the food I liked. If I had found it, believe me, I should have made no fuss and eaten my fill like you or anyone else.' These were his last words, but in his dimming eyes remained the firm though no longer proud persuasion that he was still continuing to fast.

Franz Kafka, 'A Hunger Artist'

I

I am looking, as I write of Kafka, at the photograph taken of him at the age of forty (my age) – it is 1924, as sweet and hopeful a year as he may ever have known as a man, and the year of his death. His face is sharp and skeletal, a burrower's face: pronounced cheekbones made even more conspicuous by the absence of sideburns; the ears shaped and angled on his head like angel wings; an intense, creaturely gaze of startled composure – enormous fears, enormous control; a black towel of Levantine hair pulled close around the skull the only sensuous feature; there is a familiar Jewish flare in the bridge of the nose, the nose itself is long and weighted slightly at the tip – the nose of half the Jewish boys who were my friends in

* Written in 1973, from *Reading Myself and Others* (Jonathan Cape, Ltd, London 1975 and Farrar, Straus & Giroux, Inc., New York, 1975).

high school. Skulls chiselled like this one were shovelled by the thousands from the ovens; had he lived, his would have been among them, along with the skulls of his three younger sisters.

Of course it is no more horrifying to think of Franz Kafka in Auschwitz than to think of anyone in Auschwitz – it is just horrifying in its own way. But he died too soon for the holocaust. Had he lived, perhaps he would have escaped with his good friend Max Brod, who found refuge in Palestine, a citizen of Israel until his death there in 1968. But *Kafka* escaping? It seems unlikely for one so fascinated by entrapment and careers that culminate in anguished death. Still, there is Karl Rossmann, his American greenhorn. Having imagined Karl's escape to America and his mixed luck here, could not Kafka have found a way to execute an escape for himself? The New School for Social Research in New York becoming *his* Great Nature Theatre of Oklahoma? Or perhaps, through the influence of Thomas Mann, a position in the German department at Princeton. ... But then, had Kafka lived, it is not at all certain that the books of his which Mann celebrated from *his* refuge in New Jersey would ever have been published; eventually Kafka might either have destroyed those manuscripts that he had once bid Max Brod to dispose of at his death or, at the least, continued to keep them his secret. The Jewish refugee arriving in America in 1938 would not then have been Mann's 'religious humourist' but a frail and bookish fifty-five-year-old bachelor, formerly a lawyer for a government insurance firm in Prague, retired on a pension in Berlin at the time of Hitler's rise to power – an author, yes, but of a few eccentric stories, mostly about animals, stories no one in America had ever heard of and only a handful in Europe had read; a homeless K., but without K.'s wilfulness and purpose, a homeless Karl, but without Karl's youthful spirit and resilience; just a Jew lucky enough to have escaped with his life, in his possession a suitcase containing some clothes, some family photos, some Prague mementos, and the manuscripts, still unpublished and in pieces, of *America*, *The Trial*, *The Castle*, and (stranger things happen) three more fragmented novels, no less remarkable than the bizarre masterworks that he keeps to himself out of oedipal timidity, perfectionist madness, and insatiable longings for solitude and spiritual purity.

July 1923: Eleven months before he will die in a Vienna sanatorium, Kafka somehow finds the resolve to leave Prague and his father's home for good. Never before has he even remotely succeeded in living apart, independent of his mother, his sisters, and his father, nor has he been a writer other than in those few hours when he is not working in the legal department of the Workers' Accident Insurance Office in Prague; since taking his law degree at the university, he has been by all reports the most dutiful and scrupulous of employees, though he finds the work tedious and enervating. But in June of 1923 – having some months earlier been pensioned from his job because of his illness – he meets a young Jewish girl of nineteen at a seaside resort in Germany, Dora Dymant.* Dora has left her Orthodox Polish family to make a life of her own (at half Kafka's age); she and Kafka – who has just turned forty – fall in love ... Kafka has by now been engaged to two somewhat more conventional Jewish girls – twice to one of them – hectic, anguished engagements wrecked largely by his fears. 'I am mentally incapable of marrying,' he writes to his father in the forty-five-page letter he gave to his mother to deliver. '... the moment I make up my mind to marry I can no longer sleep, my head burns day and night, life can no longer be called life.' He explains why. 'Marrying is barred to me,' he tells his father, 'because it is your domain. Sometimes I imagine the map of the world spread out and you stretched diagonally across it. And I feel as if I could consider living in only those regions that are not covered by you or are not within your reach. And in keeping with the conception I have of your magnitude, these are not many and not very comforting regions – and marriage is not among them.' The letter explaining what is wrong between this father and this son is dated November 1919; the mother thought it best not even to deliver it, perhaps for lack of courage, probably, like the son, for lack of hope.

During the following two years, Kafka attempts to wage an affair with Milena Jesenská-Polak* ...; his affair with Milena, conducted feverishly, but by and large through the mails, is even more demoralizing to Kafka than the fearsome engagements to the nice Jewish girls. They aroused only the paterfamilias longings that he dared not indulge, longings inhibited by his exaggerated awe of his father – 'spellbound,' says Brod, 'in the family circle' – and the hypnotic spell of his own solitude; but the Czech Milena, impetuous, frenetic, indifferent to conventional restraints, a woman of appetite and anger, arouses more elemental yearnings and more elemental fears. According to a Prague critic, Rio Preisner, Milena was 'psychopathic'; according to Margaret Buber-Neumann, who lived two years beside her in the German concentration camp where Milena died following a kidney operation in 1944, she was powerfully sane, extraordinarily humane and courageous. Milena's obituary for Kafka was the only one of consequence to appear in the Prague press; the prose is strong, so are the claims she makes for Kafka's accomplishment. She is still only in her twenties, the dead man is hardly known as a writer beyond his small circle of friends – yet Milena

* See above, p. 28. [Ed.]
* See above, pp. 25–7. [Ed.]

writes: 'His knowledge of the world was exceptional and deep, and he was a deep and exceptional world in himself. . . . [He had] a delicacy of feeling bordering on the miraculous and a mental clarity that was terrifyingly uncompromising, and in turn he loaded on to his illness the whole burden of his mental fear of life. . . . He wrote the most important books in recent German literature.' One can imagine this vibrant young woman stretched diagonally across the bed, as awesome to Kafka as his own father spread out across the map of the world. His letters to her are disjointed, unlike anything else of his in print; the word 'fear' appears on page after page. 'We are both married, you in Vienna, I to my Fear in Prague.' He yearns to lay his head upon her breast; he calls her 'Mother Milena', during at least one of their two brief rendezvous he is hopelessly impotent. At last he has to tell her to leave him be, an edict that Milena honours, though it leaves her hollow with grief. 'Do not write,' Kafka tells her, 'and let us not see each other; I ask you only to quietly fulfil this request of mine; only on those conditions is survival possible for me; everything else continues the process of destruction.'

Then, in the early summer of 1923, during a visit to his sister, who is vacationing with her children by the Baltic Sea, he finds young Dora Dymant, and within a month Franz Kafka has gone off to live with her in two rooms in a suburb of Berlin, out of reach at last of the 'claws' of Prague and home. How can it be? How can he, in his illness, have accomplished so swiftly and decisively the leave-taking that was beyond him in his healthiest days? The impassioned letter writer who could equivocate interminably about which train to catch to Vienna to meet with Milena (if he should meet with her for the weekend at all); the bourgeois suitor in the high collar, who, during his drawn-out agony of an engagement with the proper Fräulein Bauer, secretly draws up a memorandum for himself, countering the arguments 'for' marriage with the arguments 'against'; the poet of the ungraspable and the unresolved, whose belief in the immovable barrier separating the wish from its realization is at the heart of his excruciating visions of defeat; the Kafka whose fiction refutes every easy, touching, humanish daydream of salvation and justice and fulfilment with densely imagined counterdreams that mock all solutions and escapes – this Kafka *escapes*. Overnight! K. penetrates the Castle walls – Joseph K. evades his indictment – 'a breaking away from it altogether, a mode of living completely outside the jurisdiction of the Court'. Yes, the possibility of which Joseph K. has just a glimmering in the Cathedral, but can neither fathom nor effectuate – 'not . . . some influential manipulation of the case, but . . . a circumvention of it' – Kafka realizes in the last year of his life.

Was it Dora Dymant or was it death that pointed the new way? Perhaps it could not have been one without the other. We know that the 'illusory emptiness' at which K. gazed, upon first entering the village and looking up through the mist and the darkness to the Castle, was no more vast and incomprehensible than the idea of himself as husband and father was to the young Kafka; but now, it seems, the prospect of a Dora forever, of a wife, home, and children everlasting, is no longer the terrifying, bewildering prospect it would once have been, for now 'everlasting' is undoubtedly not much more than a matter of months. Yes, the dying Kafka is determined to marry, and writes to Dora's Orthodox father for his daughter's hand. But the imminent death that has resolved all contradictions and uncertainties in Kafka is the very obstacle placed in his path by the young girl's father. The request of the dying man Franz Kafka to bind to him in his invalidism the healthy young girl Dora Dymant is – denied!

If there is not one father standing in Kafka's way, there is another – and another behind him. Dora's father, writes Max Brod in his biography of Kafka, 'set off with [Kafka's] letter to consult the man he honoured most, whose authority counted more than anything else for him, the "Gerer Rebbe". The rabbi read the letter, put it to one side, and said nothing more than the single syllable, "No."' *No*. Klamm himself could have been no more abrupt – or any more removed from the petitioner. *No*. In its harsh finality, as telling and inescapable as the curse-like threat delivered by his father to Georg Bendemann,* that thwarted fiancé: 'Just take your bride on your arm and try getting in my way. I'll sweep her from your very side, you don't know how!' *No*. Thou shalt not have, say the fathers, and Kafka agrees that he shall not. The habit of obedience and renunciation; also, his own distaste for the diseased and reverence for strength, appetite, and health. 'Well, clear this out now!' said the overseer, and they buried the hunger artist, straw and all. Into the cage they put a young panther. Even the most insensitive felt it refreshing to see this wild creature leaping around the cage that had so long been dreary. The panther was all right. The food he liked was brought him without hesitation by the attendants; he seemed not even to miss his freedom; his noble body, furnished almost to the bursting point with all that it needed, seemed to carry freedom around with it too; somewhere in his jaws it seemed to lurk; and the joy of life streamed with such ardent passion from his throat that for the onlookers it was not easy to stand the shock of it. But they braced themselves, crowded round the cage, and did not want ever to move away.' So no is no; he knew as much himself. A healthy young girl of nineteen cannot, *should* not, be given in matrimony to a sickly man twice her age, who spits up blood ('I sentence you,' cries Georg Bendemann's father, 'to death by drowning!') and shakes in his bed with fevers and chills. What sort of un-Kafka-like dream had Kafka been dreaming?

* In Kafka's story 'The Judgment'. [Ed.]

And those nine months spent with Dora have still other 'Kafkaesque' elements: a fierce winter in quarters inadequately heated; the inflation that makes a pittance of his own meagre pension, and sends into the streets of Berlin the hungry and needy whose suffering, says Dora, turns Kafka 'ash-grey'; and his tubercular lungs, flesh transformed and punished. Dora cares for the diseased writer as devotedly and tenderly as Gregor Samsa's sister does for her brother, the bug. Gregor's sister plays the violin so beautifully that Gregor 'felt as if the way were opening before him to the unknown nourishment he craved'; he dreams, in his condition, of sending his gifted sister to the Conservatory! Dora's music is Hebrew, which she reads aloud to Kafka, and with such skill that, according to Brod, 'Franz recognized her dramatic talent; on his advice and under his direction she later educated herself in the art. . . .'

Only Kafka is hardly vermin to Dora Dymant, *or to himself*. Away from Prague and his father's home, Kafka, at forty, seems at last to have been delivered from the self-loathing, the self-doubt, and those guilt-ridden impulses to dependence and self-effacement that had nearly driven him mad throughout his twenties and thirties; all at once he seems to have shed the pervasive sense of hopeless despair that informs the great punitive fantasies of *The Trial*, 'In the Penal Colony', and 'The Metamorphosis'. Years earlier, in Prague, he had directed Max Brod to destroy all his papers, including three unpublished novels, upon his death; now, in Berlin, when Brod introduces him to a German publisher interested in his work, Kafka consents to the publication of a volume of four stories, and consents, says Brod, 'without much need of long arguments to persuade him'. With Dora to help, he diligently resumes the study of Hebrew; despite his illness and the harsh winter, he travels to the Berlin Academy for Jewish Studies to attend a series of lectures on the Talmud – a very different Kafka from the estranged melancholic who once wrote in his diary, 'What have I in common with the Jews? I have hardly anything in common with myself and should stand very quietly in a corner, content that I can breathe.' And to further mark the change, there is ease and happiness with a woman: with this young and adoring companion, he is playful, he is pedagogical, and, one would guess, in light of his illness (*and* his happiness), he is chaste. If not a husband (such as he had striven to be to the conventional Fräulein Bauer), if not a lover (as he struggled hopelessly to be with Milena), he would seem to have become something no less miraculous in his scheme of things: a father, a kind of father to this sisterly, mothering daughter. *As Franz Kafka awoke one morning from uneasy dreams he found himself transformed in his bed into a father, a writer, and a Jew.*

'I have completed the construction of my burrow,' begins the long, exquisite, and tedious story that he wrote that winter in Berlin, 'and it seems to be successful. ... Just the place where, according to my calculations, the Castle Keep should be, the soil was very loose and sandy and had literally to be hammered and pounded into a firm state to serve as a wall for the beautifully vaulted chamber. But for such tasks the only tool I possess is my forehead. So I had to run with my forehead thousands and thousands of times, for whole days and nights, against the ground, and I was glad when the blood came, for that was proof that the walls were beginning to harden; in that way, as everybody must admit, I richly paid for my Castle Keep.'

'The Burrow' is the story of an animal with a keen sense of peril whose life is organized around the principle of defence, and whose deepest longings are for security and serenity; with teeth and claws – *and* forehead – the burrower constructs an elaborate and ingeniously intricate system of underground chambers and corridors that are designed to afford it some peace of mind; however, while this burrow does succeed in reducing the sense of danger from without, its maintenance and protection are equally fraught with anxiety: 'these anxieties are different from ordinary ones, prouder, richer in content, often long repressed, but in their destructive effects they are perhaps much the same as the anxieties that existence in the outer world gives rise to.' The story (whose ending is lost) terminates with the burrower fixated upon distant subterranean noises that cause it 'to assume the existence of a great beast', itself burrowing in the direction of the Castle Keep.

Another grim tale of entrapment, and of obsession so absolute that no distinction is possible between character and predicament. Yet this fiction imagined in the last 'happy' months of his life is touched by a spirit of personal reconciliation and sardonic self-acceptance, by a tolerance of one's own brand of madness, that is not apparent in 'The Metamorphosis'. The piercing masochistic irony of the earlier animal story – as of 'The Judgment' and *The Trial* – has given way here to a critique of the self and its preoccupations that, though bordering on mockery, no longer seeks to resolve itself in images of the uttermost humiliation and defeat. ... Yet there is more here than a metaphor for the insanely defended ego, whose striving for invulnerability produces a defensive system that must in its turn become the object of perpetual concern – there is also a very unromantic and hard-headed fable about how and why art is made, a portrait of the artist in all his ingenuity, anxiety, isolation, dissatisfaction, relentlessness, obsessiveness, secretiveness, paranoia, and self-addiction, a portrait of the magical thinker at the end of his tether, Kafka's Prospero. ... It is an endlessly suggestive story, this story of life in a hole. For, finally, remember the proximity of Dora Dymant during the months that

Kafka was at work on 'The Burrow' in the two underheated rooms that were their illicit home. Certainly a dreamer like Kafka need never have entered the young girl's body for her tender presence to kindle in him a fantasy of a hidden orifice that promises 'satisfied desire', 'achieved ambition', and 'profound slumber', but that, once penetrated and in one's possession, arouses the most terrifying and heartbreaking fears of retribution and loss. 'For the rest I try to unriddle the beast's plans. Is it on its wanderings, or is it working on its own burrow? If it is on its wanderings then perhaps an understanding with it might be possible. If it should really break through to the burrow I shall give it some of my stores and it will go on its way again. It will go on its way again, a fine story! Lying in my heap of earth I can naturally dream of all sorts of things, even of an understanding with the beast, though I know well enough that no such thing can happen, and that at the instant when we see each other, more, at the moment when we merely guess at each other's presence, we shall blindly bare our claws and teeth. . . .'

He died of tuberculosis of the lungs and larynx on 3 June 1924, a month before his forty-first birthday. Dora, inconsolable, whispers for days afterward, 'My love, my love, my good one. . . .'

2

1942. I am nine; my Hebrew-school teacher, Dr Kafka, is fifty-nine. To the little boys who must attend his 'four-to-five' class each afternoon, he is known – in part because of his remote and melancholy foreignness, but largely because we vent on him our resentment at having to learn an ancient calligraphy at the very hour we should be out screaming our heads off on the ball field – he is known as Dr Kishka. Named, I confess, by me. His sour breath, spiced with intestinal juices by five in the afternoon, makes the Yiddish word for 'insides' particularly telling, I think. Cruel, yes, but in truth I would have cut out my tongue had I ever imagined the name would become legend. A coddled child, I do not yet think of myself as persuasive, or, quite yet, as a literary force in the world. My jokes don't hurt, how could they, I'm so adorable. And if you don't believe me, just ask my family and the teachers in my school. Already at nine, one foot in college, the other in the Catskills. Little borscht-belt comic that I am outside the classroom, I amuse my friends Schlossman and Ratner on the dark walk home from Hebrew school with an imitation of Kishka, his precise and finicky professorial manner, his German accent, his cough, his gloom. 'Doctor *Kishka!*' cries Schlossman, and hurls himself savagely against the news-stand that belongs to the candy-store owner whom Schlossman drives just a little crazier each night. 'Doctor Franz – Doctor

Franz – Doctor Franz – *Kishka!*' screams Ratner, and my chubby little friend who lives upstairs from me on nothing but chocolate milk and Mallomars does not stop laughing until, as is his wont (his mother has asked me 'to keep an eye on him' for just this reason), he wets his pants. Schlossman takes the occasion of Ratner's humiliation to pull the little boy's paper out of his notebook and wave it in the air – it is the assignment Dr Kafka' has just returned to us, graded; we were told to make up an alphabet of our own, out of straight lines and curved lines and dots. 'That is all an alphabet is,' he had explained. 'That is all Hebrew is. That is all English is. Straight lines and curved lines and dots.' Ratner's alphabet, for which he received a C, looks like twenty-six skulls strung in a row. I received my A for a curlicued alphabet, inspired largely (as Dr Kafka seems to have surmised, given his comment at the top of the page) by the number eight. Schlossman received an F for forgetting even to do it – and a lot he seems to care. He is content – he is *overjoyed* – with things as they are. Just waving a piece of paper in the air and screaming, 'Kishka! Kishka!' makes him deliriously happy. We should all be so lucky.

At home, alone in the glow of my goose-necked 'desk' lamp (plugged after dinner into an outlet in the kitchen, my study), the vision of our refugee teacher, stick-like in a fraying three-piece blue suit, is no longer very funny – particularly after the entire beginners' Hebrew class, of which I am the most studious member, takes the name Kishka to its heart. My guilt awakens redemptive fantasies of heroism, I have them often about the 'Jews in Europe'. I must save him. If not me, who? The demonic Schlossman? The babyish Ratner? And if not now, when? For I have learned in the ensuing weeks that Dr Kafka lives in a room in the house of an elderly Jewish lady on the shabby lower stretch of Avon Avenue, where the trolley still runs and the poorest of Newark's Negroes shuffle meekly up and down the street, for all they seem to know, still back in Mississippi. A *room*. And *there!* My family's apartment is no palace, but it is ours at least, so long as we pay the $38.50 a month in rent; and though our neighbours are not rich, they refuse to be poor and they refuse to be meek. Tears of shame and sorrow in my eyes, I rush into the living room to tell my parents what I have heard (though not that I heard it during a quick game of 'aces up' played a minute before class against the synagogue's rear wall – worse, played directly beneath a stained-glass window embossed with the names of the dead): 'My Hebrew teacher lives in a *room*.'

My parents go much further than I could imagine anybody going in the real world. Invite him to dinner, my mother says. *Here?* Of course here – Friday night; I'm sure he can stand a home-cooked meal, she says, and a little pleasant company. Meanwhile, my father gets on the phone to call my Aunt Rhoda, who lives with my grandmother and tends her and her potted plants in the apartment house at the corner of our street. For nearly two decades my father has been introducing my mother's 'baby' sister, now forty, to the Jewish bachelors and widowers of north Jersey. No luck so far. Aunt Rhoda, an 'interior decorator' in the dry-goods department of the Big Bear, a mammoth merchandise and produce market in industrial Elizabeth, wears falsies (this information by way of my older brother) and sheer frilly blouses, and family lore has it that she spends hours in the bathroom every day applying powder and sweeping her stiffish hair up into a dramatic pile on her head; but despite all this dash and display, she is, in my father's words, 'still afraid of the facts of life'. He, however, is undaunted, and administers therapy regularly and gratis: 'Let 'em squeeze ya, Rhoda – it *feels* good!' I am his flesh and blood, I can reconcile myself to such scandalous talk in our kitchen – *but what will Dr Kafka think?* Oh, but it's too late to do anything now. The massive machinery of match-making has been set in motion by my undiscourageable father, and the smooth engines of my proud homemaking mother's hospitality are already purring away. To throw my body into the works in an attempt to bring it all to a halt – well, I might as well try to bring down the New Jersey Bell Telephone Company by leaving our receiver off the hook. Only Dr Kafka can save me now. But to my muttered invitation, he replies, with a formal bow that turns me scarlet – who has ever seen a person do such a thing outside a movie house? – he replies that he would be *honoured* to be my family's dinner guest. 'My aunt,' I rush to tell him, 'will be there too.' It appears that I have just said something mildly humorous; odd to see Dr Kafka smile. Sighing, he says, 'I will be delighted to meet her.' Meet her? He's supposed to *marry* her. How do I warn him? And how do I warn Aunt Rhoda (a very great admirer of me and my marks) about his sour breath, his roomer's pallor, his Old World ways, so at odds with her up-to-dateness? My face feels as if it will ignite of its own – and spark the fire that will engulf the synagogue, Torah and all – when I see Dr Kafka scrawl our address in his notebook, and beneath it, some words *in German*. 'Good night, Dr Kafka!' 'Good night, and thank you, thank you.' I turn to run, I go, but not fast enough: out on the street I hear Schlossman – that fiend! – announcing to my classmates, who are punching one another under the lamplight down from the synagogue steps (where a card game is also in progress, organized by the bar mitzvah boys): 'Roth invited Kishka to his *house!* To *eat!*'

Does my father do a job on Kafka! Does he make a sales pitch for familial bliss! What it means to a man to have two fine boys and a wonderful wife! Can Dr Kafka imagine what it's like? The thrill? The satisfaction? The pride? He tells our visitor of the network of relatives on his mother's side that are joined in a 'family association' of over two

hundred people located in seven states, including the state of Washington!
Yes, relatives even in the Far West: here are their photographs, Dr Kafka;
this is a beautiful book we published entirely on our own for five dollars a
copy, pictures of every member of the family, including infants, and a
family history by 'Uncle' Lichtblau, the eighty-five-year-old patriarch of
the clan. This is our family newsletter, which is published twice a year and
distributed nationwide to all the relatives. This, in the frame, is the menu
from the banquet of the family association, held last year in a ballroom of
the 'Y' in Newark, in honour of my father's mother on her seventy-fifth
birthday. My mother, Dr Kafka learns, has served *six consecutive years* as
the secretary-treasurer of the family association. My father has served a
two-year term as president, as have each of his three brothers. We now
have fourteen boys in the family in uniform. Philip writes a letter on V-
mail stationery to five of his cousins in the army every single month.
'Religiously,' my mother puts in, smoothing my hair. 'I firmly believe,'
says my father, 'that the family is the cornerstone of everything.'

Dr Kafka, who has listened with close attention to my father's spiel,
handling the various documents that have been passed to him with great
delicacy and poring over them with a kind of rapt absorption that reminds
me of myself over the watermarks of my stamps, now for the first time
expresses himself on the subject of family; softly he says, 'I agree,' and
inspects again the pages of our family book. 'Alone,' says my father, in
conclusion, 'alone, Dr Kafka, is a stone.' Dr Kafka, setting the book gently
down upon my mother's gleaming coffee table, allows with a nod that that
is so. My mother's fingers are now turning in the curls behind my ears; not
that I even know it at the time, or that she does. Being stroked is my life;
stroking me, my father, and my brother is hers.

My brother goes off to a Boy Scout meeting, but only after my father
has him stand in his neckerchief before Dr Kafka and describe to him the
skills he has mastered to earn each of his badges. I am invited to bring my
stamp album into the living room and show Dr Kafka my set of triangular
stamps from Zanzibar. 'Zanzibar!' says my father rapturously, as though I,
not even ten, have already been there and back. My father accompanies Dr
Kafka and me into the 'sun parlour', where my tropical fish swim in the
aerated, heated, and hygienic paradise I have made for them with my
weekly allowance and my Hanukkah *gelt*. I am encouraged to tell Dr Kafka
what I know about the temperament of the angel fish, the function of the
catfish, and the family life of the black mollie. I know quite a bit. 'All on
his own he does that,' my father says to Kafka. 'He gives me a lecture on
one of those fish, it's seventh heaven, Dr Kafka.' 'I can imagine,' Kafka
replies.

Back in the living room my Aunt Rhoda suddenly launches into a rather recondite monologue on 'Scotch plaids', intended, it would appear, for the edification of my mother alone. At least she looks fixedly at my mother while she delivers it. I have not yet seen her look directly at Dr Kafka; she did not even turn his way at dinner when he asked how many employees there were at the Big Bear. 'How would I know?' she had replied, and then continued right on conversing with my mother, about a butcher who would take care of her 'under the counter' if she could find him nylons for his wife. It never occurs to me that she will not look at Dr Kafka because she is shy – nobody that dolled up could, in my estimation, be shy. I can only think that she is outraged. *It's his breath. It's his accent. It's his age.*

I'm wrong – it turns out to be what Aunt Rhoda calls his 'superiority complex'. 'Sitting there, sneering at us like that,' says my aunt, somewhat superior now herself. 'Sneering?' repeats my father, incredulous. 'Sneering and laughing, yes!' says Aunt Rhoda. My mother shrugs. '*I* didn't think he was laughing.' 'Oh, don't worry, by himself there he was having a very good time – *at our expense*. I know the European-type man. Underneath they think they're all lords of the manor,' Rhoda says. 'You know something, Rhoda?' says my father, tilting his head and pointing a finger, 'I think you fell in love.' 'With *him*? Are you *crazy*?' 'He's too quiet for Rhoda,' my mother says. 'I think maybe he's a little bit of a wallflower. Rhoda is a very lively person, she needs lively people around her.' 'Wallflower? He's not a wallflower! He's a gentleman, that's all. And he's lonely,' my father says assertively, glaring at my mother for going over his head like this *against* Kafka. My Aunt Rhoda is forty years old – it is not exactly a shipment of brand-new goods that he is trying to move. 'He's a gentleman, he's an educated man, and I'll tell you something, he'd give his eyeteeth to have a nice home and a wife.' 'Well,' says my Aunt Rhoda, 'let him find one then, if he's so educated. Somebody who's his equal, who he doesn't have to look down his nose at with his big sad refugee eyes!' 'Yep, she's in love,' my father announces, squeezing Rhoda's knee in triumph. 'With him?' she cries, jumping to her feet, taffeta crackling around her like a bonfire. 'With *Kafka*?' she snorts. 'I wouldn't give an old man like him the time of day!'

Dr Kafka calls and takes my Aunt Rhoda to a movie. I am astonished, both that he calls and that she goes; it seems there is more desperation in life than I have come across yet in my fish tank. Dr Kafka takes my Aunt Rhoda to a play performed at the 'Y'. Dr Kafka eats Sunday dinner with my grandmother and my Aunt Rhoda and, at the end of the afternoon, accepts with that formal bow of his the mason jar of barley soup that my grandmother presses him to carry back to his room with him on the No. 8 bus. Apparently he was very taken with my grandmother's jungle of potted plants – and she, as a result, with him. Together they spoke in Yiddish about gardening. One Wednesday morning, only an hour after the store has opened for the day, Dr Kafka shows up at the dry-goods department of the Big Bear; he tells Aunt Rhoda that he just wants to see where she works. That night he writes in his diary: 'With the customers she is forthright and cheery, and so managerial about "taste" that when I hear her explain to a chubby young bride why green and blue do not "go", I am myself ready to believe that Nature is in error and R. is correct.'

One night, at ten, Dr Kafka and Aunt Rhoda come by unexpectedly, and a small impromptu party is held in the kitchen – coffee and cake, even a thimbleful of whisky all around, to celebrate the resumption of Aunt Rhoda's career on the stage. I have only heard tell of my aunt's theatrical ambitions. My brother says that when I was small she used to come to entertain the two of us on Sundays with her puppets – she was at that time employed by the W.P.A. to travel around New Jersey and put on marionette shows in schools and even in churches; Aunt Rhoda did all the voices and, with the help of a female assistant, manipulated the manikins on their strings. Simultaneously she had been a member of the Newark Collective Theater, a troupe organized primarily to go around to strike groups to perform *Waiting for Lefty*. Everybody in Newark (as I understood it) had had high hopes that Rhoda Pilchik would go on to Broadway – everybody except my grandmother. To me this period of history is as difficult to believe in as the era of the lake dwellers, which I am studying in school; people say it was once so, so I believe them, but nonetheless it is hard to grant such stories the status of the real, given the life I see around me.

Yet my father, a very avid realist, is in the kitchen, schnapps glass in hand, toasting Aunt Rhoda's success. She has been awarded one of the starring roles in the Russian masterpiece *The Three Sisters*, to be performed six weeks hence by the amateur group at the Newark 'Y'. Everything, announces Aunt Rhoda, everything she owes to Franz and his encouragement. One conversation – 'One!' she cries gaily – and Dr Kafka had apparently talked my grandmother out of her lifelong belief that actors are not serious human beings. And what an actor *he* is, in his own right, says Aunt Rhoda. How he had opened her eyes to the meaning of things, by reading her the famous Chekhov play – yes, read it to her from the opening line to the final curtain, all the parts, and actually left her in tears. Here Aunt Rhoda says, 'Listen, listen – this is the first line of the play – it's the key to everything. Listen – I just think about what it was like the night Pop passed away, how I wondered and wondered what would become of us, what would we all do – and, and, *listen*——'

'We're listening,' laughs my father. So am *I* listening, from my bed.

Pause; she must have walked to the centre of the kitchen linoleum. She says, sounding a little surprised, '"It's just a year ago today that father died."'

'Shhh,' warns my mother, 'you'll give the little one nightmares.'

I am not alone in finding my aunt a 'changed person' during the weeks of rehearsal. My mother says this is just what she was like as a little girl. 'Red cheeks, always those hot, red cheeks – and everything exciting, even taking a bath.' 'She'll calm down, don't worry,' says my father, 'and then he'll pop the question.' 'Knock on wood,' says my mother. 'Come on,' says my father, 'he knows what side his bread is buttered on – he sets foot in this house, he sees what a family is all about, and believe me, he's licking his chops. Just look at him when he sits in that club chair. This is his dream come true.' Rhoda says that in Berlin, before Hitler, he had a young girl friend, years and years it went on, and then she left him. For somebody else. She got tired of waiting.' 'Don't worry,' says my father, 'when the time comes I'll give him a little nudge. He ain't going to live forever, either, and he knows it.'

Then one weekend, as a respite from the 'strain' of nightly rehearsals – which Dr Kafka regularly visits, watching in his hat and coat at the back of the auditorium until it is time to accompany Aunt Rhoda home – they take a trip to Atlantic City. Ever since he arrived on these shores Dr Kafka has wanted to see the famous boardwalk and the horse that dives from the high board. But in Atlantic City something happens that I am not allowed to know about; any discussion of the subject conducted in my presence is in Yiddish. Dr Kafka sends Aunt Rhoda four letters in three days. She comes to us for dinner and sits till midnight crying in our kitchen. She calls the 'Y' on our phone to tell them (weeping) that her mother is still ill and she cannot come to rehearsal again – she may even have to drop out of the play. No, she can't, she can't, her mother is too ill, she herself is too upset! goodbye! Then back to the kitchen table to cry. She wears no pink powder and no red lipstick, and her stiff brown hair, down, is thick and spiky as a new broom.

My brother and I listen from our bedroom, through the door that silently he has pushed ajar.

'Have you ever?' says Aunt Rhoda, weeping. 'Have you *ever*?'

'Poor soul,' says my mother.

'*Who*?' I whisper to my brother, 'Aunt Rhoda or——'

'Shhhh!' he says. 'Shut *up!*'

In the kitchen my father grunts. 'Hmm. Hmm.' I hear him getting up and walking around and sitting down again – and then grunting. I am listening so hard that I can hear the letters being folded and unfolded, stuck back into their envelopes, then removed to be puzzled over one more time.

'Well?' demands Aunt Rhoda. '*Well?*'

'Well what?' answers my father.

'Well, what do you want to say *now*?'

'He's *meshugeh*,' admits my father. 'Something is wrong with him all right.'

'But,' sobs Aunt Rhoda, 'no one would believe me when *I* said it!'

'Rhody, Rhody,' croons my mother in that voice I know from those times that I have had to have stitches taken, or when I have awakened in tears, somehow on the floor beside my bed. 'Rhody, don't be hysterical, darling. It's over, kitten, it's all over.'

I reach across to my brother's twin bed and tug on the blanket. I don't think I've ever been so confused in my life, not even by death. The speed of things! Everything good undone in a moment! By what? '*What?*' I whisper. '*What is it?*'

My brother, the Boy Scout, smiles leeringly and, with a fierce hiss that is no answer and enough answer, addresses my bewilderment: 'Sex!'

Years later, a junior at college, I receive an envelope from home containing Dr Kafka's obituary, clipped from *The Jewish News*, the tabloid of Jewish affairs that is mailed each week to the homes of the Jews of Essex County. It is summer, the semester is over, but I have stayed on at school, alone in my room in the town, trying to write short stories. I am fed by a young English professor and his wife in exchange for baby-sitting; I tell the sympathetic couple, who are also loaning me the money for my rent, why it is I can't go home. My tearful fights with my father are all I can talk about at their dinner table. 'Keep him away from me!' I scream at my mother. 'But, darling,' she asks me, 'what is going on? What is this all about?' – the very same question with which I used to plague my older brother, asked now of me and out of the same bewilderment and innocence. 'He *loves* you,' she explains.

But that, of all things, seems to me precisely what is blocking my way. Others are crushed by paternal criticism – I find myself oppressed by his high opinion of me! Can it possibly be true (and can I possibly admit) that I am coming to hate him for loving me so? praising me so? But that makes no sense – the ingratitude! the stupidity! the contrariness! Being loved is so obviously a blessing, *the* blessing, praise such a rare bequest. Only listen late at night to my closest friends on the literary magazine and in the drama society – they tell horror stories of family life to rival *The Way of All Flesh*, they return shell-shocked from vacations, drift back to school as though from the wars. What they would give to be in my golden slippers! 'What's going on?' my mother begs me to tell her; but how can I, when I myself don't fully believe that this is happening to us, or that I am the one who is making it happen. That they, who together cleared all obstructions from my path, should seem now to be my final obstruction! No wonder my rage must filter through a child's tears of shame, confusion, and loss. All that we have constructed together over the course of two century-long decades, and look how I must bring it down – in the name of this tyrannical need that I call my 'independence'! My mother, keeping the lines of communication open, sends a note to me at school: 'We miss you' – and encloses the brief obituary notice. Across the margin at the bottom of the clipping, she has written (in the same hand with which she wrote notes to my teachers and signed my report cards, in that very same handwriting that once eased my way in the world), 'Remember poor Kafka, Aunt Rhoda's beau?'

'Dr Franz Kafka,' the notice reads, 'a Hebrew teacher at the Talmud Torah of the Schley Street Synagogue from 1939 to 1948, died on June 3 in the Deborah Heart and Lung Center in Browns Mills, New Jersey. Dr Kafka had been a patient there since 1950. He was 70 years old. Dr Kafka was born in Prague, Czechoslovakia, and was a refugee from the Nazis. He leaves no survivors.'

He also leaves no books: no *Trial*, no *Castle*, no diaries. The dead man's papers are claimed by no one, and disappear – all except those four *'meshugeneh'* letters that are, to this day, as far as I know, still somewhere in among the memorabilia accumulated by my spinster aunt, along with a collection of Broadway Playbills, sales citations from the Big Bear, and transatlantic steamship stickers.

Thus all trace of Dr Kafka disappears. Destiny being destiny, how could it be otherwise? Does the Land Surveyor reach the Castle? Does K. escape the judgment of the Court, or Georg Bendemann the judgment of his father? "Well, clear this out now!" said the overseer, and they buried the hunger artist, straw and all.' No, it simply is not in the cards for Kafka ever to become *the* Kafka – why, that would be stranger even than a man turning into an insect. No one would believe it, Kafka least of all.

20

A Triptych for the Jackdaw

Jerzy Peterkiewicz

I

During the Thirty Years War
they built a flood-gate
under the Castle.
And they built it too late.
After the second Flood
they built a chimney
in the clouds over the Castle.
Circumstantially, it was the best
they could do.

The Jackdaw flew over and said:
I shall build a nest
inside this chimney
which has a bird's eye view
of impending disasters.

And the Jackdaw built two nests,
one against smoke, one against air;
they both fell down the chimney
and bounced into the Gräfin's chair.
She was afraid of bats.

So the Jackdaw built a third nest,
he built it upside down;
it fell out of the chimney
and bounced like a ball on the ground.

You never can win,
tossing a coin of chance,
said the Wind to the Jackdaw.
Let's go to the Castle and dance.

II

They had a ball at the Castle
to celebrate the Three Years Peace;
the Graf was in his counting-house,
counting his ribbons and tassels.

The Jackdaw stood by the door
and watched the wax on the floor.

Below, in the ballroom blue-and-grey,
quoth Margrave von A. to Marquise de Z.:
'May I have the first waltz?' 'Yes, you may,
literally speaking.' And they danced
throughout the whole Alphabet.

The Jackdaw stood by the door
and watched words waxed on the floor.

III

This is the Jackdaw's prayer,
prayed in the dead of night:

Father who are in our prison,
mind-bound yet denied by the mind,
nailed by fear with the nails of reason,
pray for the light to be late
so that we who are blind
should have time to grope our way
between the Chimney and your Castle's gate.

The Lord is in his counting-house,
counting out his grains of sand.

When sunflowers are weary of the sun,
we shall meet in the Valley of Fathers
for the trial of men and mice.

The Jackdaw is still on the run
to Paradise.

21

K. on the Moon

D.J. Enright

'If his parents love him so much, why don't they give him 30,000 gulden so that he could go off to some cheap little place on the Riviera. . . .'

Max Brod to Felice Bauer

Why is K. going to the Moon?
Because he is the thinnest person he knows
Because he neither smokes nor drinks
Because he does not care for communal life.

Off lifts the tin-beetle
Trailing its fiery slime
It looks good
(Except you can't see it).

But K. can see Fräulein Bauer
He can see Kakania, Krim and Korsika
Kreta, Kapkolonie and Kanada
They all look much as usual, only quieter.

'Dear Fräulein Bauer
I am an erratic letter writer——'

The typewriter floats above his head
Such things never happen in the office.

'Yet a letter is better
(Especially fine handwriting today, not so?)
If I arrived in person you would find me
Insufferable, and the thinnest person you knew.'

His burden he knows is weightless
But does his burden know?

'Will you marry me, dear Fräulein?
Will you marry a man who is sickly, taciturn, miserable and selfish
A man with white hair, poor prospects and palpitations
A man who is chained to invisible authorship
A man for whom even night is not night enough
A man who lives on the Moon?'

And would he want to marry a dear Fräulein –
Or anyone else who was willing to wed him?
Engagé he is but his health
Is not good enough for marriage.

'For a whole week I have seen nothing but
Outlandishly dressed Montenegrins in my sleep
Which gave me headaches . . .
When I recover my typewriter
I shall write a story called The Man Who Disappeared.'

He does not have a bent for writing
If you please, he is bent with writing.

'You read my letters carelessly. I said my uncle
Was in Madrid: you have moved him to Milan.
Is it all one to you whether I am on the Moon
Or on Mars . . .?'

The roads are long and it is easy to go astray.
He has acquired great experience in complaining.

'What have I done that you torment me so?
No letter today, no letter yesterday
And I believe it is now tomorrow.
Some diabolical official is playing about
With our letters . . .'

He runs in circles like a squirrel in a cage.
What might he not accomplish if he were free
And in good hands?
(Nothing.)

'Love me, Felice! And hate me!
Why do I torment you so?
You are my own self . . .
You are my human tribunal.
Please send a rose in forgiveness.'

*

A small step for mankind
But a giant leap for K. –
He falls on his face on the moon-rocks.
Have no fear, Felice –
Devised solely for writing, he cannot break.

Alas, the Montenegrins are there already
In their headachy garb!
A long thin butcher's knife glints in the moonlight.
Someone has been telling lies about him.
He is virtually a vegetarian.

We have a problem
(We always have a problem).

'Dearest F.
Now quickly forget the ghost that I was.
Peace will require no letters.
Try to drink less tea in future . . .
Kisses in the corner – K.'

The Moon is made of literature.

22

Kafka Without a World

Wolfgang Fischer
Translated by Chris Waller

'Because he is a writer, he has lost the world; but the world he has gained in its place ... constantly appears to him as a mirage of Hell. For to which reality does even the language correspond from which this world of his is built?'

Erich Heller*

'Don't read Kafka if you suffer from depression,' said my German teacher at my secondary school in Vienna. 'That's what I've always said to my old pupils, but the poets among them would never listen to me.'

This is my earliest Kafka memory. I can see Professor Noll before me, sitting at the dilapidated desk, leaning on her stick and, with her sharp, manly, intellectual profile, living up to her nickname 'Old Fritz' (after Frederick the Great). The courageous battles she waged at school on behalf of German literature were fought in the name of the trinity of the Good, the Beautiful and the Noble, a classical trinity in which the 'Good' was best understood as strenuous endeavour in the Goethean sense, the 'Beautiful' as the summation of all German landscapes, the homes of German tribes and literatures, in accordance with Nadler's literary ideology, and the 'Noble' as Winckelmann's hermeneutic principle, long since refuted, of the 'silent greatness and noble simplicity' of classical sculpture. A golden niche was created, the setting either for *Nathan the Wise*, idol of Freemasons, or for the Faust image of intellectual activity worshipped by German professors and privy councillors filled with establishment culture; but in this altar-recess, as may well be imagined,

---

* Introduction to Franz Kafka, *Letters to Felice*, German ed., Frankfurt a. Main 1967, p. 23.

there was no room for the cotton-reel Odradek* or for tormented Joseph K. Irony, fear and desolation had to be excluded from the world of grammar-school students in the vast Schönbrunn-yellow building of the former Imperial Institute for Officers' Daughters, for, once blighted in early youth by Kafka's negating spirit, how could anyone ever become a highly respected lawyer, a really competent doctor, a positively motivated teacher or even a shrewd graduate of Business School? In the ideal intellectual landscape conjured up by 'Old Fritz' in her German lessons there was no room for Kafka's world, not even a little corner at the edge of the road where tiny Odradek might have had a breather during his constant wanderings. . . .

No room for Kafka's world: but isn't Franz Kafka himself without a world – that is, without a world in the narrow sense of a sociological, ethnical, religious or patriotic nomenclature and classification? Allow for a moment an image to replace these philosophical concepts and to reinforce these efforts at interpretation: a swarm of black jackdaws (Kafka, or *kavka* in Czech, means jackdaw), a 'Kafka-swarm', flies over the Hradčany, crosses the Little Quarter and Alchemists' Lane, lands briefly among the weathered gravestones of the Jewish Cemetery, flutters past the famous clock on the Jewish Town Hall, the hands of which go from left to right, and vanishes over the mediaeval stone arches of Charles' Bridge behind the figure of Saint John of Nepomuk enveloped in mist:

> The crows caw in flight,
> on whirring wings move off towards the town . . .

Soon Ahasuerus, the Wandering Jew, will be coming over the bridge. . . .

Of course, the filing-cabinet, its various sub-sections researched with academic zeal and supposedly ready in their entirety to yield up the world of Franz Kafka, is full to bursting-point. Try taking a parrot, the kind which in my youth was used by itinerant sellers of lottery tickets on the bridges of the Danube Canal in Vienna, to draw the brightly coloured tickets, and up will come a winner: Kafka's Jewish world, Kafka's German cultural world, Kafka's Czech environment, Kafka's world of bureaucratic repression, Kafka's domestic world, Kafka's friends, Kafka's women etc. . . . Subjects for doctoral dissertations can be plucked just like that from the parrot's beak, but Franz K., in the swarm of Kafka-jackdaws, will elude all painstaking scholarship, will soar away, a little black speck, high above St Vitus's Cathedral, evading the straining eye of the researcher, an example of slipping the coils of rationality not unheard-of in these days of world-wide travelling among Kafka gurus, high above the Empire State Building. . . .

*From the story 'The Cares of the Father'. [Ed.]

Let's begin with the Jewish world, the paradigmatic historical representatives of which could be encountered in, say, three guises in Kafka's time: as a liberal Jew with little or no religious faith, like Kafka's father, the secular culmination of Emperor Joseph's 'Toleranzpatent'; as an orthodox Jew; or as a Zionist. In the *Letter* to his father Kafka reproaches the liberal kind of Jew for his 'insignificant scrap of Judaism'; the opening of the Ark of the Covenant reminds him of shooting-galleries, and (in the diary of 1914) he says, 'What have I in common with Jews? I have hardly anything in common with myself. . . .' Nevertheless, he attends concert and drama-evenings organized by Zionist clubs; when he goes to see the Eastern Jewish drama group giving guest performances in Prague he feels a very deep sensation of belonging to a community, and in his 'Speech on the Yiddish Language' (1912) he gives the lie to himself, for it seems as if in his loving enquiry into the idiosyncrasies of Yiddish he is paying homage to the lost dialect of his soul. His remark that Yiddish is destroyed by translation into German – *toit* would simply not be *tot* – is proof of a precise understanding of the language. In the *Letter* Kafka speaks of the trembling which swept over him as a boy when he was faced by the prospect of being summoned to read the Torah in the synagogue, and this 'trembling' remains, transformed in his work into trepidation before the power of the purely formalistic principle which, as soon as God is no longer felt to be the centre of the universe, becomes unbounded, indeterminable and Moloch-like. Transcendence becomes secular, immanent religiosity: Kafka (says Max Brod) believes in 'rightness'; as Walter Muschg writes, he becomes the 'mystic of a remote God'; to do justice to higher claims, he has to flee the daily routine of religious practice and stifling Jewish family traditions: 'A belief like the blade of a guillotine [Kafka writes, *c*. 1917], as heavy, as light.'

There are other reasons for Kafka's sense of alienation in the German world. As a Jew he is unable to identify with any typical form of German national existence – neither with the faithful members of the national students' league (with the typical duelling scars in their Teutonic faces) nor with the law-abiding Catholic supporters of the Habsburgs and their special blend of multi-national tradition. He finds it easiest to identify with the liberal-minded admirers of German culture who, as he does, attend German schools in a country with a Slav majority and who, like the two friends Kafka and Brod, wear the black-red-golden ribbon, bearing the date 1848, as members of the German students' reading-room and lecture-hall (in Prague) and perhaps undertake a pilgrimage to Weimar to 'Goethe's light' (as Kafka and Brod do together in 1912). Militant Czech nationalists, allowing no distinction between Jew and German, were openly hostile towards both groups. With deep sadness, Kafka tells Gustav

Janouch of the fate of the Jewish poet Oskar Baum, who was only a boy when he lost his sight 'as a German' in a scuffle between German and Czech primary-school children. Kafka (Janouch writes) sees Baum as a 'tragic symbol of the so-called German Jews in Prague'. But, on the other hand, it is from Prague German that the remorseless concision of Kafka's language evolves. The language philosopher Fritz Mauthner, like Kafka a German Jew (though from another part of Bohemia), laments that Prague German, ostensibly so pure, is not founded in a dialect and that consequently it remains insubstantial and lifeless: in a word, Mauthner asserts that if one has no dialect one has no mother tongue. Of course, in Kafka's work, there is no question of dialect as a prime source of popular 'coarse scenes',· nor could there conceivably be, but perhaps his language acquires its specific succinctness precisely because it lacks the liberalizing ambiguity of dialect. Kafka's German constructions seem to stand on austere Doric columns, like an ancient basilica in which the far-echoing sentences have become completely immovable.

He is separated from the Czech world not only by language, but also by the fact that Czech intellectuals take their leads from current French artistic and literary trends, in deliberate antagonism to all things German, ranging from Cubism to the Symbolists, from Baudelaire and Rimbaud to Apollinaire. Kafka however reads only the realist Flaubert. Looking for affinities, we might find them not among Czech intellectuals but among the ordinary people, represented by the Good Soldier Švejk. Day after day, on his daily round in his own royal city, Švejk confronts the proud 'Prague' Germans, meeting them always in the inferior role of servant, tailor, shoemaker, maid or cook, yet his social and national tragedy is not even a topic of German intellectual conversation. Little Odradek can again serve as an example in Kafka's work: at first his Slav name provokes laughter – any other common Czech family name would do the trick as well. But Max Brod takes the interpretation further: '. . . a whole range of Slavonic words is set ringing, which mean "renegade", renegade from one's race, renegade from the council, from the divine decree of creation.' He also believes that the elfin creature Odradek, of no fixed abode, restlessly wandering up and down stairs, might perhaps be a symbol of the hapless, eternally wandering Jewish people, a kind of Ahasuerus metaphor. Then both lines, Jewish and Czech, would have converged in the caricatured object. . . .

Kafka, like every Austrian civil servant, has the paradigm of the bureaucratic world before his eyes every day in the shape of Emperor Franz Joseph (called 'Old Procházka' by Czech wits).* Unremitting

* i.e. the Old Promenader, a nickname Franz Joseph acquired from his habit of taking solitary walks at all times of day or night. [Ed.]

devotion to duty sends him to his desk at 6 am while his imagination is kept hidden, like a painstakingly folded handkerchief beneath the hard, horsehair pillow of his most uncomfortable iron camp-bed. Kafka looks with ever-growing impatience for escape from this narrow-minded little world, and so he and Brod apply for a sort of bureaucratic sinecure with 'part-time attendance' (until 2 pm). Kafka finds even that an insufferable burden: he lacks the patient resignation of such reluctant civil servants as Stifter and Grillparzer some decades before him; he toys with thoughts of suicide when his family demands that he should supervise the 'factory' in the afternoon. But the language of the bureaucratic world he repudiates becomes a medium for his art. Knowledge of bureaucratic language and of the almost scientifically precise description of human fates and tragedies, to the exclusion of any manifestation of sympathy, as in the notoriously dry language of the Austrian Civil Code and the bureaucratic magistrates' pronouncements of verdicts, permeates Kafka's work, with the result that an apparently passionless language distends the mythological dimensions of routine office paraphernalia, like typewriters, telephones and telephone directories, into something utterly monstrous and anxiety-creating.

The final, the most demanding test, in coming to terms with this world, is provided by the world of Kafka's family and the world of women. Again and again he desperately tries to survive before their claims, and yet his very nature and his mission as the prophet of an earthly paradise of justice and 'rightness', designed according to absolute standards of other-worldly dimensions, mean that he is bound to fail. In the *Letter* he is not really settling his account with Kafka senior, but with a monotheistic God whose visible and powerful figure is not consistent with the claim of absolute love, absolute belief and absolute moral conviction. The letter never reaches the addressee, the efficient wholesale haberdasher, Hermann Kafka, and that is fortunate, because the Procrustean bed of the Job-like son's claim to absoluteness is so huge that the standard figure of the citizen Hermann Kafka – successful and highly respected by all – could not be found on it without a magnifying glass. The same is true of the women whom Kafka uses to demarcate for him the this-worldly end of the paradisical rainbow of absolute, other-worldly perfection. But while confirming in continually renewed bids for mutual simple happiness that all women are also wondrous prophets of the here and now, he at the same time demonstrates with irrefutable logic to himself and to the loved one the impossibility of achieving that happiness. In this respect Brod points to the common ground between Kafka and Kleist: both seek recognition within the framework of 'wholesome', conventional family life, but Kleist has the 'bad habit' of writing poetry instead of official documents, while Kafka goes even further: he forces bureaucratic language into the framework of his existential allegories and parables. What is more, Kafka raises (or degrades) all women who have to bear his self-justifications until they become participants in a kind of theological debate about the impossibility of measuring earthly relationships – and what is more earthly than marriage and family? – in terms of transcendental standards. Kafka, as merciless a theologian of the absolute as Kierkegaard, who also lacks humility when confronted by the flawed nature of everything earthly, knows this – the entry in his diary for 21 August 1913 reads, '... got Kierkegaard's *Book of the Judge* today ... at least he is on the same side of the world as I am. He bears me out like a friend.'

'He was neither a German nor a Jew, neither a Czech nor an Austrian (and precisely by virtue of everything which he was not, a typical subject of the House of Habsburg),' Heinz Politzer says. But all the worlds to which he was able to belong and those to which he would have liked to belong – like the world of a family, as husband and father – he destroyed masochistically, scraping away at their foundations with a kind of mysterious logic, until they crumbled into dust and then, as humus, helped to sustain that searing power which has brought his books world-wide renown as accounts of the quest for God.

Kafka's account, in defiance of those worlds of which we already have a description, always goes beyond them: only patient 'clarifying' and 'learning', in the venerable sense of the old students of the Talmud, will perhaps bring us a step nearer. The following will illustrate the point:

Out of a house in the Jakobsgasse, where we had arrived in the course of our discussion, ran a small dog looking like a ball of wool: it crossed our path and disappeared round the corner of the Tempelgasse. 'A pretty little dog,' I said. 'A dog?' Kafka asked suspiciously and slowly moved off again. 'A small, young dog. Didn't you see it?' 'I saw. But was it a dog?' 'It was a little poodle.' 'A poodle! It could be a dog, but it could also be a sign. We Jews sometimes make tragic mistakes.' 'It was only a dog,' I said. 'It would be a good thing if it were,' Kafka nodded, 'but the "only" is true for him who uses it, and for no one else. What one person takes to be a bundle of rags or a dog may, to another person, be a sign.' 'Odradek in your story "The Cares of the Father",' I remarked. But Kafka did not respond to my words and continued his train of thought with the final sentence: 'There is always something left unaccounted for.'*

Indeed, with Kafka, too, there is always something left unaccounted for.

* Gustav Janouch, *Conversations with Kafka*, trsl. Goronwy Rees, 2nd (enlarged) ed., London 1968, p. 116 [Ed.]

23

A Path in Autumn

Idris Parry

Has there ever been so convoluted a mind revealed in utterance? Kafka believed his situation was unique. Nobody else, he thought, could be so tormented by fear, the 'secret raven' he talks about in his diary. Does he exaggerate? 'I am given to exaggeration,' he writes to Milena Jesenská, 'but all the same I can be trusted.'

Art itself has been called opportune exaggeration, and what Kafka says to Milena could be taken as a note about his work as well as about his inclination. His work is this inclination expressed. He implies (and his work assumes) that the extraordinary can be trusted to have a foundation in truth.

The interplay of life in Kafka's fiction is absurd. Details on the page are precise but ridiculous. In our life, who wakes up to find he has been transformed into an insect? Where do fine horses squeeze out of miserable pigsties? Has anyone heard animals talk? Such things happen in folk-tales, not in life. In spite of absurdities, folk-tales persist in the memory. We know beyond reason that their absurdities can be trusted. We accept them as statements of a truth which subdued naturalism fails to comprehend. This is art as connection not yet visible to man.

Kafka writes folk-tales about fear. For him they are not folk-tales but personal anecdotes in various disguises. Another letter to Milena tells how his writing radiates from himself: 'I am always trying to convey something that can't be conveyed, to explain something which is inexplicable, to tell about something I have in my bones, something which can be experienced only in these bones.' Only in these bones? The recognition of readers establishes the private characteristic as generally meaningful, but Kafka is right. He is unique. There are no generalizations in life or in art, only the special event sensed to have significance.

Where is the impulse to communicate if the writer does not think his case unique? All else is repetition. Kafka sets himself a task he believes humanly impossible – the communication of the incommunicable, the utterance of the resolutely private. It is not surprising that he can refer to his writing as a form of prayer or 'a kind of closing one's eyes'. He told a friend the pen is not an instrument but an organ of the writer's. This is art as organic extension, personal growth into the unknown. The future is always unknown growth from the familiar.

Kafka often rewrites familiar legends. He acknowledges in this way the relevance of ancient insight to his problems. He acknowledges too the attraction of legendary form, the message as coded transfer, cryptic utterance. He has no faith in similes and runs metaphors into metamorphosis. The man in his story who feels like an insect is not insect-like, he is an insect, another object. Works of art are always radiations from a central intelligence, and to decode pictures made of words it is helpful to follow connections to the centre from which transformation proceeds.

Everything Kafka says can be taken down and used in evidence. He thinks it must always be evidence against him. He finds himself guilty almost before he starts. This view of Kafka from Kafka is fancifully projected in the fiction and made transparently clear in his letters. And of all his correspondents, Milena Jesenská is the one to whom he speaks without reserve. 'To you,' he says, ' I can tell the truth, for your sake as well as mine, as to nobody else. Yes, it's possible to find one's own truth directly from you.'

This intense relationship* seems to have been an attraction of opposites. Milena was further from Kafka in external circumstances than any other woman in his life. She was twelve years younger – he, at thirty-eight, thought she belonged to a different generation. She was already married, though the marriage was breaking up. She was not Jewish, and she seems to have been an extrovert. Her home was in Vienna, so she was inaccessible to the man from Prague, except through complicated and baffling arrangements. There were no simple arrangements in Kafka's life. 'Today I saw a map of Vienna. For a moment I couldn't understand why they built such a great city when after all you need only one room.'

We have the contradiction of an intimate relationship which consists largely, on his side, of painful analysis of the obstacles between them. For him any surface, even the surface of love, can generate its black swarm of disturbing possibilities. This is how life seems to him. Now obstacles grow from the ground wherever he looks – his Jewishness, passport difficulties,

* For further details see above, pp. 25–7. [Ed]

trains, lack of sleep, her husband, his own office obligations, his state of health, his sister's wedding. Disaster surrounds him like a design for living. It is the design found in his fiction. It reflects a view of life as a proliferation of obstacles which split off into more obstacles, bewildering the brain by their multiplicity and movement. His fears become almost laughable when he tells Milena he is afraid of lifting his tumbler of milk to his lips 'because it could easily explode in my face, not by chance but by design, and throw the splinters into my face'.

His letters (hers have been lost) show their relationship growing into passionate and, for him, tormented love. Who else could suffer the hostility of happiness? It could burst in his face and really consist of the fragments into which he analyses it. He reviles himself for his inadequacy, for his fears, for his corrupting influence on a life as natural and open as hers. There could scarcely be a better illustration of the catastrophe of consciousness. This happiness is too terrifying. 'Love is to me that you are the knife which I turn within myself.'

In his diary at the time he describes his own life as a hesitation before birth: 'Not yet born and already compelled to walk the streets and talk to people.' He exaggerates, as usual. It is his method. Feeling is given form. This is his way of saying life appears to be a succession of loose ends, always provisional, a hesitant progression, seemingly without connection or conclusion. Is it chance or design? He must believe in design behind the apparently accidental, or he would not assume birth beyond hesitation. He is not yet complete, not yet born. His correspondent is perhaps one who can complete him. He can address her as 'Mother Milena'. He speaks of 'your life-giving power'. She becomes for him a kind of earth-mother who can smooth into oblivion the hesitations of consciousness. 'I am tired,' he writes, 'conscious of nothing, want only to lay my face in your lap, feel your hand on my head and stay like that through all eternity.'

They met in Vienna for four days. This was the longest time they spent together. Later, Milena told a friend that Kafka forgot his fears. 'There was no need for the slightest effort,' she said, 'everything was simple and straightforward. . . .' Under her influence he could laugh at his fears. His nervousness disappeared.

But fear is not so easily lost, especially fear found in the bones. Did he really want to lose the fear which was the support of his life? His writing is an effort to find meaning in the central fact of his existence. This central fact, communicated by his consciousness, is inexplicable fear. It is the response of this organism to life. 'My life consists of this subterranean threat,' he writes to her. 'If it stops, I'll stop too. It's my way of taking part in life. If it stops, I'll give up living as easily and naturally as a dying man closes his eyes.'

The poet Rilke once explained his objection to psychoanalysis: if it rid him of his devils it could expel his angels too. Devils and angels are brothers under the human skin, computed by contrast. For Kafka the devils of fear are constant companions but his only access to the angels, as he will tell Milena.

After Vienna, alone in his room with the paper on which he writes, he abandons himself again to fear. He confesses that the possibility of living with her does not exist. Those happy days become in retrospect merely a time when 'I looked over my fence. . . . I held myself up by my hands, then I fell back again. . . .' To Kafka the torment of love was that, like practically everything else, it created an indefinite fear which threatened the bounds of his strength. It is as if relationships, to objects as well as people, are visible to him only in the hieroglyphs of fear. 'I am independent of you,' he writes to Milena, 'because the dependency goes beyond all bounds.'

When life comes to him only as emanations of fear, it is important that this fear should be accurately observed. It is the material for his work and hope. The relationship with Milena becomes especially significant because he finds that with her he can stand back and observe this fear, the basis of his existence, as it radiates from the intricacies of his life: 'You forget, Milena, that we are standing side by side, watching this creature on the ground which is me.'

Many entries in Kafka's diaries for 1921 and 1922 refer to Milena and suggest her intimate importance. At this time also, in 1922, he wrote *The Castle*; several elements of that novel – places, people, situations – can be traced to the circumstances of Milena's life and of his connection with her. In October 1921 he gave her all his diaries and never asked for them back – an almost unbelievable act of trust for such a private person. But this act was a logical consequence: in the diaries he reveals his introspective self; in the letters to Milena he exposes his fears (and therefore himself) as to no other correspondent.

He had already given her other manuscripts. One was the long *Letter* written to his father in 1919. In this essay/confession he tries to justify himself before the awful and crushing authority represented by his father, who towers over him like a combination of jealous God and ultimate court of appeal. 'My writing was all about you,' says Kafka, exaggerating as usual, but exaggerating along the lines of truth, because he is talking about fear. He could not give this letter to his father, but he could give it to Milena.

Nothing was to be hidden from her. His intention seemed so interlocked with her understanding that there was nothing to conceal, everything to discover. 'I can't listen simultaneously to the frightful voices from within

and to you,' he tells her, 'but I can listen to those and impart them to you
... to you as to nobody else in the world.'

He does seem to find his own truth from her. Not that it helps him
much. He is still a creature writhing on the ground, exposed in his pain
like a modern Prometheus. Only this time the gods are within; they are his
subjective observation. The legend of Prometheus is one Kafka rewrote for
his own satisfaction. His own conclusion is that 'legend tries to explain the
inexplicable. Since it comes from a foundation of truth, it must end in the
inexplicable.'

Where is the hope, if truth must end as it begins, in the inexplicable? Or
is this really the nature of hope? Writing is a positive and optimistic act. In
the letter about listening to the frightful voices from within, Kafka reveals
(discovers?) an irrational conviction that the fears themselves form a path
to truth. Either that, or he has no access to truth. The fears are his only
material. If there is hope, it is here, in its apparent opposite. His fear, he
tells her, is 'fear extended to everything, fear of the greatest as well as the
smallest, fear, convulsive fear of pronouncing a word'.

Writing as prayer and writing as organic extension imply faith in a
future which is both imagined and already a biological fact deduced from
the familiar. This future is not necessarily a concept in time, it is a
confession of limited perception now. The future is discovery postponed
from a fragmentary present. Optimism, the positive act of the writer, is a
declaration that the fragments do constitute a whole, even if the
connections cannot be seen yet.

'It is true,' this letter to Milena continues, 'that this fear is perhaps not
only fear but also a longing for something which is more than all the things
which produce fear.' His life is fear, but is it possible that fear is simply a
wrong interpretation of events? Kafka's work shows life in two aspects. In
one, the experienced surface seems fragmentary, disconnected and
therefore inexplicable, a source of fear. In the other, there is dream-like
acceptance of harmony beyond intellectual perception. The writings are
charged with essential fear, but also with essential hope – both together, as
they exist together in the man. He is always talking about himself. He once
told Felice Bauer, the girl to whom he was twice engaged, that she had no
cause to be jealous of the novel on which he was then working (the book
later to be called *America*). 'The novel is me,' he said to her, 'I am my
stories.'

This individual is not protected by the skin of habit and selective
awareness. He cannot lie. The books, the letters, are shaped by his
honesty. Here everything is found directly, and all quotations lead to
Kafka. Each sentence in the letters to Milena uncovers him, and one
phrase in particular, given in parentheses, seemingly an afterthought,

suddenly illuminates his work. For this writer the peripheral is also central, in a way which makes the two terms meaningless as opposites. In a complete design every component is integral. 'Sometimes,' he writes to Milena, 'I think I understand the Fall of Man better than anybody else.'

What he is telling her is that he is abnormally sensitive to the damage caused by self-consciousness. The third chapter of the Book of Genesis tells how Adam and Eve eat fruit from the Tree of Knowledge and are suddenly aware of themselves in their surroundings. This awareness is the real expulsion from Paradise. More than a hundred years before Kafka, Heinrich von Kleist implied in his essay 'On the Marionette Theatre' that the central issue of man's existence is the way self-consciousness disturbs natural response. The marionette is matter inert in space. It is integrated in the flow of its surroundings; it is therefore graceful. It does not assert itself. Man does assert himself, and this self is a creature of limited perception and so of limited knowledge. He observes, he makes categories, he impedes through definition – standing outside, he lacks grace. From the darkness of harmony man moves to the faint light of knowledge and the fractures of definable experience. This is the Fall Kafka understands so well.

But he understands it as a present situation, our condition of self-consciousness, not as an event which took place on a particular day in the remote past, when man's nature suddenly switched from insight to introspection, and integration fell to pieces. 'It is only our concept of time,' he says, 'which leads us to call the Last Judgment by that name. In fact, it's a court in standing session.' He might also have said (but did not) that it is only our concept of time which makes us think of the expulsion from Paradise as a kind of 'first judgment'. It is another court in standing session. His heroes face it every day, waking up in the morning to find they have been arrested without knowing they have done anything wrong. It is a legendary image of a perpetual human condition, now experienced by a particular individual in Prague and projected in his literary works.

Also, it is only our concept of time which makes us think of the components of the story of Eden as separate events. It is another example of our limited perception. Kafka once told a friend there are no accidents in the world but only in our way of thinking. 'Accident' is the word we use to describe an event whose cause we cannot trace. But the cause is there, even if we cannot see it. There is no world without causation, so the idea of accident merely reflects the limits of our knowledge. In the story of Eden we have divided the world of total connection into a concept of harmony and a concept of disintegration, the second being our present state of awareness, the first our sense of completion beyond our present fragmentation.

These exist together in our perception (where else can they be?). The idea of harmony can only be a projection from what we know. The duality of divine and devilish or Apollo and Dionysus is a duality only in the mind. These are two aspects of the same world. The material of harmony exists in the fragments which produce fear.

Kafka makes several references to the Fall, and consequently to his ideas on the nature of sin, in his *Reflections*, a series of aphorisms collected by himself in his notebooks from scattered sources and so (one may believe) held by him to be of special importance. His opinion here is that impatience is the chief sin: 'It was because of impatience they were expelled from Paradise, it is because of impatience they do not return there.' What he means by impatience is seen from another entry: 'All human errors are impatience, a premature breaking-off of the methodical, an apparent fencing-in of the apparent issue.' The methodical must be the continuous process of life, stepping from one organic connection to another. It is the pattern of causation which man breaks for the convenience of classification by thought. Experience is reduced to the limits of human perception, phenomena are segments fenced-in from the flow.

These segments are however our experience and our only approach. 'Accept your symptoms,' says Kafka in his diary, 'don't complain of them. Immerse yourself in your suffering.' This is characteristic of so many statements in his work which are puzzling until we realize they are, as always, a kind of legendary or pictorial form given to intimate conviction. Here he reveals his belief that the path to truth can be discovered only in the thicket of bewildering experience – of his fear which is 'more than all the things which produce fear'. Goethe knew at eighteen that hell and heaven are not separate places but a dual perception of the same world. Kafka writes to Milena, 'Nobody sings as purely as those in deepest hell. What we take for the song of angels is their song.'

Inexplicable forces must be accepted as inevitable. The apparently hostile must be turned to good account. 'Mount your attacker's horse,' says Kafka (to himself) in his diary, 'and ride it yourself. But what strength and skill this demands! And how late it is already.' Perhaps the most pathetic and inspiring of these associated comments on his need for faith is: 'Somewhere help is waiting, and the beaters are driving me there.' The beaters are his troubled experience of life, life which must be endured in every trifling detail. There is no detail which is unimportant. 'One must write into the dark,' he says, 'as if into a tunnel.'

Writing into the dark is like a return to the moment before their eyes were opened and they knew they were naked. (There is no way of writing about insight except in terms of time and successive events.) Kafka is talking about the capture of unconscious grace. 'Resign yourself,' is his advice in the diaries, 'learn . . . to rest content in the moment. Yes, in the moment, the terrible moment. It is not terrible; only your fear of the future makes it terrible.'

One striking characteristic of Kafka's fiction is the way absurdity is never regarded as accidental. When Gregor Samsa finds, at the beginning of 'The Metamorphosis', that he has become a gigantic insect, he and his family accept the situation. Of course they make a fuss, but only because his uselessness as a man is now even more apparent. Nobody gets up and says it is impossible for a man to become an insect. Nothing is impossible in the world of Franz Kafka. That world has its own rules. The first rule and the last is that the inexplicable rests on a foundation of truth.

This truth is accepted by insight. Out of the dark come absurd figures beyond human explanation. In the dark too, because again beyond human explanation, is the connection which makes an organic link with us, if we let it. Because we cannot see the causality this connection seems magical – or absurd (it depends on the point of view).

Writing into the dark is a conjuration of spirits. 'It is entirely conceivable,' Kafka writes in his diary, 'that life's splendour forever lies in wait about each one of us in all its fullness, but veiled from view, deep down, invisible, far off. It *is* there though, not hostile, not reluctant, not deaf. If you summon it by the right word, by the right name, it will come. This is the essence of magic, which does not create but summons.'

The truth is already there. Nobody makes it. It is waiting to be found along the lines of causation, beyond the accidental limits of individual perception. When Kafka describes his writing as 'an assault on the frontier' he is talking about the frontier of perception. His conjuration of spirits is an effort to follow causation across that frontier into the dark, beyond the restricted language and methods of rationality.

Patience follows from the conviction that life is greater and better than the intellect allows. But impatience is the normal human characteristic – or the story of the Fall would not exist. Kafka's fiction represents life by showing impatience and patience as a running pair, to reflect the dual aspect of experience as he finds it.

So the interminable analysis which constitutes his narrative method can include its apparent opposite, quiet acceptance. The seeming contradiction of questioning and acquiescence found in his work has its origin in the man who believes he is uniquely battered by the puzzles, perplexities, horrors and injustices of life, but can also speak of glory and claim that 'he who does not seek will be found'.

Only our concept of time makes us think there can be a graspable conclusion. 'No living thing can be calculated,' says Kafka in the astonishing *Letter* to his father. Calculation means definition and arrest. The truth that emerges from his letters to Milena is universal. He finds it difficult to utter, but his life depends on this utterance. 'There is only one truth,' he tells her, 'but it is alive and therefore has a vividly changing face.'

Sir Charles Sherrington described life as a running stream of energy. The ancients cast the same truth about effort and continuous change into the shape of Sisyphus. Kafka rewrites the legend in his usual pictorial way in one sentence from the *Reflections*: 'Like a path in autumn; scarcely has it been swept clear when it is once more covered with dry leaves.'

Milena Jesenská died in the Nazi concentration camp at Ravensbrück on 17 May 1944.

24

The Matljary Diary

J.P. Stern

In the High Tatra Mountains above M., 28.x.1944. Anniversary of the Founding of the Republic. The fifth under German occupation, and we pray it may be the last. We'd been promised reinforcements today, waited all day, at last they came. What a crew – worse than useless. As far as I can tell they are Prague coffee-house Jews, the lot of them. They all speak Czech – *of sorts* (!). It does seem to have taken them a long time to discover their patriotic vein ... Heavens, what specimens! You only have to look at them to see they don't know one end of a rifle from the other – a game of chess or rummy seems to be the only kind of exercise they're used to. Still, now they've come to join us, we must make some use of them. Better late than never, I suppose.

29.x. They all turn out to be university graduates, of course, except the one who was chef at the Hotel Paříž. We put him in charge of the cookhouse straightaway, and I must say you certainly can tell the difference. What are we going to do with the rest, I wonder. Most of them are lawyers – what else! – but there is a real doctor among them, too, and he'll come in handy soon; we've been without an M/D so far. Among the lawyers there is one, Dr F. K., they all seem to look up to – very quiet, though.

30.x. As I expected, the language question is proving troublesome and is aggravating our relations with the new lot that arrived two days ago. It's bad enough their talking nothing but German among themselves – they also organize reading groups and read German poems and stories to each other, and our chaps are furious. You can hardly blame them – after all, we're here to *fight* the Germans, not to fill our minds with their nebulous Teutonic poetry! I had to say something to Dr K. about it, simply because he seems to be the most sensible one among them – also he seems to be fairly old, though he doesn't *look* old at all – and he said he well understood why we were angry and he hoped we would bear with them. He then added that some people could not live without literature – people who hadn't much else in life, so to speak – and he thought that as long as these reading sessions didn't interfere with people's ordinary duties, we should let it pass. Fair enough, I suppose.

Somebody said Dr K. isn't really a lawyer at all but an author. *In German*, of course.

31.x. This rumour about Dr K. being an author turns out to be a lot of nonsense, as I expected. I asked him point blank and he admitted that he has hardly published anything. How can you call yourself a writer if all you've done is a few stories about animals and that sort of thing. (We read some La Fontaine at school, the year before the Germans closed all our secondary schools, but that was *in verse*.) In fact he worked in an industrial insurance office – bilking the workers of their rightful insurance money, I don't doubt. Still – he doesn't *look* like a capitalist hyena to me. As a matter of fact everybody seems to like him – I mean our chaps too – and since he is not very strong, everybody offers to help him, with the lugging of provisions etc. (They're none of them very strong, this 'Anniversary Crew', as we call them, worse luck! You don't grow muscles by moving pawns across the chess-board . . .)

I've noticed he doesn't even keep a diary, though he seems interested in the fact that I do.

1.xi.1944. There is no doubt that Dr K. is proving a useful addition to the camp. It turns out that he knows the region well – seems to have spent several months in hospital in Matljary; and even though it's *years* ago (well before I was born, I believe), he seems to remember the region quite accurately. Of course we have our Slovak liaison men who come over from the next camp and know the mountains like the back of their hand, but they're not always around. Besides, Slovaks are a bit funny, as we know to our cost – look at what happened in '38 and '39, when they left the sinking ship and set up a state of their own, with Hitler's blessing. And whatever you may think of this new lot – though they're not exactly a heroic breed, *they* won't go over to the Germans, that's for sure! Poor devils, most of their relations are in German camps anyway.

2.xi. Shared the late watch with F. K. I asked him how he came to join us. At first it sounded like the usual story. Says he was in his lodgings in

Prague one morning, still in bed, when a couple of uniformed men came into his room to arrest him. Sicherheitsdienst, I imagine, he couldn't remember their insignia (typical!), only that their uniforms were black and had pockets everywhere. He says he asked them their names (!), as if that was likely to cut any ice with the SD, and told them that they had no right to be in his lodgings, and that he had done nothing wrong, nothing that could give them the right to arrest him. He seemed at first to think it was all a joke – one of the men looked familiar, like one of the porters from his insurance office. It was a most peculiar story – I asked him whether he had forgotten about the German occupation. He said no, he remembered it all right, but that it took him some time before he realized that they really had come to take him away. Apparently he thought it had all happened before, though the way he said it I couldn't make out whether in reality or merely in his imagination. (He does seem to be a writer after all, lots of imagination and a bit slow on the uptake, I suspect.)

3.xi. First lot of snow. We spent the day improving the bivouac, sawing and piling up firewood. The sun came out at about noon and I got everybody out of their tents to do some exercises. I wonder how we're going to survive when the real winter weather comes, with this new lot to look after!

4.xi. F. K. told me that once he realized these two men had come to arrest him, he made up his mind to try to get away. 'Not like the last time,' he said (?). He quite simply pretended he had to go into the next room to get dressed and somehow managed to slip out of the house by the back stairs – a miracle he got away with it. After that he made his way into the Slovak mountains with the help of our underground network, the usual story.

'Not like the last time.' I couldn't make out what he meant by that, and so I asked him. It seems he was referring to a story he had written years before, which also began with a man being arrested. But in the story the man more or less accepted his fate, and although he was left at liberty, he actually started looking for the court of law that would be prepared to try him. Like a mouse looking for the cat that will eat it up! It sounded a most peculiar story, and I told Dr K. so. After all, he himself had said the man was innocent, that somebody had been spreading lies about him. I got a bit worked up about this – it seemed like a complete non sequitur – I had actually forgotten that what we were talking about was only a story. What could be more absurd, when you think of it, than arguing about a piece of fiction that wasn't even *published*, for God's sake. In *our* situation, with the German line in the Ukraine collapsing, and the Germans retreating westward and likely to run into us any day.

Yet I can't help feeling that this peculiar story *is* connected with our situation. And so, when he said, 'You're quite right, it was only a story, and not a very clear one at that' – I didn't want to hurt him and so didn't rub it in that the thing hadn't ever appeared in print – when he said *that*, I felt that I had somehow missed the point, and that he had really meant to say something quite different.

Then I remembered his saying that some people just couldn't live without literature – people who hadn't much else in life, I suppose – and I said I could see how important it was to him, even though it was only a story he had written ages ago. He smiled – I don't want to sound soppy over this, but he has a beautiful smile, gentle and intelligent and not a bit superior.

'Perhaps the only kind of fiction that should be written is the kind that life catches up with, don't you think?' he said. I replied that I hadn't given much thought to such things (which wasn't quite true), and that all I could think about right now was getting a chance to fight the Germans. But obviously, as far as that story of his was concerned life had not just caught up with it but had proved that the story was all *wrong*: the man should surely have resisted his arrest (not just asked those two SD thugs for their papers), he should not have let them mess him about endlessly but told them where they got off, instead of hanging about and even looking for a court that would be prepared to try him etc.

'Perhaps that's why I never published that story,' he replied – but again I had the feeling that somehow I had missed the point.

As I write this, it occurs to me that this story of the man's arrest wasn't really any *more* peculiar than Dr K.'s own arrest, or the reason why we're all here, too.

5.xi. The weather has improved. Surprise, surprise – most of our 'Anniversary Crew' turn out to be total civilians – somehow or other they managed to avoid conscription during the Republic and the only time they've ever seen a rifle being fired was in the fairground! God's mercy on us all, what *are* we going to do with them?

6.xi. I talked to F. K. about that queer story again, trying to get him to say why the man was being harassed, what he had done etc., making what I thought was a very obvious point: 'The truth is that a man cannot be guilty simply because he is what he is.'

'As you say, that is the truth. Unfortunately some stories get written by authors who just don't see the shortest way to the truth.' There was a note of irony in his voice, but I felt I would not give in.

'No, no – only a god can condemn a man for what he is. A god, or the Germans.'

He did give me a look of surprise then – I've noticed he seems to be surprised at the most obvious things people say.

7.xi. I'm doing rifle drill with them, but not firing practice. We have no ammunition to spare, and besides, we don't want to announce our presence prematurely! We are waiting for the Russian break-through, that's the time for letting the Germans know we're here.

So I spent most of the day explaining how to strip our good old Czech Bren gun, clear stoppages, assemble ammo. belts and feed them into the m.g., etc. I watched Dr K. It really is ridiculous – he has an extraordinary admiration for anyone who can strip the gun efficiently (seems to think it's a miracle to be able to do it under a minute, the Sergeant-Major does it in 45 seconds flat!) – yet he himself is not in the least clumsy, though you can see from the careful way he picks up the parts that he is not used to handling machinery of any kind.

I said something like that to him, and he grinned with pleasure. 'I'm sure you've never come across a less soldierly person than I am. I sometimes think all this is happening on another planet from the one I used to live on, sending occasional missives to the earth. A writer's imagination is unpredictable, especially in its weaknesses. But, you know, I have many reasons to be glad I am here, many reasons to be grateful.'

Several of the new lot are in a funk about being asked to handle the gun, full of lousy excuses – why, one of the lawyers actually said they ought to be regarded as 'non-belligerent partisans'!! I ask you. I told them in no uncertain terms that nobody asked them to join us in the first place, but since they were here they'd better jolly well do as they're told.

Dr K. has *not* asked for any special privileges. All the same, I don't think it's right for *him* to have to go through all this bull. I wonder why. I mean why I think so.

I wish I could read some of his stuff, even though it is in German. It appears that a lot of it was burned. By the Germans? Nobody seems to be sure.

Incidentally, I don't like the way he admires everybody and everything. Sometimes I think he behaves like some snivelling old jew, trying to make up to me.

8.xi. Truly, I've never had such weird conversations in all my life. Today it occurred to me that perhaps he really is a very important writer. I'm sure I can't think why I suddenly had this thought, but I felt I had to find out more about it. I tried to draw him out in various ways, like asking whether he had written a great deal more than he actually published, whether he was a perfectionist, what literary movement he admired, who were his favourite authors, and who influenced him most. In the end I got a bit embarrassed – I could see that he thought all these were pretty silly questions but was too polite to say so. Finally his very silence made me blurt it out: 'Are you a very important writer?' I asked and, as though that question wasn't weird enough, I added, 'You're really a sort of king among writers, aren't you?'

'You have said it,' he replied, and for a brief moment his smile became almost a grin. 'A secret king, though.'

9.xi. It's ten days since F. joined us, and somehow the atmosphere in the camp has changed. There is much less shouting and cursing and ordering people pointlessly about – it's as though everybody had become more gentle, more considerate.

F.'s smile is gentle, not a bit superior, yet there is something strange and chilling about it. Like a gleam from a treasure trove far away.

10.xi. Went over to the other side of the camp (some brilliant wit calls it 'our Kosher Reservation', I'm sick and tired of these 'jokes'), to listen to K. reading one of his stories. It turned out to be a grotesque tale about a singing mouse called Josephine. It did *not* remind me either of Aesop or of La Fontaine, nor indeed of anything else I've ever read.

It seemed to be mainly about the relationship between this prima donna mouse and her audience – and yet the precise nature of that relationship remained unclear. Was this mouse, Josephine, meant to need her public, the mouse nation, in order to perform her ridiculous singing act, or was it the public that was supposed to need *her* and her singing, so that they could feel as one nation and in that way stand up to any danger or threat from the enemy, whoever *that* was? One couldn't even make out whether her singing was meant to be any good! Half the time the narrator (?!) was saying that it was much the same sort of whistling noise that any mouse can produce, and perhaps not even as good as that, yet the other half he was saying that it was quite unique and something very special.

Anyhow, why on earth write about a *mouse*, when all he's *really* doing is writing about himself, his own writing?! As if *that* was something so very special . . . But perhaps it is?

Incidentally, I noticed quite a few of our chaps among the audience, they seemed to have come over for the reading. I was glad about that – I must confess I did feel a bit embarrassed to be there on my own.

It was quite dark when he started, the air was thick with smoke. I thought once or twice he found it hard to breathe.

Later. Embarrassed about my embarrassment, really.

11.xi. Told the Sergeant-Major that there are plenty of jobs for Dr K. to do without his having to mess about with Bren guns and getting his fingers filthy and septic. To my surprise the S/M instantly agreed. Dr K., on the other hand, said he wouldn't have it. He said he disapproved of 'Josephine' (!), with her constant petitions for recognition and for exemption from the ordinary chores of the mouse folk – it was part of her ridiculousness. (I hadn't told him I thought she was ridiculous.) He said he really wanted to be treated like everybody else and to go through with everything the others have to do. I was very glad he reacted in this way, but didn't tell him so. On coming back to my tent in the evening I found an envelope with a note from him:

> You think practical work is too coarse for me – that I am in some sense too good for it and should leave it to others. I too used to think this – used to think that not being very good at practical things was really a proof that I was good at my writing, at expressing my admiration of those who are good at practical things. The circumstances of my life – of all our lives, and mine too – were very different then. I could only admire what I was excluded from, what was done by others. I could accept that exclusion and even rejoice in it – or rather, not rejoice in it but lament it and from that lament – or perhaps it was no more than an endless complaint – draw the substance of my writing. Describing life among other people, I was describing a life determined by other people. In that way I came to have an exaggerated expectation of what happened on the other, the practical side of the world.
>
> Things are different now, so different that I look on my own writings and on my own past life as on the life and writings of a stranger. I have never been so involved as I am here and now with you all. Perhaps this is why I can no longer describe this piece of world, except to say that I am *not* too good for it.

He seems to have an eerie capacity for answering my questions before I've had a chance to put them.

12.xi. He lent me a copy of the 'Josephine' story, but I must confess that reading it didn't make things much clearer. It seems to me that everything that is said about the mouse, about her singing and her relationship to her nation-public, is contradicted and cancelled out by its opposite, so that in the end the reader doesn't know where he stands.

'Do you mean it is as if you hadn't read the story at all?' he asked.

No, I said, it was much more confusing. After all, when La Fontaine writes about a beast or a bird, a clear message emerges – about the need for cunning or wariness, or the importance of prudence.

'The importance of prudence – my father had a very clear message about that, and about many other virtues. I think that's why I so admired him. I even admired him because he believed that all my "writing" was arrant nonsense and a waste of time. Can you think of anything funnier than my trying to convince him of the opposite? Knowing all the time that the only thing that might possibly convince him would be my publisher's account books in fifty years' time?'

I remembered his saying that some people have only literature in order to make sense of their lives, and so I asked, 'You admired him for being contemptuous of what mattered to you most?'

'I admired his assurance, and I also knew that there wasn't enough of it for both of us. Of course, I could *describe* him and his immense power, and I knew he could do anything in the world except *that*, but as to having a message – any message – for other people, how could I presume?'

'It sounds like mock modesty to me.' I was suddenly afraid of having hurt him by saying that, and I realized that the last thing I wanted to do was to hurt him.

'Perhaps it is. But not because I secretly think I have a message, but because my real purpose, which is quite different, is not at all modest: to present a piece of the world, raised on a shield. Of course, it isn't the whole world, and I can't hold it up for very long.'

'You say your purpose is not really modest, yet you hide it behind a metaphor which seems to be deliberately trivial.' And I read out to him that passage in the 'Josephine' story where he writes: 'To crack a nut is certainly not an art, therefore no one would dare to call together an audience and crack nuts in front of them by way of entertainment. But if someone nevertheless does so and succeeds in his intention, then it does cease to be a matter of mere nutcracking. Or rather, it is a matter of cracking nuts, but it becomes apparent that we have overlooked this art because it was well within our powers, and that this new cracker of nuts was the first person to show us its real nature; and it might then be even more effective if he were a little less good at cracking nuts than the majority of us.'

'Perhaps it's only by arousing the reader's irritation that metaphors come into their own. Besides, when one raises the world or a part of it on a shield, one raises it only a little distance into the air. Yet it isn't like not having raised it at all.'

'You keep on speaking about the world. Do you mean our world? Frankly, I don't recognize any of it.' This wasn't really true – he was right about his metaphors being profoundly irritating.

'Don't you really? Perhaps you're just impatient, and are looking for superficial resemblances. I only describe what I see.'

'But why this game of hide-and-seek?'

'You must ask a higher authority. I only describe what I see.'

It sounded like a brush-off.

13.xi. Most of our supplies are stored in a fairly roomy cave in the rocks at the eastern end of the camp, and the C/O has given strict orders that nobody is allowed there except on duty. As F. K.'s hoarseness, or whatever it is, has been getting worse, I asked the Adjutant whether we couldn't rig up a bed for him in there, quite close to the entrance, so he'd have some protection from the weather (which is no better than what you'd expect in the High Tatra at this time of the year). To my surprise the A. said he'd already got the S/M to organize some extra blankets and a proper camp-bed. Of course K. refused, and had to be *ordered* to kip down there. 'It'll be even more confusing than out here, among you,' he said.

14.xi. Another note from F. K.: 'You are sure to have noticed how hopeless I am at talking to people – I think my bad throat must be a confirmation of my incompetence. Yet writing letters is even worse: the misunderstandings and mistakes which fill my life were all carefully prepared in the letters I have written. But I do like writing letters which aren't real letters but only envelopes for stories, like this one:

The three stages. There was a writer who was least unhappy, or so he thought, when he lived alone. And although he took little notice of the world, he discovered that in what he wrote he could foretell the future. When he wrote of war, war came upon the country, and when he wrote of pestilence, pestilence came, though not always in the form in which he had described it. He was not a stupid man, and he saw that all he was ever able to foretell were disasters, but it took him a very long time to see that. He was not a bad man, and he also saw how eager people were to make all that he foretold come true, but that too took him a long time to see. And when he wrote that the material world was real enough, but that it was only the evil in the spiritual world, his mind was divided between being pleased that what he had written turned out to be so splendidly true, and being frightened. Seeing at last how things were, he couldn't make up his mind whether to continue writing, which was all he knew, or to give it up, which seemed like giving up his life; and this hesitation made him very unhappy. This was the first stage of his life.

Then came the war and the pestilence he foretold, and he found that, whether he liked it or not, he could no longer live on his own. But as soon as he came to live with other people, partly in order to help them in the war he foretold, but largely because he needed them for his own protection, he found he couldn't write another word. There was peace of mind, he felt at first, in this silence, but it was a peace of mind he couldn't distinguish from emptiness. That was the second stage.

Now he realized that what he had to look for was the pure power of description, the art of writing without foreknowledge or intent. That, he thought, would be the third stage. He liked the sound of those words – the third stage. But everything in his world had always gone in pairs – good or evil, spiritual or material, here or there – and so there is not much hope that he will ever reach that third stage.'

15.xi. With every day that passes F.'s cough, his hoarseness and breathlessness are getting worse. It's no good putting him on patrol duty.

His face is permanently set in a smile of apology.

The M/D examined him at length and sounds very pessimistic.

There are signs – mainly intelligence gathered by our chaps when they last went down into M. village – that the German line to the east of us is at last beginning to break. Like some terrible ice floes, about to start their drift westward. It seems doubtful whether we can keep F. here much longer – the fighting may start any day.

16.xi. F. gave me his copy of the 'Josephine' story – for safe-keeping, he said. By chance I came across these lines – they seemed to jump out at me from the typed page:

'The threats that hang over us make us quieter and more modest, and more amenable to Josephine's imperiousness; we're glad to assemble and crowd together, especially as the cause of it is to one side of our tormenting preoccupation; it is as if, in great haste – for haste is essential, Josephine too often forgets that – we were drinking together a loving cup before battle.'

How terrifying a single sentence can be.

17.xi. The M/D went down to Matljary after dusk. Apparently he knows one of the doctors at the local hospital (this is where years ago F. spent some months as a patient). He got the doctor to promise to find a bed for F. if things get worse. The M/D has asked me to talk to him about it.

18.xi. From the pass above the camp where we keep a permanent patrol you can look down into the Matljary valley, and with field glasses you can make out the village. F. insisted on coming up with me – it's a climb of ten minutes and I thought he would never make it. He picked out the village with my glasses and then identified the hospital. I thought it was the right moment to break the M/D's verdict to him, but found my throat so dry with excitement that I couldn't say anything. As I was trying to get the words out, he said, 'Whatever happens, you must promise me not to put me into that hospital. What I saw there was much worse than an execution, yes, even than any form of torture. Surely, we ourselves haven't invented the tortures but have learned them from diseases – no man dares to torture the way they do.'

247

I didn't understand. He explained that during his time there he met a man who was dying of a throat disease. In the end the man couldn't talk at all and just wrote slips of paper with messages to the people who sat at his bedside. 'I've remembered what it said on those slips,' F. said, 'they were perfect sentences:

"I'd especially like you to take care of the peonies because they are so fragile.

And move the lilacs into the sun.

To think that once I could simply venture a large swallow of water.

Ask whether there is good mineral water, just out of curiosity.

Please see that the peonies don't touch the bottom of the vase. That's why they have to be kept in bowls.

Mineral water – once for fun I could

A little water; these bits of pills stick in the mucus like splinters of glass.

How trying I am to all of you; it's crazy.

A lake doesn't flow into anything, you know.

See the lilacs, fresher than morning.

You'll have to warn the girl about the glass; she sometimes comes in barefoot.

By now we have come a long way from the day in the tavern garden when we

But now enough flowers for the time being.

Show me the columbine; too bright to stand with the others.

Scarlet hawthorn is too hidden, too much in the dark.

More of the water. Fruit

Yesterday evening a late bee drank the lilac water dry.

Cut at a steep slant; then they can touch the floor.

Put your hand on my forehead for a moment to give me courage".'

I wondered how he came to remember these disconnected sentences and asked him whether he thought they were symbolical or had some special literary value.

'Forgive me, I embarrassed you,' he said; and, 'You didn't really mean to ask those questions.' And then, after another pause: 'But you are quite right. They are what I am looking for – pure description.'

19.xi. The first Very light signals from our neighbouring partisan battalion came early this morning, announcing German troops crossing the north-eastern mountain ridge. We were in readiness all day.

20.xi. Our first day of action. How can a single day bring victory and defeat?

At 8 am we received a signal: an isolated infantry detachment is entering the Matljary valley. It was a brilliantly sunny November day, the beech woods were ablaze with colours. We slithered down the mountain-side with our Bren gun carrier on patches of fresh snow, and found a good ambush directly above the road, only a few yards of which were visible from where we were. No sooner had we got our two guns in position than the first German soldiers appeared in the roadway below us: a fairly bedraggled lot. We waited till there was quite a sizeable crowd on our section of the road and then let go. Complete panic and decimation, no attempt to shoot back, they didn't even try to find out where the firing came from. They lost some twenty men, after our first burst of fire a number managed to hide in nearby houses. We would have liked to leave our ambush and get in among them, but as soon as movement on the road stopped, the C/O ordered us to pull out and we came away without a single loss. It was my first action, and of course I was terrified that I might fail (helping to feed in the ammunition belts) – but elated when I didn't; it was all over in a few minutes.

We were all immensely bucked; clambering back to camp, I was thinking of the words I would use to describe it to F. He had stayed behind with four others. Before leaving we had told them to mount a guard of two on the opposite side of the camp, the wooded part at the end of a steep little path that leads up from the valley to the west of us. We didn't really think there was any danger from that side.

They were all dead. How the Germans came to discover that path – how many they were, whether they got detached from the rest and lost their way – we shall never know. The guards had undoubtedly put up a fight – one could see that from the positions of the bodies, and their magazines were empty. What had happened to the others wasn't clear. F. had been shot through the forehead, slumped over the last remaining Bren gun. The Germans had taken most of our food stores, tried to set fire to the camp, but only in a half-hearted way.

They had taken the ammunition belts but left the gun in position, with F. spread-eagled over it. The barrel was clean, but it seemed that he had tried to fire it. We shall never know for certain. I think he would have wanted to fire it. Not from any hatred or warlike feeling – as he himself once said, he was the least soldierly person you can imagine. But he did, in the end, make his choice, he wanted to be involved. 'Not like last time,' he had said.

21 xi. We buried them this morning on the eastern pass, close to the spot where F. had looked down into the valley with my field glasses. One of our chaps, a carpenter, made two crosses and three stars of David from the sweet-smelling wood of the mountain pine. No names.

The C/O spoke at some length, first on the 'no difference of race or creed' line, then on 'death to the Fascists', the word 'German' was never mentioned. Every inch the professional officer.

Our friendship was so short – sometimes it seems as if it had never been. Like a gentle ghost passing in our midst. Strange: since it happened I have hardly thought about his writing – only about the man. Would he have liked that?

The Sergeant-Major talked about him on the way back from the pass. He said there was something special about him, everybody seems to have felt that. I wonder what it was. Perhaps a kind of grace, a way of making us feel that there is something special about each of us. The S/M would have understood that, but I didn't say anything.

List of Contributors

* The author's contribution is especially written for this volume.
†The author's contribution is especially translated for this volume.

*JOACHIM BEUG teaches German at the University College of Cork, has written on the Austro-Hungarian novelist Joseph Roth, and is co-editor (with Erich Heller) of an anthology of extracts from Kafka's writings on the art of writing (1969).

*ALLAN BLUNDEN Lately Fellow of Fitzwilliam College, Cambridge, has taught German at the University of Virginia and in Canada, now a free-lance translator and writer living in Cornwall.

*FRANK W. CARTER teaches geography at University College, London and has written extensively on the demography of continental cities, including Cracow, Sophia, Prague, and *Dubrovnik-Raguse – a classic city-state* (1972).

*JOYCE CRICK teaches German at University College London, has written on Thomas and Heinrich Mann.

*ROSEMARY DINNAGE is a writer of essays and a regular contributor to the *Times Literary Supplement* and the *New York Review of Books*.

*D.J.ENRIGHT is a writer, poet and professor of literature in various Far Eastern and European universities, now a publisher in London. Among his books are *Selected Poems* (1969), *Paradise Illustrated* (1978), *Figures of Speech* (1965), *The Apothecary's Shop* (1957), *Conspirators and Poets* (1966), *Memoirs of a Mendicant Professor* (1969) and, most recently, *A Faust Book* (1979).

*WOLFGANG FISCHER is an Austrian novelist and poet, and London art dealer. *Interiors* (1971) and *Lodgings in Exile* (1979) are the first two volumes of a trilogy published in an English translation.

*ROY FULLER is a poet, novelist and essayist. His novel *Image of a Society* (1956) contains among its main characters one whose remarkable affinities with Kafka have served as the basis for the present contribution. *Collected Poems* (1962), *New Poems* (1968), *Professors and Gods*: last Oxford lectures on Poetry (1973), *Poor Tom* (1977).

*ERICH HELLER is a native of Bohemia, now teaches German at Northwestern University, Evanston, Illinois; among his books are *The Disinherited Mind* (1952), *The Ironic German: a study of Thomas Mann* (1958), *The Artist's Journey into the Interior and Other Essays* (1965) and the *Kafka* volume of the Fontana: Modern Masters series (1974). Chapter VII of *The Disinherited Mind* ('The world of Franz Kafka') is one of the first important critical writings on the subject.

FRANK KERMODE teaches English at Cambridge and has written on Shakespeare, John Donne, Milton, D.H. Lawrence, T.S. Eliot, Wallace Stevens and other subjects. Among his most recent books: *The Sense of an Ending* (1967), *Continuities* (1968) and *The Classic* (1975). His contribution is reprinted from the Charles Eliot Norton lectures he gave at Harvard in 1978.

*IDRIS PARRY is Professor Emeritus of German in the University of Manchester. Has written *Animals of Silence; Essays on Art, Nature and Folktale* (1972), *Stream and Rock* (1974), and on aspects of German language and literature.

*ROY PASCAL is Professor Emeritus of German in the University of Birmingham. Author of *The Social Basis of the German Reformation* (1933), *Shakespeare in Germany, 1740–1815* (1937), *The German Sturm und Drang* (1953), *The German Novel* (1956), *Design and Truth in Autobiography* (1960), *From Naturalism to Expressionism* (1973), *Culture and the Division of Labour* (1974), *The Dual Voice* (1976).

*JERZY PETERKIEWICZ is a poet and novelist, originally Polish, who now writes in English. Among his books: *The Knotted Cord* (1953), *Future to Let* (1958), *Five Centuries of Polish Poetry* (1960, 1970), *The Other Side of Silence* (1970), *The Third Adam* (1975). *Eastern Vigil and other poems* (1979) are translations of poems by Karol Wojtyla.

PHILIP ROTH is the author of *Portnoy's Complaint* (1969) and many other best-selling novels on American Jewish themes. He has returned to the Kafka theme in *Professor of Desire* (1977).

*WALTER H. SOKEL teaches German at the University of Virginia in

Charlottesville, Virginia. His books include *The Writer in Extremis: Expressionism in Twentieth-Century German Literature* (1959), *Franz Kafka: Tragik und Ironie; zur Struktur seiner Kunst* (1964) and on the same subject in Columbia Essays on Modern Writers (1966).

*J.P.STERN is a native of Prague who now teaches German at University College, London. Has written on Ernst Jünger (1952), G.C. Lichtenberg (1959), A. Hitler (1975) and Friedrich Nietzsche (1979), and other topics.

*SHEILA STERN teaches French and German at Cambridge.

*ANTHONY THORLBY teaches comparative literature at Sussex; among his writings are *Gustave Flaubert and the art of Realism* (1956), *A Student's Guide to Kafka* (1972); he has edited *The Romantic Movement* (1966) and is co-editor of *Literature and Western Civilization* (1972–   ).

†JOHANNES URZIDIL (1896–1970) was one of the few Prague German writers who did not sympathize with the national socialist regime. Among his many books is *Goethe in Böhmen* (1962), *Da geht Kafka* (1966), *Prager Triptychon* (1960), *Die verlorene Geliebte* (i.e. Prague) and *Hollar, a Czech émigré in England* (1942). He died in New York.

†KLAUS WAGENBACH is a Berlin publisher and author of an unfinished Kafka biography, the first volume of which, *Franz Kafka: A Biography of his Youth* (i.e. up to 1912) was published in 1958.

†MARTIN WALSER is among the most prolific post-war novelists of Federal Germany; e.g. *Ehen in Philippsburg* (1957, English 1971), *Das Einhorn* (1966), *Halbzeit* (1962); *Plays* (vol. I, 1963); his contribution is a series of extracts from his PhD dissertation *Beschreibung einer Form: Versuch über Franz Kafka* (1961).

FELIX WELTSCH (1884–1964) was a classmate of Max Brod who introduced him to Kafka in 1914; Zionist and writer of philosophical and theological books, including *Organic Democracy: A Jurisprudential Study of the Representative System and Parliamentary Suffrage* (1918) and *Grace and Freedom* (1920). He died in London.

J.J.WHITE teaches German at King's College London. *Mythology in the Modern Novel: a study of prefigurative techniques* (1971). His contribution is the opening of his essay in *On Kafka: Semi-Centenary Perspectives*, ed. Franz Kuna (London 1976).

Index

F.K. = Franz Kafka

Adler, Friedrich, 50
Adorno, Theodor W., 181
Aesop, 104, 112
Against a Misunderstood Realism (*Wider den missverstandenen Realismus*) (Lukács), 181–2
Aktion, Die (periodical), 35
Alchemists, 64
Alchimistengasse (Alchemists' Lane), Prague, 23, 61, 224
Allgemeinbildung (universal culture), 38
Altstädter Deutsches Staatsgymnasium (German Grammar School), Prague, 13, 37
America, 17, 18, 92, 98, 200; black frock coated officials, 95; construction, 100; enemies in, 94; first chapter published as 'The Stoker', 18; 'the novel is me', 233; posthumous publication, 161
America, United States of, 56
Anders, Günther, 183–6
Anthroposophy, 16
Anti-Semitism, 48, 67
Assicurazioni-Generali, 15
Auden, W. H., 169
Augustine, Saint, 106–7
Austro-Hungarian empire, 24, 30, 42–3

Bar Kochba, 36, 42
Bauer, Felice: correspondence with M.

Brod, 73; with F.K., 18–9, 21, 23, 71–7; with Julie Kafka, 73; engagements, 19, 20, 23; first meeting with F.K., 17, 70; and graphology, 125; meeting at Bodenbach, 21; at Munich, 23; at Prague, 24; visited in Berlin by F.K., 19, 20
Baum, Oskar, 15, 27, 35, 50; blindness, 58, 226; at F.K's funeral, 60
Beethoven, Ludwig van, 108, 195
'Before the Law' parable (*The Trial*), 90, 114, 120–1, 138
Benjamin, Walter, 175, 176–8, 180
Bergmann, Hugo, 42, 58, 60
Bezruč Petr, 179
Berlin, 19, 20, 28, 61, 205, 207
Berlin Academy for Jewish Studies, 207
Berlin Jewish People's Centre, 23, 28
Bible, 52, 107
Binder, Hartmut, 146
Blau, Sigmund, 50
Blériot, Louis, 16
Bloch, Grete, 19–20, 22, 26
'Blumfeld, an Elderly Bachelor', 92, 116, 200; Freudian interpretation, 153–6
Bodenbach (Ústí nad Labem), 21
Bohemia, the Kingdom of, 30, 32, 48, 50
Bohemia (newspaper), 35
Book of Roads and Countries, The (Codex Cordova), 64

Brahe, Tycho, 61
Brand, Karl, 57
Brecht, Bertolt, 178–81
Brescia, 16
Breuer, Josef, 145
Brno, 61
Broch, Hermann, 161, 163, 167
Brod, Max, 5, 30, 50, 58; meets F.K., 14;
  biography of F.K., 175, 192, 194, 306;
  compares F.K. and Kleist, 227; and
  Czech culture, 59; death in Palestine,
  203; on F.K., 71, 73, 175; at F.K's
  funeral, 60; on F.K's work with
  Workers' Accident Insurance Institute,
  192–3; holidays with F.K., 16;
  introduces Felice to F.K., 70; and
  literary clubs, 35; refuses to destroy
  F.K's diaries and other papers, 125; on
  'Odradek', 226; and periodicals, 35;
  persuades F.K. to publish, 207;
  posthumous publication of F.K's novels,
  161; and Prague cafés, 34; on *The Castle*,
  84, 168; visits F.K. on death bed, 29; and
  Zionism, 42.
  Works: 'Richard and Samuel' (with
  F.K.), 35; *Tycho Brahe's Way to God*,
  63; *Zauberreich der Liebe* (*The Magic
  Realm of Love*), 175
Brod, Otto, 16
Brooks, Van Wyck, 159, 161
Buber-Neumann, Margarete, 204
Büchner, Georg, 186
Budapest, 21, 61
Bunyan, John, 170
'The Burrow' ('Der Bau'), 77–8, 115, 142,
  156, 207–9

Cabbala, 65–6
Cafés in Prague, 16, 34, 42
Camus, Albert, 100–1
Čapek, Karel, 64
'Cares of the Father, The' ('Odradek'), 224,
  228
Carossa, Hans, 161
Čas (*Time*) (Prague newspaper), 35
The Castle: Brod on, 168; Castle as
  opposing order, 98–9, 101; connection
  with Milena, 232; deleted fragment,
  77–8; disturbances in, 99; father's
  influence on, 13; Heller on, 114;

'humming and singing', 109; Muir on,
  161–2, 168; narrative method, 88–90; as
  parable, 114; posthumous publication,
  161; power of authority in, 98, 117–8;
  real-life correlatives, 79–84; setting
  based on Osek?, 81–4; villagers as a
  group, 91–2, 96; villagers' function, 92;
  and visit of F.K. to Friedland, 16, 27
Castle Hill, Prague *see* Hradčany
Charles IV, Emperor, 63
Charles Bridge, Prague, 62, 63, 224
Chotek's Park, Prague, 37
Christianity, 52
'Civilized Sexual Morality and Modern
  Nervous Illness' (Freud), 148
Coleridge, S. T., 169, 170
Conversations with Kafka (Janouch), 191,
  196, 197, 225–6, 228
Counter-Reformation, 62
'Country Doctor, A', 23, 24, 62, 128, 134
Crime and Punishment (Dostoyevsky), 5,
  104
Croce, Benedetto, 87
Czech nationalism, 47–8, 225
Czech University, Prague, 38, 62
Czech Young Men's Club (Klub mladých),
  36
Czechoslovak State, 24, 42

Dance of the Just, The (Liwa ben Bezalel),
  66
Dante Alighieri, 145, 172, 180
Danton's Death (Büchner), 186
Darwin, Charles, 14
David, Josef, 25
Day Lewis, Cecil, 169
De Generatione Rerum Naturalium
  (Paracelsus), 64
'Description of a Struggle', 149, 157
Deutsch, Ernst, 37
Dialectics of Concreteness (Kosík), 186–7
Diamant, Dora, *see* Dymant, Dora
Dobson, Austin, 191
Don Giovanni (Mozart), 37
'Dora' (Freud), 145
Dostoyevsky, Fedor, 5, 104
Doubek, Eduard Knight of, 82
Dymant, Dora, 28–9, 60–1, 70, 170, 204–9;
  father's reception of F.K's proposal, 206;
  lives with F.K., 28–9, 205–9

Eddington, Sir Arthur, 175-6
Eden, Garden of, 108, 234
Einander (One Another) (Werfel), 58
Eisner, Pavel, 34
Eliot, T. S., 4
'The Emperor's Message', 118-9
'Er' ('He'), 139
Existentialism, 183, 186
Expressionism, 59
Ezechiel ben Juda Landau, Rabbi, 68

Fackel, Die (periodical), 35
Fanta, Berta, 145
Faust, Johannes, also *Historia*,
    Frankfurt/M, 1587, 63
Faust (Goethe), 63, 66
Feuchtwanger, Lion, 161
Fiegl, Fritz, 38
Flaubert, Gustave, 226
Fontane Prize for Literature, 22
Franz Ferdinand, Archduke, 20
Franz Joseph, Emperor ('starý Procházka'),
    226-7
Franz Kafka: an interpretation of his Works
    (Tauber), 196
Freeman, The (periodical), 159, 161
Freud, Sigmund: *Angst*, 148; concept of
    Eros, 147-8; concept of repression, 150;
    differences with F.K., 146; dreams,
    150-1; the ego, 150-1; influence on
    F.K., 145-6; parapraxes, 151-2, 154;
    preconscious system, 150; projection,
    153-7; psychoanalysis, 146-7, 151;
    repression, 149-53; on symptoms, 152;
    unconscious system, 150; universal
    obsessional neurosis, 140, 143
Friedland, in Western Bohemia, 16
Frye, Northrop, 170
Fuchs, Rudolf, 50, 60-1

Gans, David, 40
'German and Austrian State Law, Common
    Law and Political Economy' (F.K's
    thesis), 39
German Casino, Prague, 50
German Progressive Party, 35
German Student Debating and Reading
    Club ('die Halle'), 36, 49
German Theatre, Prague, 36, 49

German University, Prague, 14-5, 38, 48;
    fraternities and clubs, 48-9; *voelkisch*, 48
'Give it up', 113
Gmünd, village in Southern Bohemia, 26
Goethe, Johann Wolfgang von, 14, 17, 63,
    169
Goethe and the Jews (Teweles), 49
Goldschmied, Professor, 38
Goldstücker, Eduard, 7
Golem, 61-8; animation of lifeless matter,
    64-5, 67; created by Rabbi Liwa ben
    Bezalel, 67-8
Golem (novel by Meyrink), 63
Good Soldier Švejk, The (Hašek), 35, 179n,
    180
Gosse, Edmund, 191, 194
Great Wall of China, The, 23, 118, 130-1
Gross, Otto, 145

Haas, Vilém, 34-6; on ballet, 37; on decline
    of Austro-Hungarian Empire, 42; on
    F.K., 36
Haeckel, Ernst, 14
Haggadah, 178
Halakah, 178
Hamburger, Michael, 169
Hamlet, 107
Hamsun, Knut, 196
Hardt, Ludwig, 160
Hašek, Jaroslav, 35, 36, 179
Hauptmann, Gerhart, 161
Heidegger, Martin, 148
Heine, Heinrich, 51
Heller, Erich, 114, 169-70
Herderblätter (periodical), 35
Herzl, Theodor, 49
Hibbert, George, 30
Hochland, Das (periodical), 35
'Homecoming', 113-4
Homer, 122
Homunculi, 64
Hradčany, Prague Castle, 46, 61, 62, 63,
    224
Huebsch, Ben, 161
'Hunger Artist, A', 27, 109-10, 131, 202,
    206
Hus statue, by Ladislav Šaloun, 62
Husserl, Edmund, 144
Hussite Wars, 39
Hyperion (periodical), 35

Ibrahim ibn Jakub, Rabbi, 39, 64
Image of a Society (Fuller), 197–9
'In the Penal Colony', 103–4, 134, 207;
   F.K's public reading, 23
Interpretations of Dreams (Freud), 145, 156
'Investigations of a Dog, The', 104–111,
   116–7, 200–1; alienation of dog, 105–6,
   110; compared to Tonio Kröger, 105;
   concert in, 110; fable or parable? 104;
   and Fall of Man, 105–11; music in,
   108–11; nature of dog in, 104–6
Italy, 56

Jackdaw (*kavka*), 11, 196, 218–9, 224
Jakobson, Roman, 39
James, Henry, 136–7
Janouch, Gustav, 191, 196, 197, 225–6, 228
Janowitz, Franz, 57
Jeiteles, Dr., 40
Jesenská-Polak, Milena, 25–7, 35;
   character, 204; death, 237; relationship
   with F.K., 70, 229–37; writes F.K's
   obituary, 59, 204–5
Jewish People's Centre, Berlin, 23, 28
Jewish Town Hall, Prague, 16
Jews in Prague, 31–3; anti-Semitism, 48,
   67; Bar Kochba, 36, 42; education, 37–8;
   emancipation, 1848, 79; in German
   Theatre, 49; Germanisation, 41, 47–8,
   53; ghetto abolished, 33, 41; history,
   39–42; importance, 39; journalists, 50;
   language and, 52–5; loss of identity as
   Jews, 51, 106; poets, 49–50; religion and,
   52–3; restrictions, 40–1; revival of
   Jewish awareness, 50–5; in Trollope
   novel, 46
Jokes and their Relation to the Unconscious
   (Freud), 145
Josefov (Josefstadt) (Jewish quarter of
   Prague), 31, 32
Joseph II, Emperor, 40, 41, 47
'Josephine, the Singing Mouse', 126–7,
   129, 132, 142, 243–5
Juarez, Benito (Pablo), 58
'The Judgment', 17, 71, 103, 130, 136; and
   tuberculosis, 139; and Freud, 146, 156

Kafka, Bruno, 50
Kafka, Elli, 12, 21, 28, 148
Kafka, Franz,

Life and background: background, 2;
   Jewishness, 2, 207, 225; birth, 11;
   unsettled childhood, 12–13; 'three
   worlds', 13; education, 12, 13–15,
   38–9; thesis, 39; graduation, 15; visits
   Munich, 14; works on first novel, 15;
   sanatorium in Zuckmantel, 15; early
   affairs, 14, 15, 17, 19; compulsory year
   of legal experience, 15; works at
   Assicurazioni-Generali, 15; first work
   published, 15; works at Workers'
   Accident Insurance Institute, 6, 15–6,
   191–7, 200, 203, 227; 'double life', 16,
   194; official report for Institute, 194;
   promotions, 194; air display, 16; at
   Prague Technical High School, 39;
   attends anarchist meetings, 16; in
   Paris, 16; in Friedland, 16; holidays
   with Brod, 16, 17; sanatorium at
   Zurich, 16; and Yiddish actors, 16;
   Yiddish evening, 17; and Jewish
   culture, 17; learns Hebrew, 66, 207;
   and family asbestos factory, 16, 17, 21;
   writes for periodicals, 35; and literary
   clubs, 35–6; and political clubs, 36;
   and Prague cafés, 34; at health farm,
   Goslar, 17; writes *America*, 17–8, 20;
   contemplates suicide, 17, 227; writes
   'Metamorphosis', 18; and rejects
   illustrations of 'Metamorphosis', 22;
   insomnia, 18, 26; sanatorium in Riva,
   19; rents a room, 21; turned down by
   army, 20; and Fontane Prize for
   Literature, 22; headaches, 22; public
   reading in Munich, 23; tuberculosis,
   23, 74, 139, 209; stays with Ottla,
   23–4, 27; influenza, 24; in Schelesen,
   24, 25; at Merano, 25–6; begins *The
   Castle*, 27; sanatorium at Matljary,
   26–7; in Spindlermühle, 27, 79;
   contemplates emigrating, 28; at
   Müritz, 28; moves to Berlin, 28, 205;
   sanatoria in Vienna and Kierling, 29;
   orders Brod to destroy papers, 125,
   207; last visit of Brod, 29; death, 29;
   funeral, 29, 58, 60–1; obituary by
   Milena, 59, 204–5; effect of his death
   on Prague writers, 59.
Character and relationships: alienation,
   106, 125, 225; and *Angst*, 147–8, 181;

appearance, 38, 202; and awakening of Jewish consciousness, 55; character, 5–6, 69; condemns sexuality, 147; and death, 131–2; and deprivation, 4; disagrees with Freud's ideas, 146–8; extremism, 126; fear, 205; fear of artistic failure, 192–3; friendliness, 185; humour, 5–6; influence of family background on, 41–2; inherited characteristics, 12; as jackdaw, 196; love of solitude, 3, 16, 19, 73, 125; and marriage, 76–7, 126, 204; 'mystery', 1; mysticism, 178; necessity to work, 195–6; opinion of graphologist's analysis, 125; as outsider, 105–6; relationship with Brod, *see* Brod, Max; with Dora, 28–9, 60–1, 70, 170, 204–9; with father, 12, 25, 77, 83; with Felice, 17–24, 70–6, 125–6; with Grete Bloch, 19–20; with mother, 24–6; with Milena, 70, 229–37; religiousness, 170, 175–6, 187; and sex, 76–7; tension between mystical and physical experiences, 176–7; torment of relationship with women, 69–78, 227, 232; as torturer, 69; uniqueness, 229–30; 'unreality' of his concept of Felice, 72, 74

Diaries: against marriage, 19; 'autobiographical investigations', 124–131; begins *The Trial*; Brod quoted in English translation of, 192; on death, 131–2; on Felice, 19, 20, 70–1, 197–8; on health, 195; on 'The Judgment', 71; on Kierkegaard, 228; Milena given them, 232; not destroyed after F.K's death, 124–5; on second engagement, 20; on self-perception, 123; on work in the Workers' Accident Insurance Institute, 193; 'writing into the dark', 235–6

Letters: to Baum, 27; to Brod, 5, 22, 24, 74, 76, 79, 128, 131, 140; to Elli, 148; to Felice, 18–9, 21, 23, 71–6, 125; to Grete Bloch, 20, 26; to Robert Klopstock, 28; to Milena, 205, 206, 229–237; to Ottla, 23, 27, 28; to Pollack, 14, 15, 149; 'Letter' to his father, 1919 (never delivered), 83, 126, 135, 146, 204, 225, 227, 232; on

marriage, 25, 126, 204; on 'one illness', 147; on Workers' Accident Insurance Institute, 195n; from Zürau, 24

Writings: affinities with Rilke, 2; ambiguous message of writing, 139, 142; animal writings, 128, 178; astonishment as theme, 180; *Ausweg* (way out), 115; characters maimed, 117; characters obsessive, 115–7; construction and deconstruction, 142–3; contradictory attitude to writing, 135; depersonalization, 97; destruction of pseudo-concreteness, 187; distraction figures, 92–3, 96; economical characterisation, 91, 95; endings and non-endings, 102, 130; and Fall of Man, 103, 111, 234–6; fantastic writings, 149–57; fear in, 229; freedom as deprivation, 183; and Freud, 145–57; and Freudian image of man, 145; Freudian projection, 153–7; Freudian repression, 149–53; guilt in, 183–5; guilt of central characters, 103–4; hearings and examinations in, 98; hero as narrator, 88; identity/function relationship, 93, 95; immortal longings, 114; imperative to write, 124, 127, 134; inner vision, 129–30; knowledge of Osek, 81; language, 133–144; literal use of metaphor, 137–8; literary *persona*, 87; manner anticipated by Trollope, 44–6; Marxist-Leninist view of, 178–80; metaphorical language, 141–3, 230; metaphors, 4; moral questions, 104; music in, 108–9, 110–1; myth-like character of stories, 140–2; narrative method, 88–90, 85, 140–2, 149, 162; nihilism, 58, 185; officials, 95–7; parables, 112–9, 178; 'patchwork' writing, 129–30, 134; political significance of work, 6; prophetic quality, 180; and psychoanalysis, 145–7; rejection of conversation, 129; rhythm, 99–100; Rilke's writing compared, 3–4; symbol and allegory, 169–70; thesis, 39; 'timeless world', 182; and Tower of Babel, 141–2; uniqueness, 181; unintelligibility, 133; use of German language, 226; women characters, 76, 94;

words as spears, 136; 'world of phenomena', 196; 'writing as a form of prayer', 134; 'writing as fun and despair', 135; writing as suffering, 21; *see also* under the names of novels

Kafka, Hermann, father, 4, 17, 227; character, 12–13; irony, 13; opposes F.K's engagement to Julie Wohryzek, 25; opposes Ottla's engagement, 25; parentage, 11, 79; relationship with F.K., 12–3, 25, 77, 83, 204; youth, 11 *see also* Kafka, Franz: Letters

Kafka, Jakob, 79–81, 83

Kafka, Julie (née Löwy), mother, 11–2, 73, 204

Kafka, Ottla, sister, 12, 23, 79; relationship with F.K., 70; wishes to marry, 25

Kafka, Valli, sister, 12, 21, 70

'Kafka and Psychoanalysis' (Binder), 147

Kafka 'family-book', 79

Kafka – pro und contra (Günther Anders), 183

Kafka's Friend Milena (Margarete Buber-Neumann), 59

Kbelnice, village of, 80, 82

Kepler, Johannes, 61

Kestenberg-Gladstein, Ruth, 40

Kierkegaard, Sören Aaby, 1, 70, 168, 181, 228

Kierling, sanatorium at, 29, 57

Kinský Palace, Prague, 37

Kisch, Egon Erwin, 30, 35, 42, 50; and Golem legend, 64

Klee, Paul, 177

Kleist, Heinrich von, 70, 227, 233

Klepetář, Otto, 35

Klopstock, Robert, 26–7, 29

Kmen (periodical), 35

Kohen, Gershom, 40

Kornfeld, Paul, 50

Kosík, Karel, 186–7

Kraus, Karl, 16

Kuntstwart, Der (periodical), 14

La Fontaine, Jean de, 104

Lenin, Vladimir, 56

'Lese- und Rede-Halle' (Debating and Reading Club of the German Students), 36, 47

Liblice Conference, 1963, 7

'Little Fable, A', 113

'Little Woman, The', 116

Liwa ben Bezalel, Rabbi (High Rabbi Loew), 64, 66; and creation of Golem, 67–8; and Rudolf II, 66–7

Löwy, Alfred, 12

Löwy, Esther, 11

Löwy, Jacob, 11

Löwy, Jizchak, 16

Lucerne, 16

Lukács, Georg, 114, 181–2

MacDiarmid, Hugh, 164

Mann, Thomas, 14, 105, 148, 203

Mareš, Michal, 16

Maria Theresia, Empress, 40, 41

Marienbad, 5, 22

Mark, St., the Gospel of, 121

Marriage of Figaro, The, 37

'Married Couple, The', 76

Marx Brothers, 5

Masaryk, Thomas G., 35

Matljary, 26, 29

Mauthner, Fritz, 226

Maximilian, Emperor of Mexico, 58

May Festival, Prague, 36–7, 49

Mein Kampf (Hitler), 57

Merano, 25–6

Městský sad (Stadtpark), Prague, 37

'Metamorphosis, The', 4, 18, 74, 137, 207, 236; cover design, 118; its relation to Golem legend, 64; Freudian interpretation of, 150–2, 155; illustration of, 22; movement from supernatural to natural, 150; published, 22; Todorov on, 149–50; violin playing in, 109, 207

Meyrink, Gustav, 63

Milton, John, 108, 191

Moldau River, *see* Vltava

Monkhouse, Cosmo, 191

Mozart, Wolfgang Amadeus, 37

Mozarteum (Bertram Villa), Prague, 37, 160

Muir, Edwin, 159–173; affinities with F.K., 159; and Brod's German texts, 167; and Brod's interpretation, 168; early language experiences, 164; F.K. criticism, 161–2, 167–73; F.K's negative theology, 170–1; method of translation,

162–3; natural translations, 165–7; in
Prague, 160; as translator, 161–3
Works: *Essays on Literature and Society*,
171–2; 'The Law', 171; *Poor Tom*, 163;
Scott and Scotland, 163–4; 'Sonnet to
Franz Kafka', 172; *The Structure of the
Novel*, 162
Muir, Willa, 159–67; and Brod's German
texts, 167; in Dresden, 160; method of
translation, 162–3; quality of
translations, 161–2, 165–7; in Prague,
160
Munch, Edvard, 4
Munich, 14, 23

Národní listy (newspaper), 35, 59
National Theatre, Prague, 36–7
Nature of the Physical World, The
(Eddington), 176
'Neighbour, The', 116
Neill, A. S., 160–1
Neruda, Jan, 62
Neumann, Angelo, 36–7, 49
Neumann, S. K., 36
Nietzsche, Friedrich, 14, 107, 142; on God
and grammar, 140
Nijinsky, Vaslav, 37
Nina Balatka (Trollope), 44–6
Noll, Professor ('Old Fritz'), 223

'Odradek' ('The Cares of the Father'), 224,
228; as symbol of Jewish people, 226
Odysseus, 122–3, 132
Old-New Synagogue, Prague, 40, 52, 64, 68
Old Town Square, Prague, 38, 62, 63
Osek (Wossek), 30, 79–83; Castle, 81–3

Paracelsus, 64
Paris, 16
Pasley, Malcolm, 167, 194
Pavillon d'Armide (ballet), 67
Perutz, Leo, 35, 50
Petrouchka (ballet), 37
Pharaoh's Hard Heart (Liwa ben Bezalel),
66
'Philosophical Suicide' (Camus), 101
Piaristenschule (German Primary School),
Prague, 38, 51, 81
Pick, Otto, 38, 50
Pilgrim's Progress (Bunyan), 114, 168
Planá, village of, 27, 79

Platowski, Franziska, 79–80
'Political Party of Moderate Progress within
the Law', 36
Pollak, Oskar, 14, 15, 149
Prager Jüdische Zeitung (periodical), 35
Prager Tagblatt (newspaper), 35, 50
Prague, 2, 30–43, 56–61; *Allgemeinbildung*,
38; *Altneuschul* (Old-New Synagogue),
40, 52, 64, 68; ballet, 37; cafes, 34; coffee
houses, 34, 35; Czech anti-Semitism, 48,
67; Czech University, 38; development,
30–1; educational system, 13, 37–8,
50–1; ethnic divisions, 32, 36; in
Frankfurt Faust *Historia*, 63; German
Casino, 50; German element, 32;
German University, 14, 38;
germanisation of Jews, 41, 47; Golem
myths, 64–5; Hebrew printing works,
40; history and importance of Jews in 31,
32, 39–42; industrialisation, 32, 37;
influence on writers of, 30; Jewish ghetto
(Josefov), 62, abolished, 33, 41; Jewish
Town Hall, 16; journals and newspapers,
34–5; lack of cultural class distinction,
36; Lichtenstein houses, 40; literary
clubs, 35–6; Little Quarter (Malá
strana), 40, 62, 63, 224; May Festival,
36–7, 49; mixed cultures in, 2; as new
state capital, 160; New Town (Nové
město), 40, 63; not a tourist centre, 61;
nicknames of, 30, 41, 51; Old Town
(Staré město), 40, 62, 63; physical
environment, 30–1; Pinkas Synagogue,
40; political clubs, 36; population
figures, 30, 31–2, 41; 'Prager-Deutsch',
164; Prague Spring of 1968, 7, 186;
suburbs, 33; Technical High School, 39;
theatres, 36–7, 49; 'Toleranzpatent' of
1782, 40; trams, 32; in Trollope novel,
44–6; unmentioned by F.K., 44;
Wenceslas Square, 34; Zionist
movement, 42
Prague Linguistic Circle (der Prager Kreis),
35, 143
Prague-German School of writers, 32
Preisner, Rio, 204
Přemysl Otakar II, King of Bohemia, 39
Prometheus legend, 233
Psychopathology of Everyday Life, The
(Freud), 145

R.U.R. (play by Karel Čapek), 64
Radomyšl, village of, 80
Ravensbrück Concentration Camp, 237
'Reflections on Sin, Pain, Hope and the
    True Way', 235, 237
'Report for an Academy', 115
'Richard and Samuel' (Brod and F.K.), 35
Rieger, Prague Park, 37
Rilke, Rainer Maria, 1, 30, 50; biographical
    affinities with F.K., 1; background, 2;
    and deprivation, 4; marriage, 77;
    objections to psychoanalysis, 232; and
    prodigal son, 3; rejection of 'Prague'
    German, 4; style compared with F.K's
    3–4
Rimsky-Korsakov, Nicholas, 37
Riva, 16
Rosenheim, J., 49
Rowohlt, Ernst, 17, 36
Royal Vineyards (Královské vinohrady), 37
Roztoky, village near Prague, 33
Rozvoj (periodical), 35
Rudolf II, Emperor, 61, 63, 64, 68; and
    Rabbi Liwa ben Bezalel, 66–7
Rudolfinum Palace, 37
Russia, 56

Saint Vitus's Cathedral, 44, 62, 224
Salus, Hugo, 50
Sartre, Jean-Paul, 90
Sauer, August, 14
Schéhérezade (Rimsky-Korsakov), 37
Schelesen (Želizy), 24, 25
Schiller, Friedrich, 14, 51, 108
Scholem, Gerhard (Gershom), 176
Schönborn Palace, Prague, 62
Schopenhauer, Arthur, 14, 104, 107, 153–4
Selbstwehr (periodical), 35
Shem, 65, 67–8
Sherrington, Sir Charles, 27
Sinyavsky, Andrey, 183
'Sirens, The Silence of the', 122, 179
Sisyphus, 237
Spectre de la Rose, Le (ballet), 37
'Speech on the Yiddish language', 225
Spindlermühle, mountain village, 27, 79
'Spring of Nations' movement (1848), 33
Šrámek, Fráňa, 36
Stagmoat of Prague, the 61
Stekel, Wilhelm, 146

Steiner, Rudolf, 16
Sternheim, Carl, 22
Stevens, Wallace, 191, 193, 194–5
'Stoker, The' (first chapter of *America*), 18
Stories from the Little Quarter (Neruda), 62
Strakonice, village in south-western
    Bohemia, 81
Strašnice Cemetery (Prague), 60, 67, 224
Stravinsky, Igor, 37
Studies in Hysteria (Freud and Breuer), 145
Supernatural powers, 65–6
Szafranski, Kurt, 40

Tábor, town in Southern Bohemia, 80
Talmud, 53, 64, 207
Tauber, Herbert, 196
Tears of God, The (Liwa ben Bezalel), 66
'Test, The' ('Die Prüfung'), 106
'Testimonials' ('Fürsprecher'), 119
Teweles, Heinrich, 49, 50
Thieberger, Friedrich, 60; and golem
    myth, 65
Three Essays on the Theory of Sexuality
    (Freud), 145
Thus Spoke Zarathustra (Nietzsche), 14
Todorov, Tzvetan, 149–50
'Toleranzpatent', 1782, 40, 225
Tolstoy, Count Leo, 5
Toman, Karel, 36
'Tonio Kröger' (Thomas Mann), 15, 105
Town Moat (Ditch), Prague ('Příkopy'), 34,
    63
Trakl, Georg, 4
Trial, The: 20, 87–100, 134, 207; action in
    three strands, 100; bank clerks as
    distractions, 92–3; 'Before the Law'
    parable, 90, 114, 120–1; 138; defendants
    as a social grouping, 90–2, 96;
    defendants' function, 92;
    depersonalisation, 97; economical
    characterisation, 91; enemies, 94, 96;
    F.K's divided self in, 157; F.K's
    engagement to Felice and, 137; function
    of parable in, 138; influence of father on,
    13; Joseph K. as defendant, 91; officials,
    95; as parable, 114; parapraxis in, 156–7;
    posthumous publication, 161; power of
    authority in, 98, 117–8; 'Der Prozess',
    137–8; setting, 44; whipping of Franz,
    74, 97

Tribuna (newspaper), 34
Troja Pomological Institute (near Prague), 32
Trollope, Anthony, 46
Tucholsky, Kurt, 40
Tycho Brahe's Way to God (Brod), 63
Tyl, J.K., 30

Umělecký měsíčník (periodical), 35
'The Uncanny' (Freud), 150
Ungar, Hermann, 50
Upward, Edward, 169
'*Ur-Mythus*', 107

Venice, 18
Verdi, Giuseppe, 37, 58
Vienna, 18, 21, 26, 58, 59, 61, 230–1
'Village Schoolmaster, The' ('The Giant Mole'), 115–6
Vltava (Moldau) River, 30, 37, 62
Vom Judentum, anthology, 36
Vrchlický, Jaroslav, 36

Wagner, Richard, 37, 49, 58
Warner, Rex, 169
Weimar, 16, 225
Weiss, Ernst, 50

Weissen Blätter, Die (periodical), 35
Weltsch, Felix, 14, 15, 38, 58; at F.K's funeral, 60
Werfel, Franz, 30, 34, 35, 42, 50; on F.K., 58
Wilson, Woodrow, 56
Winder, Ludwig, 35, 50, 60
Wir sind (*We Are*) (Werfel), 58
Wittgenstein, Ludwig, 144
Wohryzek, Julie, 22–6
Wolff, Kurt, 22, 36
Workers' Accident Insurance Institute (Arbeiter-Unfall-Versicherungs-Anstalt für das Königreich Böhmen in Prag) also WAII, 6, 15–6, 27, 191–7, 200, 203
Wossek *see* Osek
Wuthering Heights (E. Bronte), 162

Yetzirah, 64
Yiddish Theatre Group, 2, 16
Yitzchak bin Simson Cohen, Rabbi, 67

Zauberreich der Liebe, *see* Brod, Max
Zionism, 42
Žižkov, 36
Zuckmantel (Silesia), 15
Zürau, 23–4
Zurich, 16